GODDESSES
for Every Day

OTHER WORKS BY THE AUTHOR
(AS JULIE GILLENTINE)

The Hidden Power of Everyday Things

Messengers

Occult Symbology & the Metaphysics of Number

Tarot and Astrology, Linking the Archetypes

Tarot and Dream Interpretation

GODDESSES
for Every Day

Exploring the Wisdom & Power
of the Divine Feminine
around the World

JULIE LOAR

New World Library
Novato, California

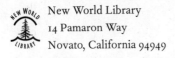

New World Library
14 Pamaron Way
Novato, California 94949

P. v, epigraph: Excerpted from Betty De Shong Meader, *Inanna, Lady of the Largest Heart* (Austin: University of Texas Press, 2000), 174.

Text design by Tona Pearce Myers

Library of Congress Cataloging-in-Publication Data
Loar, Julie, date.
Goddesses for every day : exploring the wisdom and power of the divine feminine around the world / Julie Loar. — 1st New World Library ed.
    p.   cm.
Includes bibliographical references and index.
ISBN 978-1-57731-950-4 (pbk. : alk. paper)
1. Goddesses. I. Title.
BL473.5.L63 2011
202'.114—dc22   2010035641

First New World Library edition, January 2011
ISBN 978-1-57731-950-4
Printed in Canada on 100% postconsumer-waste recycled paper

New World Library is a proud member of the Green Press Initiative.

10 9 8 7 6 5 4 3 2 1

In honor of Her

You of the bountiful heart
You of the radiant heart
I will sing of your cosmic powers.

— From "The Exaltation of Inanna"
by Enheduanna, High Priestess of Sumeria,
Daughter of Sargon of Akkad,
Princess Imperial of Sumer and Akkad,
circa 2300 BCE

Enheduanna is the first author
of either gender mentioned in world literature.

CONTENTS

PREFACE

*E*very woman wants to feel like a goddess. Strong. Wise. Brave. Loving. Who better than powerful goddesses to be role models? *Goddesses for Every Day* presents a collection of 366 goddesses, diverse examples of the Divine Feminine through time and across cultures. This book of days holds up a mirror so you can try on a new goddess every day, seeing your own nature reflected through timeless examples of women's wisdom and feminine power. These goddesses are meant to act as daily guides, way-showers through the passages of life, engaging the sacred feminine within you.

Goddesses for Every Day is arranged as a loop, a meditative journey through the year, with the goddesses organized within the zodiac signs. Every culture on earth has marked time by tracking the motions of the moon and the paths of the planets against the background of the stars. The Babylonians and Egyptians used the zodiac thousands of years ago. This circle of stars, which has been called the Girdle of the Goddess, seemed an appropriate frame for the year. The goddesses are also linked with seasonal cycles. Goddesses of dawn and new beginnings are aligned with spring, goddesses of birth with summer, goddesses of the harvest with autumn, and goddesses who preside over death with the dark time of year in the Northern Hemisphere.

Sacred feminine symbols such as birds, trees, serpents, and spirals are found in almost all cultures around the world, and I perceived that these icons are aligned with the familiar twelve zodiac signs. Because this book chronicles feminine power, I chose one of these symbols to represent each zodiac sign. For example, Libra is symbolized by the Dove, and Taurus is represented by the Tree of Life. I call these goddess signs. A short explanation precedes each chapter's list, briefly describing the characteristics of the sign, why I chose the particular symbol and goddess sign, and why the specific goddesses were selected for that section.

The many facets and myriad manifestations of the goddess embody a seeming paradox. Like life itself, her expressions can be alternately gentle or fierce, nurturing or punishing, or creative or destructive. The goddesses who appear in this book are often complex, even contradictory, so they did not always conveniently fit into one zodiac sign. I placed them where they resonated most, based on what I perceived to be their dominant quality.

Women understand cycles because our lives are framed by them, and there is an intrinsic ebb and flow to the feminine experience. The stages of a woman's life are demarcations of menstruation: prepuberty, the childbearing years, and the cessation of menstrual flow. Each month of an adult woman's life is a

Goddesses for Every Day

complete cycle of birth and death, a microcosm of life itself. As women age, their cycles change and life takes on a different character. The wheel of the year symbolically relates to the stages of women's lives, commonly expressed as the triple goddess: maiden, mother, and crone or elder. This trinity of the sacred feminine existed in ancient cultures long before the male trinity we recognize from the Bible. The triple goddess was symbolized by a triple crown that was formed by the phases of the moon: waxing crescent, full orb, and waning crescent. This crown, worn by Isis and many others, was the symbol of creation, generation, and regeneration. Most ancient cultures honored the crone or elder as a woman who had come fully into her power. In Western culture we seem to revere youth and fear age, and in this way we lose the wise voice of experience.

Goddesses for Every Day relates the myths of 366 goddesses. The word *myth* comes from the root word for "mouth," as storytelling was originally an oral tradition. Myths are sacred stories, and they have been the way that people transmitted their holiest truths, their understanding of our relationship to the Divine, for thousands of years. The well-known Swiss psychoanalyst Carl Jung observed that archetypes — the intrinsic patterns of human consciousness such as maiden, mother, and crone, queen and princess — do not cease to exist if we ignore or devalue them. Rather, they become submerged in what Jung termed the collective unconscious, becoming strong forces that emerge in dreams, complexes, or even psychoses. Archetypes are building blocks of human nature. Myths, legends, and fairy tales, which contain principles and morals, are structured with the symbolic language of archetypes.

In Western culture we have devalued, even demonized, aspects of the feminine for nearly four thousand years, effectively pushing these archetypes beneath our conscious awareness.

Serious scholars of myth have noticed that the tenor of the stories began to change nearly four millennia ago. Symptoms of this shift in Greek myths included an increasing glorification of war, accompanied by a deteriorating value assigned to agriculture and cyclical time. The importance of the Great Goddess diminished and has been essentially buried for four millennia. The loss of half of the Divine has resulted in a rupture between mind and heart that has reverberated through centuries, evidenced by violence, alienation, and growing environmental devastation. Western culture no longer moves in harmony with natural cycles, and I believe our lack of balance with the natural seasons of earth and sky has brought us to a precarious place.

Humanity has a deep need to revere the feminine side of the Divine, and this unmet need is resurfacing in our time in such examples as the phenomenal popularity of the film *The Da Vinci Code*. Apparitions of Mary, mother of Jesus, are on the rise around the world. One of the best-documented instances in recent times took place in Zeitoun, Egypt, where hundreds of thousands of people of diverse beliefs stood side by side over a period of twenty-three years, watching as Mary appeared over a small church in a suburb of Cairo. Millions make annual pilgrimages to Fatima, Lourdes, and the basilica of Our Lady of Guadalupe in Mexico each year. The site in Mexico is the second-most-visited Catholic site; only the Vatican draws greater numbers. The tremendous outpouring of love and concern in response to the death of Diana, Princess of Wales, also spoke to our need to revere a feminine archetype.

Writing this book has been a profound journey for me, a personal reunion with the Divine Feminine. The process has been a labor of love that taught me a great deal about the nature of guidance. Hundreds of goddesses revealed their deep wisdom about the quality of feminine power, speaking in the timeless language of symbols, myths, and archetypes. I have been amazed by the depth and breadth of wisdom I discovered and am continually awed by a creative process that has drawn me along as a willing, if sometimes dazzled, participant.

As I researched and wrote this book, I was often spontaneously transported into an altered state, where I experienced a different realm of awareness. Sometimes a goddess declared her intention to be included in the circle by drawing me to a book. As if by magic, or by the mysterious mechanism of synchronicity, my eyes were drawn to a previously unknown goddess who aligned perfectly with the place in the calendar I was working on. At other times, guidance came through a provocative dream. Sometimes the goddesses seemed to come to life and move around the wheel, revealing something deeper about their natures than I had originally perceived. In this spirit, *Goddesses for Every Day* can be used as an oracle by setting an intention, or asking a specific question, and letting the pages fall open in a seemingly random way, allowing a goddess to speak to you.

The predominant view in religion today is of God as a singular, authoritarian father figure, although many gods fill the myths of the world. It is my hope and prayer that *Goddesses for Every Day* will serve in some way to restore the overarching principle of the goddess to her rightful place as the feminine half of the Divine. She has been known as Queen of Heaven and Great Mother in many cultures, and it seems right for her to reclaim the throne. I invite you to enter this sacred circle and embrace this ancient wisdom, taking these truths into your heart and soul. I hope you will get to know the powerful feminine beings represented here. Ancient Egyptians said every woman was a *nutrit*, a "little goddess" who partook of the nature of the powerful goddess Nut. And, as you embark on your own journey around the sacred wheel, I hope you will be empowered to become the goddess you are, consciously embodying love, strength, courage, compassion, inner beauty, and receptivity. That's the way we'll save the world: one empowered woman at a time.

SIGNS AND SEASONS

The astronomical phenomenon known as precession of the equinoxes, apparently caused by the earth's wobble on its axis, gives us the great wheel of the astrological ages. This slow movement of the heavens has always been understood as a vast circle of time, and it lasts approximately twenty-six thousand years. As the wheel turns, time cycles through each of the ages, coloring each period of roughly twenty thousand years with the overarching energy of the prevailing zodiac sign. At this point on the wheel, we are leaving the age of Pisces and moving into the age of Aquarius.

Five thousand years ago, during the age of Taurus, cultures were more agricultural, and fertility and the earth's growing cycle were held in high esteem. Time was experienced as circular, and daily, monthly, and yearly cycles repeated. Sexuality was seen as sacred, and all aspects of fertility were honored where the Great Goddess was revered. Seasonal festivals celebrated the annual ebb and flow of life, and people moved in conscious resonance with shifting cycles of light and dark, life and death. In ages past, women were revered as givers of life, and the beginning of each stage of a woman's life was viewed as an important crossroad, or rite of passage. Ceremonies and rites of initiation were conducted to usher a woman into the next phase.

Every year, earth makes a full circle around the sun. Earth's orbital motion causes the sun to appear to move in the sky in a path called the ecliptic. Astronomically, the zodiac is a circular band of sky, ranging from eight degrees above to eight degrees below the ecliptic, that contains the familiar zodiac constellations, from the Ram to the Fishes. Temporally, the zodiac also marks the apparent journey of the sun, based on our motion relative to the sun, and it has four main subdivisions. These are the so-called cardinal points of the year, the equinoxes and solstices. Although Western astrology now uses a measure of time that begins at the spring equinox in the Northern Hemisphere, the names of the zodiac signs are still the same as those of the constellations from which they originally drew their names.

The twelve signs of astrology are organized into what are termed the four "elements," or phases of expression, and arranged according to the three ways these elements act: initiating, consolidating, or alternating. According to tradition, the elements are fire, earth, air, and water, and the modes of expression are cardinal, fixed, and mutable. The elements are said to describe phases of expression, from pure energy to matter, in the same way that water can be a liquid, solid, or gas. Each of the twelve signs combines one element and one quality. For example, Aries is said to be a cardinal fire sign, intense and initiating. The zodiac is a cycle of experience that provides the template of evolution through which earth receives the influences of the sun and planets.

This constantly repeating circle of the year is separated into twelve equal divisions, which represent successive phases of experience. The borders, or divisions, of the zodiac signs are not consistent every year. I used the dates that occurred most frequently over the past ten years, so at times the signs and dates may not match certain birthdays. Because the seasons of the year actually shift a bit from year to year, a person born at the cusp of two signs may find that his or her birthday falls in the preceding or following sign in the book. And just as the energies of the two signs blend at the cusp, so do the qualities of the goddesses, so call on both, instead of one, to bless the day of your birth.

The book is organized according to the calendar and begins with January 1. However, the sign of Capricorn begins at the winter solstice, December 21, so for the sake of convenience the introduction to the goddess sign of Capricorn appears both at the beginning of the year and again before December 21.

The zodiac signs have been described as being like stained-glass windows that "color" the solar and planetary influences. I have endeavored to present the goddesses, and what they represent, within this ancient frame, as well as in a new light.

CAPRICORN GODDESSES
The Spinning Wheel

THREADS OF DESTINY ARE SPUN
BY CHOICES AND DEEDS

*C*apricorn anchors the winter solstice and combines the principles of cardinal initiating energies with the grounding influence of earth. In this sign, matter organizes itself into perfect forms. Capricorn's energy expresses itself as governing and conserving, focused on achievement, integrity, recognition, and responsibility. Capricorn natives are fueled by tremendous ambition, and their lessons stem from learning the motive that underlies their drive to climb. Capricorn is the tenth sign, and it represents the stage of the spiritual journey in which our aspiration turns inward to the clear mountain air of our spiritual nature. It also represents the principle of ambition, whether this is directed outwardly to the world of accomplishment or turned toward the spiritual path.

The goddess sign for Capricorn is the Spinning Wheel,

representing crone goddesses who are weavers of fate. Spinning, weaving, and looms are the province of wise elder goddesses who pronounce our destiny and measure and cut the threads of our lives. While Scorpio spins the threads out of the substance of the goddess's belly, it is in Capricorn, the sign of form, that the threads take shape and are woven into the tapestry of our lives. Mountains symbolize the spiritual quest in numerous traditions, so Capricorn is traditionally symbolized by the Sea Goat, a mountain goat with the tail of a fish or dolphin. And so, ancient mountain goddesses are included in Capricorn, along with goddesses who embody structure, organization, time or duration, endings, the dark of winter, and the wisdom of old age.

JANUARY I

White Tara

ETERNITY

White Tara (TAR-ah), called She of the White Lotus, is one of the manifestations of the Great Goddess Tara, who originated in India as a Hindu goddess. Tara has 108 names and many aspects or qualities. Worship of Tara was incorporated into Buddhism; she is Buddhism's most revered female bodhisattva. Her name means "star" in Sanskrit and also "she who brings forth life." White Tara is a three-eyed goddess of the day and is pictured with the wheel of time on her chest. She travels across the ocean of existence in a celestial boat, and her countenance is filled with love and compassion.

As Yeshe Dawa, or Moon of Primordial Awareness, she was a princess from millions of years ago who attained *bodhichitta*, the "awakened heart." She resolved to be incarnated only in female form until all the wounds of humanity are healed. Then, as the embodiment of Tara, she will manifest the supreme *bodhi*, or spirit of enlightenment in the world. In Japan, temple bells are rung 108 times in her honor at midnight on New Year's Eve to help counteract humanity's sins and hasten her manifestation of enlightenment.

CONTEMPLATION

As the eternally revolving wheel of the seasons starts the cycle of the calendar again, I set my sights on noble endeavors and vow to serve.

Chomolungma

DEVOTION

Chomolungma (cho-mo-LUNG-mah) is the Nepalese goddess embodied by the mountain we now call Everest. Her name is the original name of the mountain, bestowed by the indigenous people who live there. She is the goddess of the mountain itself and is considered to be the mother of the world, since she reaches so close to heaven. Chomolungma is the consciousness that abides through countless eons. When we approach her, or what looks like a mountain to us, we should adopt an attitude of devotion.

Today, when native Sherpas accompany those who would climb to the summit of the twenty-nine-thousand-foot mountain, one of the highest on earth, they pray and string colorful flags, honoring her at every stage of the ascent. They are Buddhists whose relationship with this austere goddess is one of humility and deep respect for the challenges she presents.

CONTEMPLATION

*I climb to the peak of the mountains of my life
in a spirit of humility and vigilance.*

Konohana Sakuya Hime

CHARACTER

Konohana Sakuya Hime (koh-no-HAH-na sah-KOO-yah hee-may) is the Shinto goddess of Mount Fuji in Japan. Her name means "blooming flower princess." Fuji is the tallest and most famous mountain in this country of volcanic islands. The serenity of the snowcapped mountain symbolizes the peace that comes only in meditation, when the restless activity of the mind is stilled. But of course this stillness is broken at times by the powerful eruptions of human life.

Her myth tells of her husband's jealousy and his doubt about her faithfulness. To prove her innocence, she entered into a fire while pregnant with their unborn son and emerged unscathed. As a result, fire ceremonies are performed each year. The people light flames on altars in their homes, and torches in public ceremonies, to honor Konohana Sakuya Hime. Women also call upon her to ease the pain of childbirth.

CONTEMPLATION

*By quieting my mind, I can still the quakes
and reverberations of my unruly consciousness.*

JANUARY 4

Ninhursag

TALENT

Ninhursag (nin-HER-sag) is a Sumerian creator and mother goddess who is one of the seven major deities of Sumer worshipped five thousand years ago. Her name means "lady of the sacred mountain," and she is generally depicted with a horned headdress and tiered skirt similar to those of the goddesses of Crete. She was the tutelary goddess to several Sumerian rulers who called themselves "children of Ninhursag."

Ninhursag, sometimes along with Marduk, chief god of the Babylonian pantheon, molded the first humans out of clay or mud. This myth precedes the much-later, similar biblical account. She shaped Enkidu to be the rival of the hero Gilgamesh. Some stories say she also gave birth to Gilgamesh. She created all vegetation and was also a goddess of childbirth. Serpents were sacred to her as symbols of continual regeneration.

CONTEMPLATION

I am the sculptor of my future and the weaver of my destiny.

Jord

STRENGTH

Jord (yord) is a Norse or Teutonic goddess who was worshipped on the tops of mountains, where it is believed she once mated with the sky, bringing heaven to earth. *Jord* is the word for the earth in the old Norse language, so this powerful goddess may have embodied all the strength and endurance of our planet. Her father was thought to be an ancient giant, so Jord, as befits the earth, is considered a giantess.

Some stories say she is a wife of the Norse god Odin and the rival of his other wife, Frigg. She was the mother of Thor, the god of thunder and lightning. This makes Jord an important figure in Norse cosmology, as she gave birth to thunder, lightning, and the rain that follows, fertilizing the fields and making all life on earth, which is her body, possible.

CONTEMPLATION

*If I close my eyes and open my imagination,
I can feel I am as big as the whole earth.*

La Befana

DUTY

La Befana (lah bay-FAH-nah) is the Italian Lady of the Twelfth Night, January 6, and the Feast of the Epiphany, which is twelve days from December 25. Her name has been corrupted from the original Italian, *epifania*, which means "epiphany." In the Christian tradition this date is when the Magi visited the infant Jesus. The goddess La Befana visits every child in Italy on the night before January 6, filling stockings with candy. And in a very familiar theme, bad children are said to get coal instead. La Befana is usually depicted as an old woman who rides through the sky on a broom, not a sleigh, and it is often said she will also sweep the house clean when she visits.

The legend of La Befana tells how the Magi asked her for directions to Bethlehem while on their journey following the star. They spent a night with her and invited her to join them. Although she declined to make the journey, she was made the symbolic mother of every Italian child. Between December 25 and January 6, a Roman festival takes place, during which toys, candles, and charcoal are sold.

CONTEMPLATION

*Sometimes the wisdom of ages comes cloaked
in simple garb, bearing priceless gifts.*

Parvati

RENUNCIATION

Parvati (PAR-vah-tee) is a Hindu goddess also called She of the Mountains, especially the mountain Annapurna, which is located in central Nepal and is the tenth-highest peak in the world. Parvati is a consort of Shiva who won his affection through acts of devotion and self-denial. Shiva is the third aspect in the Hindu trinity that consists of Krisha, the creator; Vishnu, the sustainer; and Shiva, the destroyer. Parvati's practice caused her body to become so pure it developed a golden glow. She is the mother of Ganesha, the beloved Hindu elephant-headed god, and is revered for her obedient nature, her loyalty, and her kindness to those in need.

It is said in the *Soundarya Lahiri*, which means "waves of beauty," a famous spiritual book about the goddess, that Parvati is the source of all power in the universe, and that Lord Shiva derives all his power from her. The energy of her sacrifice and renunciation is said to be transformed into a blessing for humanity.

CONTEMPLATION

*Where can I unleash untold power through
a conscious act of renunciation?*

JANUARY 8

The Fates

DESTINY

The Fates, or Moirai in Greek, are goddesses of fate, which was thought to be fixed. Destiny, on the other hand, could be altered by choice or acts of will. The Fates are three daughters of the goddess Nyx, whose name means "night." The daughters are called Clotho, meaning "spinner"; Lachesis, "apportioner"; and Atroposy, "cutter." Their names suggest their roles in casting the fate of a mortal. Clotho spins the material of the thread, Lachesis decides the length of life, and Atroposy cuts the thread and seals the fate. In myths, the Fates are often shown in opposition to Zeus, which hints at their remarkable power. They assisted Hermes, Greek god of writing and the divine messenger, with the invention of the alphabet. As the Roman Parcae, their Latin names are Decima, Para, and Nona.

The Norns are three Norse goddesses of destiny who are similar to the Fates. They are Urd, meaning "fate"; Verdandi, "necessity"; and Skuld, "being." Sometimes called the Wyrd Sisters, they lived beneath the roots of Yggdrasil, the great World Tree, which grows at the very center of the cosmos. The Norns controlled the destinies of both deities and humans, as well as overseeing the unchanging laws of the universe. Each person's life was one string in their loom, and the length of the string determined the length of the person's life.

CONTEMPLATION

I make the most of the portion allotted to me today.

Paivatar

RELEASE

Paivatar (pie-VA-tar), a Finnish goddess of light, appears in Finland's national epic poem, the *Kalevala*. The *Kalevala* describes her as "residing in heaven, resplendent on a shaft-bow of the sky." Finnish myths, told as oral poems, date back many centuries. Part of Paivatar's myth is similar to that of the Japanese Amaterasu, and it tells of the annual release of the sun from the cave where her mother, a powerful sorceress named Louhi, holds her captive while she passes her tests of initiation. Courage and cleverness are required to win this annual battle. These stories promised the annual return of light during the dark times of the year and contained the deeper message that strength of character would eventually bring enlightenment.

Paivatar is a solar virgin, a solitary principle of light without a mate. She is the daughter of the sun and the arctic cold, and she spins daylight from her perch on the arch of the rainbow. She possesses a silver reed, from which she spins the threads of destiny, and a golden shuttle, with which she weaves a glorious cloth of gold from threads of daylight. Paivatar's work is similar to that of her cognate, the Hindu goddess Parvati, who spins the colored threads of fate.

CONTEMPLATION

*Do I hold my own brilliance captive
in a cave of my own creation?*

Nott

DARKNESS

Nott is a Norse goddess who is seen as the personification of the night. The daughter of the giant called Norvi, Nott had several marriages, each of which produced a child. The stories vary, and the relationships can be confusing, but Nott is usually identified as the mother of Jord, the earth, but sometimes the earth is Nott's sister. Dagr, the day, is Nott's son, but sometimes Dagr is feminine and her daughter. Nott rides in a black chariot pulled by a dark horse named Hrimfaxi, meaning "frosty mane." Frozen dew, which covers the ground in a white sheet, is said to drip from his mane as they gallop across the land.

Dagr, the day, rides around the world in a chariot of light, and the foam from the chariot horse, named Skinfaxi, brings the next day's dawn. Both Nott and Dagr circle the earth, pulled by their magic horses, as the cycle of light and dark shifts, bringing night and day in turn.

CONTEMPLATION

In the deep dark of winter,
I turn within and learn to know myself.

Louhi

CRYSTALLIZATION

Louhi (LOU-vee) is a goddess of Finland and Lapland. Her realm in the Arctic North is called Pohjola in the *Kalevala*, an epic poem compiled from Finnish folklore. Her name means "magic" and also refers to a trance or alternative state of consciousness. The people who live in this part of the world were often feared for their shamanic powers. Anthropological research suggests that the original shamans were female, so it's no surprise that Louhi is a powerful sorceress who can shapeshift and cast spells.

Louhi is sometimes depicted as a winged creature and, like other goddesses of power, is often cast in a negative light. The more powerful a goddess was, the more she was feared and maligned as the patriarchy increased in power. In the *Kalevala*, Louhi challenged one of her daughter's suitors to forge a *sampo*, a magic mill that could continuously grind salt, flour, and gold. Then a hero challenged Louhi for the priceless artifact, and the drama of the tale unfolded. Despite many tests, Louhi managed to keep the mill.

CONTEMPLATION

*The mill of my life grinds out grain and salt,
as well as the gold of my heart's desire.*

Nortia

RULES

Nortia (NOR-tee-ah) is a goddess of the Etruscans, who inhabited the part of Italy now known as Tuscany. The meaning of her name is linked to both the word *north* and the direction, the symbolic place of wisdom and the direction of the spiritual quest. Nortia had a temple in the Etruscan city of Velsna.

Her symbol is a large nail, which was ritually hammered into a block of wood on the New Year to symbolize the idea of ending, or permanently establishing, what had passed in the previous year. When the hammer fell and the nail sank into the wood, the situation, or fate, was seen to be unalterable. The rules could not be changed. What had gone before was no longer in motion or in play, and a new fortune governed the future, or the new year to come. The custom survived into Roman times in the temple dedicated to Juno, Jupiter, and Minerva.

CONTEMPLATION

The universe operates according to laws. Once a course is set in motion, it's wise to make the best of it.

STRUCTURE

Seshat (sah-shet)* is the Egyptian goddess of architecture, sacred structures, books, and records. She recorded the name of each new pharaoh on the sacred Persea tree at the time the king took the throne. As goddess of writing and recording, she is called Mistress of Books. She was also known as Lady of Builders in the ritual called "drawing the cord" that she performed with the assistance of her priests. The ritual precisely aligned the axes of Egyptian temples to certain stars when the foundations of the structures were laid.

Seshat is the wife of the god Thoth, who was known as Hermes to the Greeks, and she is also credited with inventing mathematics and hieroglyphics. Seshat measures the cord that determines the length of a person's life, making her also a goddess of fate. Her iconic headdress is a seven-point star, a geometric figure that has to be drawn by trial and error and that is not an equal division of the circle. This symbol, as a result, is said to be an emblem of spiritual work.

CONTEMPLATION

As I lay the foundation for what I desire to build,
I set my sights on the stars.

---

* In pronunciation guides with no capitalized syllable, each syllable is given equal emphasis.

Bertha

KINDNESS

Bertha, known as the White Lady, is a goddess of the New Year who is identified by various names in the snowy climate of Holland, Germany, and Scandinavia. She was thought to have a somewhat homely appearance, but Bertha was revered for her inner qualities, especially her kindness and sweet nature. Because Bertha's true beauty was recognized as internal, it is everlasting and evergreen.

One of Bertha's responsibilities was to watch over the souls of unborn children, who are called the Heimchen. She also takes special care of the souls of babies who die before baptism. Bertha is sometimes seen as the feminine form of the Norse god Odin, and then she is called Frau Gode.

CONTEMPLATION

A woman's path to enlightenment is a journey of unconditional love and compassion.

JANUARY 15

Amalthea

SUSTENANCE

Amalthea (ah-mall-THEE-ah) is a goddess of ancient Crete. In later myth she was a magical nanny goat who nursed Zeus in a cave at Lyktos on the island of Crete. When Zeus grew up, he broke off one of her horns and an abundance of milk and precious gifts poured out of it, providing sustenance. This is the origin of the cornucopia, which was said to contain enough substance to feed all of humanity. The story foreshadows the later myths about the unicorn.

In other versions, one of Amalthea's horns flows with nectar and the other with ambrosia, the divine substance that bestows immortality upon the gods. Subsequently in myth, Amalthea, with only one horn, was transformed into a collection of stars and became the constellation Capricorn, where she is eternally suspended between earth and sky.

CONTEMPLATION

I recognize the abundance of support and the unseen sustenance that continually flows into my life.

Skadi

ACCEPTANCE

Skadi (SKA-dee) is a Scandinavian goddess of winter and mountains who is now also one of the moons of Saturn. Her name is the origin of that of the Scandinavian peninsula, and she is also equated with the darkness and cold of winter, the shadow time, and the state of hibernation associated with the dark time of the year. It is said that she gives hunters the gift of the bow and the knowledge of how to use it wisely. Skadi is a giantess with a fierce side, just like winter, and because she is a goddess of such a stark place, where in the past survival could be assured only through hunting, blood rites were believed to be necessary to propitiate her.

Skadi's myth tells of her having to choose, while blindfolded, a god to be her mate. Since she could see only the feet of her prospective mates, she picked the one with the feet that looked the strongest. It proved to be an unhappy alliance, as she and her partner had nothing in common. Her next choice was a god of winter, with whom she could share her joys. We must each face our true nature and bring what's hidden into the light.

CONTEMPLATION

In the darkness of winter,
I go deep within to face my shadows.

Uma

DEDICATION

Uma, the Bright One, is a form of the crone aspect of the Great Goddess in India. Her name means "light." She is a goddess of spiritual wisdom, and the experiences she brings are intended to provide wisdom. Ironically, she is known as the Mother of the Dark Season, since the light of this time is internal. Uma is also a goddess of the Himalayan mountains, where she dwells with the spirit of her sister, Ganga, who became the great Ganges River of India.

Uma is depicted as golden and said to embody beauty and wisdom. Sometimes she is seen as a mediator between heaven and earth. Uma is said to have inspired all the gods with her dedication. She is also said to be the reincarnation of Parvati, who burned herself in a sacrificial fire.

CONTEMPLATION

I sit in silence and cultivate a single point of stillness like the silence of a mountaintop.

Aega

SHIELD

Aega (EE-jah) is a pre-Hellenic goddess from the region that later became Greece. She is the daughter of Gaia and Helios, earth and sun, and her title is Daughter of the Sun. Her name means both "gust of wind" and "goat." In some stories, Aega took the form of a goat, and, in her goat form, she was a nurse to the infant Zeus. She is also a goddess of domesticated animals. Her sisters are Circe and Pasiphae, and together the three of them form an ancient manifestation of the triple goddess. This archetype of maiden, mother, and crone appeared in cultures around the world long before the male trinity of the Bible. When the Titans attacked Mount Olympus, Gaia protected Aega by hiding her in a cave to conceal her beauty and blinding light.

By the time Zeus took over as the king of heaven, he had a sacred shield called the Aegis, which was made from a goat hide. Some stories say it was the skin of Aega, retrieved after she had been slain in a battle. *Aegis* is also the word for "goatskin." The Aegis was a symbol of great power and was formerly worn by priestesses of Athena, before Zeus took possession of it. Aega also appeared as a concealing storm cloud that surrounded Zeus's famous thunderbolt. Later she was placed in the sky as the star Capella, the Little She Goat.

CONTEMPLATION

Truth and illumination are powerful forms of protection shielding me from darkness.

JANUARY 19

Xmucane

TIME

Xmucane (SCHMU-kah-nay) is a Mayan corn goddess. She is called Grandmother of the Sun or Grandmother of Light. According to the Popol Vuh, the great Mayan creation epic, Xmucane, together with her partner, Xpiayoc, created the first humans. Xmucane and Xpiayoc are the oldest of the Mayan gods and are considered to be the divine grandparents of the Maya. They molded the first people from white and yellow corn, then Xmucane made a broth that brought the people to life.

Xmucane and her mate are also the day keepers of the Popol Vuh and, as a result, are connected with the Mayan calendar and the principle of time. Although they are often mentioned as a couple, Xmucane is the primary character in the mythic interaction with the famous Mayan Hero Twins, a story in which she is called Grandmother. Like other great crone goddesses, Xmucane is associated with the waning moon and dark cycles of time.

CONTEMPLATION

Give us good life,
Grandmother of the Sun,
Grandmother of the Light,
Let there be dawn, let the light come.

— FROM THE MAYA DAWN PRAYER,
IN *Popol Vuh: The Maya Book of the Dawn of Life*

AQUARIUS GODDESSES
The Spiral

WHAT SEEMS LIKE A STRAIGHT LINE
IS A NEVER-ENDING SPIRAL

quarius is a fixed air sign. In the Aquarian stage, the unfolding sequence of the zodiac is expressed in the form of group consciousness. During this stage it is possible for human beings to be unified by a common ideal. Aquarians look for truth in all things and desire to unite with others on a universal level. Aquarians are forward thinking, and they can be mental pioneers, blazing conceptual trails toward new utopian possibilities that people of more earthbound signs can't envision. However, this energy is mentally fixed, so Aquarians tend to see things only their way and may also rebel against the status quo or object in principle to structures that don't seem to work or that appear to them to be outmoded.

Aquarius is traditionally symbolized by the Water Bearer and said to rule the ancient discipline of astrology. The goddess sign for Aquarius is the Spiral, which can be seen in hurricanes, pine cones, sea shells, and the whirling galaxies of deep space. The spiraling motion represents the spiraling nature of reality, which eternally spins and evolves. The spiral also represents the cycles of nature and the sky, including the arms of our Milky Way, which invite us to look up and beyond our limited scope and widen our view. Aquarius goddesses are connected to the sky, space, and knowledge of the alchemical principle of "Above." This refers to the realm of super-consciousness and the higher mind — the domain of abstract thought. Aquarius goddesses reach toward heaven and the realm of the higher mind, connecting to the stars, celestial themes, and the ancient wisdom of astrology.

JANUARY 20

Hebe

ATTITUDE

Hebe (HEE-bee) is the Greek goddess of eternal youth and the freshness of spring. Sometimes she is called the Downy One, as she represents the downy, green shoots of spring. Her sanctuary was generously decorated with cuttings of ivy. Hebe was the original cupbearer to the Olympian gods, an important position, as the magic potion contained in the cup was ambrosia, the elixir of immortality. She also guarded the Tree of Life, which bore magic apples, the fruit that produced the nectar of immortality. Heroes could become immortal simply by living in her garden.

Hebe, like other goddesses who lost their once-powerful status, was later replaced. In this case, the beautiful young male Ganymede, a goatherd Zeus became enamored of, usurped her position. Afterward, Hebe was placed in the stars, becoming the constellation of Aquarius.

CONTEMPLATION

*I choose to be playful today and revel
in a sense of childlike wonder.*

JANUARY 21

Yngona

FORESIGHT

Yngona (ing-OH-nah) is a Danish goddess whose sacred day is January 21. She is a crone goddess whose role is to destroy old and outworn forms, and she removes what should not proceed into the lengthening days of the new year. Her festival came at the point where the sun moves into the sign of Aquarius. She was later Christianized, becoming Saint Agnes; the root of the name Agnes means "sacred." The original goddess, Yngona, must have been potent, and her worship well entrenched, as Saint Agnes is one of only seven females, excluding Mary, who are commemorated by name in the canon of the Catholic Mass.

Young girls still pray to her as Saint Agnes, performing rituals on the eve of her special day to obtain visions of their future mates. This custom was immortalized in a poem by Keats. Ironically, in the lore of Saint Agnes the martyr, she was beheaded for refusing to marry, and yet she is now invoked by virgins looking for mates and by victims of rape to aid in their healing.

CONTEMPLATION

*If I could see into my future,
would I change my present course?*

Bau

SPACIOUSNESS

Bau is a Babylonian sky goddess. She is called Goddess of Dark Waters, a reference to the night sky. Bau may be the predecessor of the goddess Tiamat, as the latter was called Eldest of Heaven. Bau's name actually means "space." She was invoked to bless the crops because her goodwill was considered essential for a bountiful harvest. She was also seen as a goddess of the dog, which may link her cosmologically, like the Egyptian Isis, to Sirius, the Dog Star.

Although Bau was thought to have healing powers, she was also called upon to curse those who trampled the rights of others. A prayer to Bau discovered by archaeologists, a translation of which appears in *Myths of Babylon and Assyria* by Donald A. Mackenzie, was meant to be said on the occasion of a lunar eclipse and entreated her to counteract any evil influences caused by such an eclipse. One line reads, "O, Bau, mighty lady who dwellest in the bright heavens."

CONTEMPLATION

All the stars I can see on a clear, dark night represent but an infinitesimal fraction of the galaxies in our universe.

Tanith

HEAVEN

Tanith (TAN-it) is a Phoenician goddess who was the chief deity of Carthage, where her temple was called the Shrine of the Heavenly Virgin. Ba'al-Hammon is her consort, but she was represented as being superior to him. Tanith is a celestial goddess who rules the sun, moon, and stars. Some scholars associate her with the Egyptian Hathor in her role as a goddess of light.

Called Queen of the Stars, Tanith was symbolized by a triangle topped by an orb and a crescent. The palm tree was another of her symbols, as it is a life-giving tree of the desert. Many inscriptions have been found with her name, and she has been called Parent of All Things and Highest of the Deities. The Romans destroyed Carthage, but they still called Tanith Heavenly Goddess and took her rites to Rome, where they pictured her with wings and a zodiac above her head.

CONTEMPLATION

Look up at the sky so you can bring heaven to earth.

Uni

WHOLENESS

Uni (OO-nee) is the supreme and cosmic goddess of the Etruscans, and the goddess of the city of Perugia, Italy. Uni's scope is so vast that we can think of her as the "Uni-verse," the one who contains everything and is the source of all. The Etruscans lived in what is now northern Italy about four hundred years before the Romans. They were strongly influenced by the Greeks and Phoenicians. Uni is thought to be the predecessor of the Latin Juno and is also compared to the Greek Hera. Scholars have noted that her name sounds the same as *yoni*, a term for the feminine sexual organ and gateway of life.

Uni, her husband, and their son formed a great trinity. In earlier times it would have been the goddess in her triple form, the threefold manifestation of maiden, mother, and crone, who would have composed this trinity. The sky goddess Uni, not her husband, threw thunderbolts across the sky. She also gave blessings on the occasion of new births.

CONTEMPLATION

*Can I imagine my heart growing big enough
to contain the whole universe?*

Cliodna

RESONANCE

Cliodna (KLEE-nah) is an Irish and Scottish goddess and is one of the Tuatha De Danann, the Celtic people of the goddess Danu. Cliodna is a deity of beauty who also rules the pattern that recurs in ocean waves. It is said that every ninth wave represents her, and that this wave is stronger and higher than the rest in its cycle. The wave symbol of Aquarius can be felt in this image.

Cliodna can shape-shift into a wren; birds are Celtic symbols of the afterlife. She is often accompanied by three birds who eat magic apples and are able to heal the sick with their birdsong. Their magic apple tree has silver leaves and bears golden fruit. Cliodna is also the goddess of copper and possesses an emerald cup that can turn water into wine. In her myths, she lured human lovers to the fairy realm, from which they could not return. As a result, she was ultimately sent to the Otherworld, where she now has dominion over the afterlife.

CONTEMPLATION

Everything moves in resonating and repeating cycles,
breathing in and breathing out.

Lemkechen

FIXITY

Lemkechen (lem-KEK-en) is a stellar goddess of the Berber people of North Africa who call themselves Amazigh. She lives in the polestar and is seen as standing perfectly still, holding the reins of a young camel as its mother is milked. We know these camel constellations as Ursa Minor, the Little Bear, and Ursa Major, the Great Bear. Lemkechen believes that the other stars want to kill her, so she remains fixed while the rest of the sky moves around her.

The Amazigh people regard Lemkechen as a great mother goddess. Their culture is ancient, dating back more than five thousand years. These African people are mostly Muslim now, but they still practice some of the old ways. People who live in the desert revere the stars and also believe in magical spirits of the desert, called djinns. The English word *genie* comes from *djinn*. A geological formation on the planet Venus has been named Lemkechen Dorsa.

CONTEMPLATION

*What is the fixed point of orientation
around which my whole life revolves?*

Zigarun

KNOWLEDGE

Zigarun (zig-ah-ROON) is an Akkadian goddess whose name means "heaven" or "mother who has begotten heaven and earth." She has dominion over the watery abyss that was called Deep Apsu, or the House of Knowledge. In Babylonian and Sumerian myth, this was the source of all things. The root of the word *apsu*, a deep abyss, expresses the same concept that appears in the biblical book of Genesis, where God is said to "brood upon the waters of the deep."

Zigarun was also known in Babylon as Apsu. As time passed, Apsu became a male god and was portrayed as the dragon mate of the goddess Tiamat. But in the earliest versions of this story, Apsu was feminine in nature and the source of all things that emerged from the watery abyss of potential knowledge. The later male god Apsu appeared in the Enuma Elish, or The Seven Tablets of Creation, the Babylonian creation epic, circa 600 BCE. Cisterns of holy water were also called *apsu* and were kept for ritual purposes in courtyards in Assyrian and Babylonian temples.

CONTEMPLATION

*If I don't have the wisdom of a loving heart,
what does it matter if I gain all the knowledge in the world?*

The Pleiades

SISTERHOOD

The Pleiades (PLEE-ah-dees) are the seven daughters of the Titan Atlas and the sea nymph Pleione. The sisters were born in Arcadia and followed Artemis the huntress in her escapades. Some scholars say Pleione was not a mere sea nymph but was actually the goddess Aphrodite. When Atlas was forced to carry the world on his shoulders, this left Orion the hunter free to chase after the sisters. To keep them safe, Zeus first transformed them into doves and then placed them as stars in the sky.

All the Pleiades consorted with other gods to produce divine offspring, except for Merope, who consorted with a mere mortal and, as a result, shines less brightly than her sisters. The Pleiades star cluster is known and revered around the world in a wide range of myths. As stars, the Pleiades were central to the Babylonians' agricultural year. To the Egyptians, the Pleiades were the seven Hathors, judges of humans.

CONTEMPLATION

I rejoice and honor the priceless treasure
of sisterhood in my life.

Nephele

DISCRIMINATION

Nephele (neh-FELL-ee), whose name comes from *nephos*, which means "cloud," is the Greek goddess whom Zeus, the sky god, created out of clouds. Zeus meant for Nephele to be an exact replica of Hera, his wife. Hera had alerted Zeus that a certain king had made advances and wanted to ravish her. Zeus needed to be sure before he acted, so he molded Nephele to serve as a decoy. King Ixion, who indeed had evil intentions, was fooled by the ruse and raped Nephele. This cruel act gave birth to the entire race of centaurs, which fell as drops of rain from a thundershower on Mount Pelion.

Ixion was subsequently punished, chained to a wheel of fire for eternity, but it was too late — the rapacious and rowdy centaurs had already been born. Nephele later married Athnmas, the king of Orchomenus in Greek myth, and gave birth to twins. The family subsequently figured in the famous myth of Jason and the Argonauts and their quest for the golden fleece.

CONTEMPLATION

I hone my perception so I see what is truly there and am not fooled by illusion.

JANUARY 30

Ixchel

MEMORY

Ixchel (ISH-ell) is a Mayan goddess of water and rain. Like many goddesses, she also ruled over childbirth and weaving, and so she is involved with fate. Called Old Woman of the Moon, she represents the wisdom of the waning crescent. She is also called Grandmother, and she is still honored by the Maya. The origin of the name Ixchel is uncertain, although the word *chel* in Mayan can mean "rainbow." In the *Dresden Codex*, one of the few surviving Mayan texts, she is depicted emptying a large water vessel, which is thought to bring about a great flood. Perhaps the rainbow is formed in the water she pours from her vessel.

Mayan women who desired a fruitful marriage would make pilgrimages to her shrine on the island of Cozumel. A smaller nearby island was named Isla de las Mujeres, the "Island of Women," because statues of Ixchel were found there. Ixchel has dominion over the ritual of the sweat bath, which women used before and after childbirth to purify themselves.

CONTEMPLATION

Today I can seek out a grandmother and drink deeply of her memories and experiences.

JANUARY 31

Nut

AWAKENING

Nut (noot) is the Egyptian sky goddess and one of the original nine deities. She is the mother of both Isis and Osiris. With her body, she physically supports the sky, and paintings on the ceilings of temples picture her with her hands and feet on earth and her body forming the arch, or vault, of heaven. Her name means "night," and she is represented by the starry night sky. Nut was also seen as a great cow whose milk created the Milky Way. As mentioned in the preface, ancient Egyptians said every woman was a *nutrit*, a "little goddess," after the great goddess Nut.

All the stars and heavenly bodies were seen as Nut's children. She gave birth to them and swallowed them again in an ever-repeating cycle. One of her more illustrious titles is She Who Holds a Thousand Souls, and one of the more mundane and amusing epithets is Pig Who Eats Her Piglets. Nut also swallowed Ra, the sun, at each sunset and gave birth to him again each dawn. Osiris, god of resurrection, was said to use a sacred ladder, one of Nut's symbols, to ascend to her domain in the sky.

CONTEMPLATION

*Each night brings another forgetting, and each dawn
a new promise, a new chance to remake my world.*

Goddesses for Every Day

Brigid

BECOMING

Brigid (breed), meaning "bright" or "fiery arrow," is a goddess of the Irish Celts. She was Brigantia to the English, Bride to the Scots, and Brigandu in Celtic France. Devotion to her was so pervasive that the Catholic Church converted her to Saint Brigid and canonized the fictional saint, complete with all her goddess attributes. One legend says Brigid invented both whistling and the sound of mourning called keening.

Brigid is a goddess of healing, metalsmithing, poetry, and music. As the muse of poets, she is called the High One, describing the realm from which inspiration comes. Her feast is Imbolc, or Candlemas to Christians, which marks the halfway point between the winter solstice and the spring equinox. At Imbolc, the sap begins to run in the trees, and buds form as the energy of life flows again. Groundhog Day is a dim reminder of former ceremonies honoring the shift in the balance of light and dark. On the eve of Imbolc, women hung a pure white wool cloth outside on a tree. The cloth was believed to absorb the energy of the goddess, and, sanctified in this way, it would serve as an altar cloth or special talisman.

CONTEMPLATION

Like a pure white cloth of pure potential, I feel Brigid's energy flowing within me today as the seasons and inner cycles of life open, becoming outer expression.

Dou-Mu

CONSTANCY

Dou-Mu (dow-moo) is a Chinese mother and sky goddess. Her name means "mother of the great wagon," and the seven stars of the Big Dipper are her children. The Chinese pictured this group of stars within the larger constellation of Ursa Major as a wagon or a plow. Dou-Mu supervises a register in which the life and death of each person are recorded. She is said to save people who call on her from many evils and troubles. Depicted in art as seated on a lotus throne, she has four heads, each facing one of the four cardinal directions. Each head has three eyes, a concept that seems related to the twelve signs of the zodiac, and she has eight far-reaching arms.

Dou-Mu is an important deity in the Taoist hierarchy. There are famous temples dedicated to her in China at the White Cloud monastery in Beijing, and at Shandong, Qian Mountain, and Yunnan.

CONTEMPLATION

I behold the constancy of the northern stars,
which eternally circle the vault of heaven
and anchor my sense of direction.

Ha Hai-i Wuthi

CONSCIOUSNESS

Ha Hai-i Wuthi (hah high-ee WOO-thee) is a spirit being of the Hopi. She is called Pour Water Woman, and she holds a water jug that has been blessed in ceremony. For a culture that depends on life-giving waters and asks for rain in virtually every prayer, this blessing is paramount. She pours out her many blessings and the water of life on humanity. She is seen as nourishing all beings on every level of existence, whether they are the *katsinas*, the beneficent Hopi spirit beings who live in the San Francisco Peaks in Arizona, or other forms of life, including plants, animals, humans, and even the rocks of the earth. The Hopi see her as the spiritual mother of the *katsinas*.

Ha Hai-i Wuthi is important in several of the seasonal ceremonies performed on the Hopi mesas, especially the bean dance and the night dance. She is carved in the form of a traditional three-dimensional *katsina*, and she is also formed as a flat cradle doll, which is the first gift given to a new infant, placed near the baby to protect it. This same sort of cradle doll is also placed in the cages of captive eagles.

CONTEMPLATION

*The quality of my life is determined by the positive
or negative state of my consciousness,
just as the quality of water is affected by mountain snows.*

Pali Kongju

LIMITATION

The Korean goddess Pali Kongju (pah-lee KONG-goo) is the lineal ancestor of all the shamans, or Mudang, in Korea today. Most of these shamans are women, and they go through a complicated and difficult initiation process. The Mudang see themselves as disenfranchised descendants of the once-powerful royal houses of Korea of the distant past. Pali Kongju was the seventh daughter of a king who desired only one son. Unwanted, she was cast into the sea but miraculously survived. She traveled to the North Pole to collect magical water from the westernmost part of the sky.

Pali Kongju's myth is a difficult rite-of-passage story in which she undertook the most important quest, usually performed by the eldest son. Against all odds and many obstacles, she fulfilled her quest and returned to heal her parents and her people. Today Pali Kongju still resides in the heights of heaven and comes when invoked to rescue souls from the gates of hell.

CONTEMPLATION

Whatever obstacles have been placed in my path because I am a woman, victory over them makes me stronger than before.

FEBRUARY 5

Aataensic

LETTING GO

Aataensic (EE-yah-tah-HEN-sick) is a great sky goddess of the Huron people, who originally lived along the Great Lakes. Their creation myth tells of a time before the earth or humans existed, and of Aataensic falling through a hole in the sky. Some versions say she had married a powerful sorcerer, one who became jealous because her magic was stronger, and she was trying to escape him. Other stories say she was searching for medicine for her husband when she fell. She tried to hold on to a tree branch but eventually had to let go, allowing herself to fall into the darkness. With the help of two geese she landed on the back of a great turtle renowned for its wisdom. All the animals brought roots and mud to create what became Turtle Island, or the earth, which the Hurons believe is the center of everything.

Aataensic was pregnant when she fell through the hole in the sky and eventually gave birth to twin boys, one good and one evil. One son gives corn, life, and good weather, and the other causes death and misfortune. Aataensic has the ability to become a beautiful young girl whenever she desires and can still appear at ceremonies disguised as a human.

CONTEMPLATION

No matter how frightening the leap into the void may be, there is always a place to land.

Anahita

PURIFICATION

Anahita (an-a-HEE-tah) is an ancient mother goddess from Persia, in what is now Iran. Her name means the "immaculate one." Rivers and lakes were sacred to her, as they were thought to be the waters of birth. She is also a sky goddess who has domain over fertilizing waters and the great spring among the stars, the Milky Way, which was thought to be the origin of all earthly rivers. Anahita was called Mother of the Gods and has a mythic link to Fatima, who is recognized in Islam.

According to the Avesta, the holy texts of Zoroastrianism, Anahita and Ahura Mazda conferred kingship on mortals. In Iran, beautiful rock art reliefs that depict such scenes remain along what was once the ancient Silk Road through the Middle East. Anahita purified the seed of all males, sanctified women's wombs, and purified their breast milk. Women called upon her during childbirth for protection. She carries a water jar, and her crown has eight points, like the phases of the moon, with one hundred diamond stars. She wears a golden mantle and a beautiful gold necklace.

CONTEMPLATION

I can imagine bathing in the purifying waters of the Milky Way, the cosmic river of stars.

Ananke

NECESSITY

Ananke (eh-NUN-key) is the Greek goddess of necessity and is said to have emerged self-formed from primeval Chaos in serpentine form. Her mate is Kronos, the principle of time. Together they coiled themselves around the cosmic egg and constricted their coils until existence split into sky, earth, and ocean. Their spiraling embrace drives the rotating cycles of the heavens and the movement of time itself. The ancient myth of the cosmic egg anticipates modern science in the sense that it describes the universe as once having been contained in a very small space, a singularity. Ananke represents what modern physicists see as the unavoidable response to what is called the "big crunch" of the previous universe, before the "big bang" that began this one.

Ananke was worshipped by the Orphic mystery cult and was perceived as the representation of a necessity, or of a course of action that could not be altered. The Greek playwright Euripides, famous for his tragedies, believed that Ananke was the most powerful of all deities because she rules the only real choices we have in certain circumstances. She was mother of the Fates, the goddesses believed to influence our destiny. Ananke is now also the thirteenth moon of Jupiter.

CONTEMPLATION

And yet the true creator is Necessity,
who is the mother of invention.

— PLATO, *The Republic*

FEBRUARY 8

Nisaba

LEARNING

Nisaba (nee-SAH-bah) is a Sumerian goddess responsible for architecture, record keeping, and writing. Nearly five thousand years ago, she was a patron goddess of scribes. She is sometimes shown in the important role of chief scribe of the goddess Nanshe. Every scribe finished his or her composition with the words "Nisaba be praised." She had a temple at Eresh called the House of Stars and had other shrines that honored her wisdom.

Nisaba had a keen knowledge of the stars and was depicted with a tablet made of lapis lazuli, which may have contained a sort of sky chart. Nisaba also possessed what has been translated as "measuring lines," with which she measured the distances of heaven. She was a tutelary deity, or teaching goddess, who instructed kings and other gods, including Babu, the son of Marduk, one of the high-ranking Sumerian gods. One image of her found at Lagash, in modern Iraq, shows her crowned, and with long, flowing hair, holding sheaves of corn and a crescent moon.

CONTEMPLATION

The words of my mouth and my pen are
as true and constant as the stars of heaven.

The Dakinis

INTENTION

Dakini (dah-KEEN-ee), or in Sanskrit, Kandroma, translates as "she who traverses space" or sometimes "sky dancer." A Dakini is not an individual goddess but a spirit of the air, according to Buddhism. Dakinis are similar to Celtic fairies and the air spirits who serve the Hindu goddess Kali. Like angels or elves, Dakinis are supernatural beings thought to act as initiators of spiritual tests, challenging our commitment. They appear at critical moments, or turning points, when our choices are paramount.

The heavenly realm of the Dakinis is called Khechari, meaning "Dakini land," a state of enlightenment achieved through specific Tantric yoga practices. There are five orders of Dakinis, and these are organized by color and attribute. Dakini priestesses, like hospice workers, take care of the dying, and they are said to take the last breath of the dying into themselves, thereby easing the dying person's transition and helping him or her to achieve a conscious death.

CONTEMPLATION

I resolve to stay the course no matter how tempting the diversion may appear to be.

Bixia Yuanjin

ADAPTABILITY

Bixia Yuanjin (BIX-ee-ah WAN-jin) is a Chinese weather goddess who lives in high places. Clouds are her special domain. One of her lovely Taoist titles is Princess of the Azure Clouds. The clouds we see overhead are thought to be guardians or signposts along the routes to temples. Rural Chinese women honor Bixia Yuanjin as they make the long ascent to her temple at the summit of Tai Shan mountain.

Bixia Yuanjin has dominion over destiny and is seen as bringing the returning light each year from the womb of the earth, just as new life emerges from a mother's womb. Clouds of incense evoke her nature, and as the incense moves, the goddess is thought to transform into different shapes.

CONTEMPLATION

The beliefs I hold in my mind should be able to change like pictures in the clouds.

Feng Po-Po

AIR

Feng Po-Po (fung PO-po) is a Chinese wind and weather goddess with the illustrious title of Madame Wind. She rides a great tiger across the sky on a path made of the clouds themselves, and she carries in her arms a large bag filled with wind. When the days are calm, it is believed that Feng Po-Po has generously gathered all the winds into her bag, but when the weather is blustery it's because she has released the contents of her bag into the sky. Sometimes she is in the mood to stir up a good storm.

Feng Po-Po is thought to embody all the manifestations of the element of air and is depicted as a wrinkled old woman. Maybe she is windblown from spending too much time in her own element and needs to experience more elemental balance.

CONTEMPLATION

*A strong wind helps me set my sail in the direction
I wish to go, but a gale can end my journey in disaster.*

Iris

ESSENCE

Iris (EYE-rus) is a Greek goddess whose physical form is the rainbow. Before Hermes/Mercury was the messenger of the gods, Iris had this role, and her words were never doubted. She was able to fly around the world, and from the heights of heaven to the depths of the sea, connecting humanity to the Divine. She is depicted in art as a beautiful young woman with golden wings, usually standing by Hera or Zeus. Like the goddess Hebe, she also served as a cupbearer to the gods, dispensing the magical elixir ambrosia that gave the gods their immortality.

Her sisters are the winged Harpies, who were once beautiful maidens, but who, like certain other goddesses, were later maligned and turned into ugly creatures. Iris's consort is Zephyrus, the west wind. She was especially loyal to the goddess Aphrodite. One of her duties was to lead the souls of deceased women to the afterlife at the Elysian fields. As a token of constant thanks, the ancient Greeks always planted purple irises on women's graves.

CONTEMPLATION

Is my life's vision colored by my negative emotions or infused with the radiance of divine light?

Ayizan

VIRTUE

Ayizan, or Ayizan Velekete (EYE-zan VELL-ah-keet), is a goddess, or *loa*, of the system called Vodun. We are more familiar with the term *Voodoo*. She is a powerful goddess and is present at the initiation ceremony called Kanzo. In fact, Ayizan is said to be Mother of All Initiates. She is imagined as a woman going to market, wearing a white dress and an apron with very deep pockets containing candles, coins, or candy to give to her children. The earthly plane of existence is seen as a great marketplace and melting pot.

Ayizan is a Mambo, a high priestess, in her religion. Most of her rites are secret because of the nature of initiation, but she is associated with cleansing, blessing, and empowering. A variety of geometric designs, called *veves*, are drawn to invoke the *loas*, who are the powerful spirit beings of Vodun. The Yoruba people of western Africa, after they were taken as slaves, usually overlaid their spirit beings with Catholic saints, and Ayizan became associated with Saint Claire.

CONTEMPLATION

When I am ready to face the truth,
the next stage of my journey will begin.

Psyche

SOUL MATES

Psyche (SIGH-key) is a Roman goddess who was said to represent the immortal soul in its quest for spiritual union with the human heart. This is epitomized in myth by Psyche's relationship with her lover, Cupid (Eros to the Greeks). Their love story seems appropriate for Valentine's Day. Psyche was a mortal more beautiful than the goddess Venus. Bewitched by Psyche's beauty, people stopped venerating Venus, and the world became barren. Cupid, Venus's son, was sent to put a spell on Psyche with one of his arrows, but he fell in love with her instead. In some versions of the story, Cupid hid her in a secret garden, where he came to her each night in darkness. Perhaps this symbolizes the incomplete nature of romantic love that lacks the conscious connection of two souls.

Psyche was curious to learn the identity of her lover, so she lit a forbidden lamp, and Cupid took flight. Instead of the male hero, as in most stories, it was Psyche who set out on a quest, following her heart. After an arduous journey filled with tests and trials, Psyche was finally reunited with her lover in the higher consciousness of heaven, satisfying her spiritual longing. They had children named Love and Delight.

CONTEMPLATION

I must first recognize the divine within myself
before I can join the divine in me with that of another,
linking heart and soul.

Ceridwen

WONDER

Ceridwen, or Keridwen (CARE-ah-dwen), is a Welsh goddess of poetic inspiration. She possessed a magic cauldron in which she stirred the heady brew of divine inspiration. With this potent concoction, she intended to make her own son the wisest and most clever bard. She left a mere mortal to guard the cauldron, however, and he accidentally consumed some of the contents when a few drops splashed on his hand. Ceridwen pursued the mortal by shape-shifting into many forms. She finally caught and consumed him, became pregnant as a result, and gave birth to the famous Welsh bard Taliesin.

Ceridwen's magic cauldron is called *amen*, and in an intriguing linguistic connection, Muslims, Christians, and Jews end their prayers with the word *amen*. To the Egyptians, Amen was the Hidden One, a deity of great power. It may be that the sound of *amen* relates to an ancient chant that invokes the hidden power symbolized by Ceridwen's cauldron.

Ceridwen's story is perhaps meant as a metaphor for the intense and sometimes painful process of creation, which unfolds when we are captured by a muse. At a deeper level, Ceridwen is a goddess of initiation, embodying the tests and trials that this entails.

CONTEMPLATION

*The cauldron of my life's experiences becomes
the hidden vessel of my transformation.*

Saraswati

WORDS

Saraswati (sa-RAH-swa-tee) is a Hindu goddess of knowledge and all aspects of literary tradition. Her name means "one who flows." In India, people worship her in libraries by offering fruit, flowers, and incense. Saraswati is credited with inventing the alphabet, speech, literature, poetry, and the complex patterns that occur in Indian music. Ironically, on her feast day complete silence is observed and no reading is allowed. Some sources say she also discovered *amrita*, the elixir of the gods that confers immortality.

In Hindu belief, it is only through the pursuit of knowledge that we can attain freedom from the wheel of rebirth. The sacred waters of Saraswati's inspiration are said to originate in the snowy heights of the Himalayas and then course down the river named for her, flowing all the way to the ocean. Saraswati is depicted as a beautiful and graceful woman with a crescent moon on her forehead, riding on the back of a peacock, called a *hamsa*. Swans are sacred to her.

CONTEMPLATION

I take care that only truth and words of power emerge from my mouth.

Crystal Woman

INSIGHT

Crystal Woman is the mythical goddess of the crystal skulls. She is said to transmit information between the dimensions, especially to medicine people. Numerous American Indian tribes, including the Maya, have stories about the skulls. These indigenous people say the skulls can speak or sing. The best-known legend says the goddess possessed thirteen sacred skulls with movable jaws, but that the skulls were separated from each other and protected by shamans until the time came for them to be rediscovered.

A few of the skulls that have been found are made of quartz and are "crystal clear." Some are life-size and made from a single piece of quartz. The origin and manner of creation of the crystal skulls are unknown and controversial, and the mystery only deepened with their investigation via modern technology. They have enigmatic properties of refraction. In 1964, scientists at Hewlett-Packard, the leaders in the manufacture of crystal oscillators at the time, said it should not be possible for the skull they examined to exist.

CONTEMPLATION

The voice of the goddess speaks
when I open my inner eye to light.

Atargatis

ORIGINALITY

Atargatis (at-ar-GATE-is) is a Syrian sky goddess usually depicted as a mermaid, since she sometimes appears in the form of a fish. Atargatis is said to have fallen from heaven in the shape of an egg, which then hatched into a woman with the tail of a fish. When she is shown as a sky goddess, her face is lightly veiled with what look like clouds, and eagles surround her head. At her temples, sacred pools were filled with oracular fish that only her priests were permitted to touch.

Eating fish or doves (her daughter, Semiramus, became a dove) was forbidden, as it still is in certain belief systems in Egypt and the Middle East. Some sources say the constellation Piscis Austrinus, the Southern Fish, whose mouth receives the waters from the urn of Aquarius, was placed in the sky to honor her. She was honored by the Romans as well, and she also appears in the Talmud.

CONTEMPLATION

I can learn to be comfortable in multiple elements,
reaching to the sky and plumbing the depths.

PISCES GODDESSES
The Grail

AN AWAKENED HEART IS FULL OF COMPASSION

*P*isces is a mutable water sign and can be seen as the universal solvent, both dissolving the boundaries of separation created by all the preceding signs and creating the fluid environment in which the seeds of a new cycle can germinate. In Pisces the sorrows and joys of others are keenly felt, and under this sign compassion is born. More than with any other sign, the Piscean must lose the sense of personal self and serve something higher. Pisces contains the knowledge of the underlying unity of all things, which is the reality behind the world of manifested forms.

The goddess sign for Pisces is the Grail, the chalice that contains the waters of collective consciousness. The grail is a symbol of the quest for immortality and conscious union with the Divine. Pisces is traditionally symbolized by two fish swimming in opposite directions in the ocean of existence, but tethered at the tails. Pisces can represent illusion, not seeing clearly or refusing to see, and divine inspiration. This stage of the journey requires faith. Pisces endows one with the knowledge of the alchemical principle of "Below," the deep reservoir of collective existence, sometimes called the collective subconscious, which engenders empathy. Pisces goddesses include mermaids, fish deities, and mother-creators from the sea, as well as those who embody the principles of sacrifice and compassion.

Kwan Yin

COMPASSION

Kwan Yin, who is called Mother of Mercy, is the Chinese bo-dhisattva and embodiment of the principle of compassion. In Sanskrit, the word for "compassion" is *karuna*, and *karuna* is understood to be a state of intense connection to others in which we feel their sorrows or joys as if they were our own. *Karuna* is related to the idea of weeping on behalf of others. Kwan Yin is greatly revered wherever Buddhism has spread. In Japan, this same goddess is called Kannon; in Bali, Kannin; in Korea, Gwan-eum; and in Thailand, Kuan-eim. Her full name means "observing the cries of the world."

Kwan Yin is usually depicted in a flowing white robe, holding an urn containing a substance called the water of life in one hand and a weeping willow branch in the other. She is often shown standing on a dragon, just as the Virgin Mary is shown on a serpent. One legend says Kwan Yin has a thou-sand arms with which to reach out and respond to the count-less cries of humanity. In China, fishermen pray to her to ensure safe voyages.

CONTEMPLATION

Oh, you who hear the cries of the whole world,
have mercy on me.

Korobona

EMPATHY

Korobona (core-oh-BONE-ah) is a water goddess of Central and South America whose story bears some similarity to that of the Wawalag Sisters of Australia. Korobona is one of two sisters who walked by a sacred lake and decided to bathe in the waters. While doing so, she became entranced by a piece of wood standing upright in the lake. She grasped the wood, and this broke the spell of enchantment that held a powerful water spirit entranced and captive below. He emerged and took her to his home at the bottom of the lake.

As in most myths, the child of this union created much strife in the family, and the symbols of the story include the potency and taboos relating to water and menstrual blood. The story of mother and son is central to the entire creation legend of the Carib, Arawak, and Warau peoples of Central and South America. Korobona's son, who was half serpent, became a sacrificed savior and was later resurrected to become the first of the Carib Indians and a mighty warrior.

CONTEMPLATION

If I pause, look deeply, and resist the urge to judge,
I can feel the pain of another's path.

Ganga

ABSOLUTION

Ganga (GONG-gah), whose name means "swift goer," is the Hindu goddess whose body is the holy Ganges River in India. The origin of her waters is believed to be in heaven, where she circles the celestial Mount Meru three times. In art, Ganga is depicted as a crowned mermaid or a great white queen. When beautiful Ganga was born, she danced in heaven but was cursed by a sage for laughing too much. He said she must be born as a river in which everyone would bathe to purify themselves.

Part of her karmic destiny was to flood a certain ashram, freeing sixty thousand souls from their ashes and absolving them of their karma. Ganga is seen as a Ma Ganga, Great Mother, and in this way, the author David Kinsley, in *Hindu Goddesses*, has said, Ganga is "the distilled essence of compassion in liquid form." In iconography she is depicted with a full vessel, which symbolizes her life-giving potential as well as her cleansing waters.

CONTEMPLATION

As fire consumes fuel so this stream consumes error.

— EXCERPT FROM THE GANGA LAHAN,
HYMN OF PRAISE TO GANGA, BY JAGGANATHA

Britomartis

WOUNDS

The goddess addressed as Britomartis (brit-oh-MAR-tis), or Sweet Maid, is from ancient Crete, and she entered Greek legend by way of King Minos. *Sweet Maid* is thought to be an epithet for the maiden aspect of the trinity of the triple goddess and does not reveal her true name. She had an earlier and more powerful aspect as Mother of Mountains, wielding the Cretan double ax and holding sacred serpents. Britomartis became a goddess of fishing and hunting called Lady of Nets, which links her to Artemis, who may have placed her in the heavens as a star.

According to the later legend, King Minos, imitating Zeus, pursued her, and she leaped into the ocean to avoid him. She was saved, or captured, by the very fishing nets she had gifted to mortals and was then carried by fishermen to the island of Aegina. Although scholars suspect Britomartis may have once been the greatest goddess of the Minoan culture, she was "netted" and thereby tamed by the patriarchal Greeks, which reduced her power and made her an ugly demon, who was depicted on coins of the later period.

CONTEMPLATION

I exercise caution in my choices so that I do not swim into a prison that masquerades as a sanctuary.

Hel

ENDINGS

The goddess Hel is described as the "hidden," or "one who hides," from the Norse word *hel*, which means "to conceal." She is a goddess of death and the afterlife, and her name may have been the origin of the English word *hell*. Hel has a dual nature, in that the top part of her body is alive and the bottom half decaying, perhaps suggesting that earthly life can be a living death. Meeting Hel was inevitable for everyone, even gods. She rode a black horse through the night, calling out the names of those who would die before dawn of disease, old age, or other causes. She lovingly wrapped her arms around them and carried them off to her ninefold domain.

In the early stories, her realm was more like a cauldron of rebirth, and Hel was seen in a more positive light. She also ruled over the land of shadows, or "shades," where all souls gather after leaving their bodies. She was sometimes called Brunhilde, meaning "burning Hel," and was leader of the Valkyries. In later myth, those who died in battle or heroically were carried off by the Valkyries.

CONTEMPLATION

*If I release the shadows of the past with courage,
knowing all things must eventually die,
I can face the future with hope.*

Nammu

POTENTIAL

Nammu (nah-MOO) is the ancient and primeval Sumerian goddess of the sea who appears in the Babylonian myth of creation called Enuma Elish. She is the mother of all the gods, including the high god An, whose name means "heaven," and Ki, who is the earth. Nammu may have become represented in the sky as the constellation we call Cetus, the Whale, to represent the idea of the "Deep," the vast watery potential from which all existence emerged, and which the Sumerians called Apsu, meaning "fertile waters." For this reason, she has been compared to the goddess Tiamat.

Nammu was also responsible for creating humans by molding them from clay to be servants of the gods. This creative act occurred thousands of years before Genesis. Nammu is represented by a symbol that depicts the sea.

CONTEMPLATION

What resides as potential in the deep parts
of my consciousness that I desire to bring into form?

Oba

FEELINGS

Oba is a great goddess of the Yoruba people of western Africa, who were savaged during the period of slave trading. The Yoruba were taken to sugar plantations in the Caribbean, where they were forcibly baptized. The goddess is represented by the waters of the river Oba. Some say she is jealous of her sister, Oshun, who lives in another river, named after her. As proof of this jealousy, worshippers have pointed out that, at the place where the two mighty rivers meet, the waters are turbulent and dangerous, reflecting the volatile nature of the two goddesses' relationship.

Oba is seen in other accounts as a goddess of culture and science who brings wisdom. She provides life-giving waters that are critical for drinking water and crop irrigation. The Yoruba syncretized their beliefs by overlaying Catholic saints onto their spirit beings, or Orishas. The result has been called Santeria, or the "Way of the Saints." The Yoruba believe that they enter a realm of the ancestors after death, and they make annual pilgrimages to the grave sites of their families to pay homage.

CONTEMPLATION

Unchecked, my feelings can run high and wild
like a river in spring, flooding its banks
and spilling into my life in harmony or discord.

Lorop

MYSTERY

Lorop (LOR-ahp) is a sea goddess and creator deity of the Yap people of Micronesia. This area of the Pacific is composed of thousands of small islands and is divided into eight nation-states and territories. Lorop is the daughter of the creator deity Liomarar, who threw sand into the ocean to form the first islands of what became Micronesia and then gave birth to Lorop. Lorop bore three children, one of whom went on to become a hero figure.

Each day, Lorop secretly dove into the ocean. Finally one of the children, curious about her activities, followed her and discovered her filling her basket with fish from the depths of the sea. This discovery meant she had to remain below the waves, but she still came to the surface each day to feed her family. In modern times, Lorop had the honor of appearing on a 1997 postage stamp, in the series Sea Goddesses of the Pacific issued by Palau and Micronesia, two republics that were once protectorates of the United States. The stamp pictured her diving deep into the ocean with a basket to procure fish.

CONTEMPLATION

*Sometimes mystery is its own source of power,
and knowing the secret spoils the magic.*

Thetis

VULNERABILITY

Thetis (THEE-tis), who was known as the Silver-Footed Daughter of the Ancient One of the Sea, is a Greek goddess who possesses the gift of shape-shifting. She is one of the Nereids raised by Hera, which suggests that she is an ancient and powerful goddess. Some sources believe Thetis was one of the earliest deities worshipped before the time of the Greeks. Naturally, in Greek myth, Zeus desired her, but an oracle had prophesied that if she bore a son he would be more powerful than the gods. This too suggests that this goddess had great power.

Because of the prophecy, Thetis was condemned to marry a mortal, and it was at her wedding to Peleus that Eris, goddess of discord, tossed her golden apple of discord among the guests. The apple was marked "to the fairest," and some versions of the story say this provoked an argument between Aphrodite, Athena, and Hera. The mortal Paris was appointed to decide which of the three was the fairest. He chose Aphrodite because she promised him Helen of Troy, who was already married. In myth, this incident sparked the Trojan War. Later Thetis gave birth to the hero Achilles and immersed him in the river Styx so he would be invincible. Unfortunately, as she did so, her hand covered his heel, which remained vulnerable and eventually became his undoing.

CONTEMPLATION

It is wise to know where I am vulnerable
and whether openness or protection is the best defense.

Ma Tsu

SECOND SIGHT

Ma Tsu (mah tsoo) is an ancient Chinese Taoist goddess of the sea. Her name means "mother ancestor," and she is revered as a patron saint. She protects fishermen, sailors, and all who travel on the ocean. Ma Tsu is worshipped by over one hundred million people in the coastal areas of southeastern China, and her devotees come from seafaring lineages. More than fifteen hundred temples are dedicated to her.

Ma Tsu's legend begins with a mortal girl who would later became a goddess. According to one story, Lin Mo, whose name means "silent girl," demonstrated such an amazing spirit that a Taoist master took her as a pupil at the age of thirteen. She developed second sight and was able to calm storms and rescue those in danger at sea. She was later proclaimed to be a bodhisattva, a person who has attained enlightenment. After her death, she was elevated to the status of a goddess, as Ma Tsu.

CONTEMPLATION

By entering a deep state of silence,
I see my true course revealed.

SACRIFICE

Sedna is a goddess of the Inuit people of the frigid Arctic North, who were once called Eskimo. Her myth is a story of a beautiful girl tricked by a potential mate who was actually a monster. He appeared to her as a handsome young man. Sedna went to live with him and later discovered his true nature. She appealed to her father for help, and he came in his boat to rescue her. But his fear for his own safety caused him to betray her. He threw her in the water, then cut off her fingers and then her hands as she clung to their boat. Sedna and her appendages slowly sank into the ocean and became the seals, walruses, and whales of the deep Arctic Ocean.

As Queen of the Sea, Sedna is responsible for all the aquatic food the Inuit must hunt. Only shamans can undertake the dangerous journey to ask her indulgence so they may pursue her aquatic children, and great courage and sacrifice are required on their part. Once the shamans reach the icy realm known as Adlivum, the Inuit land of the dead, or underworld, they comb her long hair and massage her limbs. In recent times, Sedna's name was given to a newly discovered dwarf planet in the icy outer reaches of our solar system, in an area known as the Kuiper Belt.

CONTEMPLATION

What precious thing would I be willing to sacrifice
for the greater good?

Maya

ILLUSION

The Hindu and Buddhist goddess Maya (not the Greek Maia) is the universal creator of all forms in existence, and she is the divine power that allows the evolution of the world. She is worshipped as Mother of Creation and Weaver of the Web of Life. Although the word *maya* is generally translated as "illusion," Maya represents the continual exchange of matter and energy, and she is the embodiment of Einstein's famous equation $E = mc^2$. She embodies the quantum reality that connects all life.

Maya is the very substance of the One Limitless Power that changes shape and form into what we perceive as manifested reality. As we experience her, she is like a cloak that veils the underlying and unifying energy of manifestation. Illusion is not the same as deception, and her deeper lesson is that we may choose to identify with our ego and our impermanent lives, or to understand that forms are fleeting and that we are souls moving through eternity.

CONTEMPLATION

Of all the forms of Maya, woman is the most important.

— SUTRA FROM MAHAYANA BUDDHIST SCRIPTURE, QUOTED BY JOSEPH CAMPBELL IN *The Masks of God: Oriental Mythology*

MARCH 2

Amphrite

MAKING WAVES

Amphrite (am-FRI-tee) is a Greek goddess who ruled the sea but is perhaps better understood as the very embodiment of the ocean. She is described as "all encircling," suggesting how the oceans embrace the land. Amphrite appears among the chief goddesses listed in archaic sources. Later Greek myth diminished her by assigning her the role of wife of Poseidon, who married her in order to become god of the sea.

In Greek art, Amphrite is depicted in a chariot drawn by *hippokampi*, fish-tailed horses, and sometimes she wears a crown embellished with crab claws. She especially loved dolphins and seals, who were among her children. This suggests a much earlier origin, as she gave birth to the creatures of the sea. Sadly, it was a dolphin, later transformed into the constellation Delphinus, who persuaded her to wed Poseidon. Her special domain was underwater caves, where she stored her treasures.

CONTEMPLATION

My emotions can be like the gentle lapping
of a calm tide or the raging swells of a storm at sea.
It's up to me to master these powerful and shifting currents.

MARCH 3

Hsi Wang Mu

RECEPTIVITY

Hsi Wang Mu (sigh wang moo), known as the Queen Mother of the West, is a Chinese Taoist goddess whose domain is immortal life. At a deeper level, she represents the balance and cycles of life and death. She is the embodiment of the principle of yin, the feminine side of creation. In the yin-yang symbol, yin is called "haven" and "darkness," and yang is called "earth" and "light." The two are seen as opposite and complementary, continually waxing and waning, like the feminine and masculine principles of life.

Hsi Wang Mu lives in a golden palace beside a turquoise lake on Mount Kun-Lun, a mountain of jade, and she is the keeper of the list of immortals. In this guise she was called Golden Mother of the Shining Lake. She is also the guardian of the sacred peach tree, P'an-t'ao, which yields the peaches of immortality. This priceless fruit takes three thousand years to grow and another three thousand to ripen. Hsi Wang Mu has no husband and is a powerful independent presence who is not subject to masculine authority. She was immensely popular in China roughly two thousand years ago. In her oldest aspect she was said to be responsible for plagues and pestilence and determining whether or not those evils were to be released.

CONTEMPLATION

*All life ebbs and flows in an eternal cycle of darkness
and light. I learn to practice patience,
waiting for the tide to turn in its own time.*

Goddesses for Every Day

Hina-Ika

RESPECT

Hina-Ika (HEE-nah-EE-kah), a Hawaiian goddess known as Lady of the Fish, is regarded as the mother-creator of the island of Molokai. In Polynesia she is known as Ina, and in New Zealand she is Hine-tu-a-maunga, meaning "goddess of waters." Hina-Ika makes a special cloth from bark, and she taught this skill to humanity. As Ina she kept an eel in a jar, but her prisoner grew too large and tried to attack her. She killed him and then buried his head on a sandy beach in punishment for the attack, and the first coconut palm grew on the spot. However, other variations of this story, similar to other myths, tell that the serpent was really her lover.

Hina-Ika is the guardian of the sea and all its creatures, because her worshippers believe that all life emerged from the oceans. The whales are her siblings and she protects them, retaliating when they are killed. She is an aspect of the overarching goddess, who in Tahiti is the first being from whom all others were born.

CONTEMPLATION

I learn to respect all life and never take more from nature's bounty than I need, realizing that extinct is forever.

Ningyo

SOLITUDE

Ningyo (nin-ghee-OH) is a Japanese fish or mermaid goddess depicted in art as a beautiful woman with long black hair and the tail of a fish. Stories of her appear in *Nihonshoki*, a historical record of Japan. She is believed to bring good fortune, and statues of her are found in both Shinto and Buddhist temples throughout the country that honor Ningyo Shinko, the "Mermaid Religion."

Legends say that when Ningyo cries, her tears become precious pearls of great value. She is elusive and lives deep in the ocean, but sometimes she can be seen by mortals. In a rather macabre bit of lore, any woman who succeeds in capturing her and taking a bite of her flesh is said to acquire perpetual youth and beauty. No wonder Ningyo doesn't show herself.

CONTEMPLATION

At what cost to others, including the creatures of the sea, would I pursue youth and beauty?

MARCH 6

Wah-Kah-Nee

ATONEMENT

Wah-Kah-Nee is a spirit being of the Chinook Indians, whose home lies along the Columbia River in the Pacific Northwest. The Chinook lived on the river and depended on fish for their livelihood. One year, the legend says, the people endured a never-ending winter. The elders convened a council and decided the icy weather had been sent as punishment for killing a bird. A young girl sadly confessed to throwing a stone that had killed a bird. The Chinook dressed her in her finest clothes and laid her out on the ice as a willing sacrifice. She slowly froze.

Her atonement appeased the spirit beings, and the ice began to melt, and the river ran once more. The following year the block of ice in which Wah-Kah-Nee was encased thawed, and miraculously she was revived. For the rest of her life she served as a shaman for her people. It was said that from that day on she could walk unprotected in the coldest of weather.

CONTEMPLATION
*Every action has a reaction,
and every choice has a consequence.*

Nyai Loro Kidul

AMENDS

Nyai Loro Kidul (NEE-eye LORE-oh KEY-dull) is a mermaid goddess of Java in Indonesia. Java, once home to powerful Hindu kingdoms, is the most populous island in the world, lying between Bali and Sumatra. Nyai Loro Kidul lives in the heart of the sea and controls the sometimes treacherous waves of the Indian Ocean. Her long, flowing hair is green and is filled with shells and seaweed. The Javanese people never wear green in the water for fear of offending her. Sometimes the lower part of her body is serpentine, and then she is described as a nagini, a female serpent being.

In her Cinderella-like legend, Nyai Loro Kidul was once a beautiful princess who became a victim of spite and jealousy. Her wicked stepmother poisoned Nyai Loro Kidul's bathwater, and she was left cursed with a skin disease. When she was magically healed, she was transformed into a mermaid.

CONTEMPLATION

I will not seek retribution but will ask others to forgive me when needed. Revenge escalates, and the backlash can cause great harm.

Andromeda

FORTITUDE

Andromeda (an-DROM-eh-da) is the human daughter of Cepheus, the king of Joppa. In her myth, her mother, Cassiopeia, claimed that her daughter was more beautiful than the sea nymphs. Naturally, the daughters of the sea god Poseidon were offended. In retribution, Poseidon demanded that Cepheus offer Andromeda as a sacrifice. She was chained to a rock to be devoured by Cetus, the sea monster. Fortunately, the hero Perseus came by in the nick of time and rescued her.

Some scholars believe Andromeda originated earlier, since her name means "ruler of men" and her story has parallels to that of Marduk and the goddess Tiamat, and that of Ba'al and the goddess Astarte. Like many other goddesses who were later redesignated as merely wives of gods or heroes, Andromeda became the wife of the hero Perseus, and her power was diminished. She was later raised to the stars by Athena, and the entire myth is retold each year as the constellations move through their annual cycles. The Andromeda Galaxy is our closest galactic neighbor, and astronomers believe our own Milky Way Galaxy is similar to it in form and characteristics.

CONTEMPLATION

Whatever comes my way, no matter how unfair it seems,
I can hold myself with dignity.

Sequana

SANCTUARY

Sequana (see-QUAW-nah) is the Celtic goddess of the river Seine, the most famous river in France. Sequana is the Latin name for the river, which flows from its source high in the mountains west of the Alps, through Paris, and into the English Channel. The goddess is represented in the water that flows both on the surface of the land and in deep underground streams and wells.

Recently, relics have been found in marshes at the site of an ancient healing sanctuary at the source of the river. The artifacts are thought to have been gifts or offerings to the goddess brought by worshippers who came on pilgrimage and sought solace and healing at her holy sanctuary. During Sequana's annual festival, the people pulled a boat along the river carrying the figure of a duck with a berry in its bill. A statue with similar details on display at the Dijon Archaeology Museum is thought to be of Sequana. This statue is a figure of a woman dressed in a long gown and crowned with a diadem, who stands in a boat shaped like a duck.

CONTEMPLATION

*Today I take time to turn within
and create a sense of sacred sanctuary.*

Hat-Mehit

CONFIDENCE

Hat-Mehit (hat-may-hit) is a prominent predynastic goddess of ancient Egypt who is generally represented by a fish. Sometimes she is seen as a dolphin, which takes her significance beyond the river and into the great ocean. She was worshipped in the Nile Delta at Mendes, where she was seen as the personification of the Nile itself. *Mehit* means "great flood," and the goddess's name translates as "house of Mehit." She is a mother goddess who was also called Foremost of the Fishes.

Hat-Mehit is pictured with a fish on her head, the symbol of the Nome, which is like a province or state, where she reigned. That she carried the symbol of the area indicates how powerful she once was. Later, when the cult of Osiris arose, she was regarded as his wife and the one who gave him his authority; she was later diminished. Pottery remains have been found outside what is believed to have been her temple.

CONTEMPLATION

I cast my net into the deep waters of my consciousness.
The promise of finding treasures long submerged
gives me confidence.

Chalchiuhtlicue

FORGIVENESS

Chalchiuhtlicue (chal-chee-WEE-til-quay), called Emerald Lady, or She of the Jade Skirt, or sometimes Petticoat of Blue Stones, is the Aztec goddess of lakes and streams. Sometimes she is seen as the mate of the hero-god Quetzalcoatl, whose name means "feathered serpent." Another of her titles is She Whose Night-Robe of Jewel-Stars Whirls Above. Like other goddesses, she has both a benign and a dark aspect. In her benevolent demeanor, she is a wide, flowing river with a bountiful prickly-pear cactus growing on the banks, representing a generous and open heart. She also blessed those who fished in her waters.

Chalchiuhtlicue had dominion over the fourth world, the one that existed before our own, where the sky was made of water. The fourth world was destroyed by a great flood, which she released. However, she transformed the deserving into fish and built a bridge to the fifth world; the bridge now appears in the sky as a rainbow. Chalchiuhtlicue is also associated with flowers and with hallucinogenic mushrooms used in initiation ceremonies. This shows her role in altering and expanding consciousness.

CONTEMPLATION

Clinging to past hurts and losses only holds me back.
Today I forgive the past and face the future.

Junkgowa Sisters

DREAMTIME

The Junkgowa (junk-OW-ah) Sisters are marine goddesses of the Australian Aborigines who live in the Dreamtime. Like other sister trios around the world, the Junkgowa Sisters represent the triple aspect of the Great Goddess: maiden, mother, and crone. The Junkgowa Sisters created all the creatures of the oceans and rivers, as well as the first people. To explore the ocean waters, the sisters built a canoe and set out, singing as they paddled. Everywhere they dipped their oars, the creatures of the sea appeared.

When the Junkgowa Sisters reached land, they began a walkabout. Every place they touched their staffs to the ground, a water hole appeared, releasing the waters of a sacred spring. These openings are seen as portals into the world of the spirits. The sisters are still imagined as traveling together in a canoe above their watery domain. They appeared in this way on a postage stamp in the Sea Goddesses of the Pacific series.

CONTEMPLATION

Every act can be a potent meditation connecting me with collective wisdom, and I can tap into that wisdom through my dreams.

Lady of the Lake

RECLAMATION

Viviane is the name most frequently given to this Celtic goddess who appears in several guises. To the medieval Celts, she was the Lady of the Lake, and she appeared in the legend of King Arthur. Her name means "life." In some stories, she lives on the enchanted isle of Avalon with her eight sisters, similar to the Muses. Avalon is the mystical underwater land of the dead, and the mythical place where Arthur was taken after his death.

As the Dame du Lac, she was the foster mother of Lancelot and raised a great hero of the day in the same way the Greek Thetis fostered Achilles. The Lady of the Lake was also said to guard the Hallows of Kingship, which were sacred objects related to the principle of sovereignty. In this capacity she gave Arthur his famous sword, Excalibur. As the mythical Viviane, she lured her teacher, Merlin, into a perpetual enchantment to keep him with her in their magical student/mentor relationship. But a deeper look at this story reveals the initiatory period that wizards were required to spend in the Land of the Fairies to learn the mysteries of life and death.

CONTEMPLATION

What objects in my life are sacred
and seem to be filled with power?

Goddesses for Every Day

Ran

UNDERCURRENTS

Ran (rahn) is a Scandinavian goddess of the ocean who is known as the Queen of the Drowned. This goddess also has dominion over storms at sea. She was thought to love gold, so sailors always kept a gold coin in their pockets in case they were swept overboard during bad weather. In this way they gained admittance to her paradise. In the *Eddas*, a compilation of Scandinavian myths in two volumes, this practice is called "faring to Ran."

Ran's mate is the sea god Aegïr, with whom she had nine daughters. These daughters are the waves of the ocean and the "Claws of Ran." Sometimes the daughters were seen as mermaids. Superstitious sailors believe Ran has a big net in which she traps men and brings them to the bottom of the ocean as companions for her daughters. However, those she brings to her underwater realm she cares for tenderly. Anyone who drowns and is then seen as a ghost at his or her own wake is said to be in the good care of Ran.

CONTEMPLATION

*I chart my course and set sail in calm waters,
lest I become swept overboard by the currents
of my unexpressed emotions.*

Glispa

AFFIRMATION

Glispa (GLUH-spa) is a Navajo goddess who gave the Dine, or "the people," as they call themselves, their sacred chant of beauty and healing. After a dangerous journey, which was shamanic in nature, Glispa met a shaman of the Snake People who became her lover and teacher. He lifted the surface of a magical lake, which was the entrance to the underworld, allowing her to enter. Serpents are guardians of wisdom in mythology around the world and are almost always seen in a positive light. Snakes are also frequently connected to the element of primordial water.

Glispa spent two years with the Snake People, who lived by the Lake of Emergence in the underworld. She learned their beautiful and elaborate chant, which she taught to the Navajo when she emerged from the underworld to visit her family. Navajo chants are thought to bring healing and to restore balance and harmony.

CONTEMPLATION

On the beautiful trail I am.
With it I wander.

— EXCERPT FROM *Navajo Beauty Way Chant*

MARCH 16

Modjadji

SECRET POWERS

Modjadji (mod-JAD-jee), which means "ruler of the day," is a rain goddess of South Africa and a manifestation of the goddess Mwari. She is known by the title Khifidola-maru-a-Daja, which means "transformer of the clouds." The rain queen is thought to possess the secret of creating rain by interacting with cloud spirits. The goddess gave birth to a lineage of human queens bearing the honorary title Modjadji, and these successive queens have ruled over the Lovedu people of South Africa. They are said to embody the power of the goddess, and they trace their lineage and rainmaking abilities to her.

The modern story began when a young princess fled with her followers from the Karanga empire in Zimbabwe and established a new community. She became the first in a lineage of human rain queens drawing power from the goddess. Afterward, even the Zulu and Swazi warriors were awed by her. There is now a nature preserve called Modjadji, named after this Rain Queen with mysterious powers. This queen also inspired the famous book *She*, by H. Rider Haggard.

CONTEMPLATION

Today I call upon the cloud spirits to bring cleansing and purifying rain to the parched areas of my life.

Erish-Kigal

DORMANCY

Erish-Kigal (err-ish-KEY-gaul), a Sumerian goddess and queen of the domain of Arallu, the Land of No Return, is known as the Great Lady under Earth. She is a psychopomp, one who leads the souls of the dead to the underworld, in this case her palace made of lapis lazuli, whereas her sister, Ishtar, lives in heaven. When heaven and earth separated and the world was created, Erish-Kigal was carried below. As in the myths of many goddesses around the world, her domain is the time of year when the earth is dormant.

Once long ago, Erish-Kigal ruled alone in a western wilderness at the end of the world that was enveloped in gardens of rainbows. Later she actually received the dead into herself in a sort of cosmic recycling program. Sometimes she is shown as lion-headed and seen as dark in color. Several myths concerning Erish-Kigal appear to grapple with the never-ending cycles of life and death.

CONTEMPLATION

During the dark time of the year, I can gestate new creations and turn within to my inner light.

Kauri

TENDERNESS

Kauri (COW-ree) is a pre-Vedic goddess of India who dispenses *karuna*, which in Tantra includes love in all its forms. Tantra is an Asian body of beliefs in which the goddess Shakti is worshipped and the universe is seen as the loving play of Shakti and the god Shiva. Kauri's love encompasses everything from physical affection and sexuality to a mother's unconditional love for her child. Psychological research has proven how vital touch, especially a mother's affection for an infant, is to emotional health and well-being. Kauri was seen as the virginal, or power-in-potential, aspect of Shakti, which empowered the gods and without which they could not act.

Karuna is usually understood to mean compassion with wisdom, or mercy, especially as a kindness offered to those who suffer. *Kauri* sounds the same as *cowrie*, the name for the vulva-shaped shell prized as a talisman and used for jewelry all over the world. The shell is seen as an emblem of the female reproductive organ and its generative properties.

CONTEMPLATION

Intense love does not measure. It just gives.

—— MOTHER TERESA

MARCH 19

Ixtab

VALOR

Ixtab (ISH-tab), a Mayan goddess known as She of the Rope, is the guardian of those who die by suicide, especially hanging. The ancient Maya believed that those who committed suicide went directly to heaven, and that hanging was an honorable way to die. Ixtab is a psychopomp deity who led such souls directly to paradise, where they dined under the Yaxshe, the Pleasant Tree, and rested in its shade. She also collected women who died in childbirth, sacrificial victims, and those who died in battle.

Ixtab appears in the *Dresden Codex*, one of the few surviving Mayan texts, hanging from a rope in the sky and looking like a corpse. She is depicted with tables that record eclipses, so she no doubt has astronomical significance related to eclipses of the sun and moon. Solar eclipses particularly can be seen as emblems of death and rebirth, as the sun seems to disappear completely for a time behind the orb of the moon.

CONTEMPLATION
*Am I facing up to my situation,
or looking to take what seems to be the only way out?*

ARIES GODDESSES
The Double Ax

COURAGE IS ACTING IN SPITE OF FEAR

*A*ries is a cardinal fire sign that, in the Northern Hemisphere, begins at the spring equinox, the time of equal day and night. The character of the time of Aries is the initiating force emerging out of the collective nature of the twelfth sign, Pisces. Aries is irresistible force, and it represents the principles of resurrection and individualization, the symbolic point of all beginnings, and the onset of the circle of the seasons. Aries has traditionally been represented by the Ram, and its energy, like spring after winter, tends to be pioneering, initiating, headfirst, impulsive, and adventurous.

The goddess sign for Aries is the Double Ax of Crete, called a *labrys*, a ritual implement wielded by a priestess. The *labrys* was a symbol of royal power and was not a weapon, although it may have been an implement of sacrifice. The word comes from the same root as *labyrinth*. The earliest labyrinths were found in southern Europe and date to four thousand years ago. Aries are pathfinders, and walking the sacred path of a labyrinth, wielding the double ax, seems a fitting metaphor for the pioneers of the zodiac.

Aries goddesses include gentle goddesses of spring who embody new beginnings, the light of dawn, cyclical renewal of the earth, and the rebirth of life. They are also courageous leaders, pioneers who blaze new trails, and fierce warriors who have the will to do battle. Aries goddesses are independent, possessing a keen sense of adventure. The quality of an Aries's vision, which enables her to move forward on a new path, is vital.

Tefnut

VISION

Tefnut (TEF-noot) and her brother, Shu, are Egyptian deities worshipped in their role as the Twin Eyes of the sun god Ra. The left eye was the moon, the eye of night, and the right eye was the sun. The siblings were created in the beginning from the primeval god Atum and were the first divine couple of the Ennead, the nine original gods of Heliopolis, the city of the sun in northern Egypt. Tefnut is the sun's left eye and is also associated with the *ureaus*, the rearing cobra symbol of royalty and mastery worn on the brow of the pharaoh. She was also known as the Ureaus on the Heads of all the Gods.

The goddess was worshipped at Leontopolis, in ancient Egypt, in her red lion form, or in her lion form with a sun disk and *ureaus* on her head. At Heliopolis she was seen as a creative force, occupying a space between heaven and earth, and as the means of bringing life into the world. Although Tefnut was called Lady of the Flame, her name is related to the moisture of the morning dew, and it was through her mysterious grace as a solar principle that moisture came to Egypt. Along with Shu, Tefnut supported the arch of the sky and received the newborn sun each morning.

CONTEMPLATION

*When my vision is clear, my creations are
divinely inspired and have the power of the sun.*

Aditi

ORDER

Aditi (ah-DEE-tee), whose name means "limitless," is the Hindu goddess clothed with the sun. She is the self-formed Mother of Worlds. Two of her titles are Cosmic Space and Supporter of the Sky. Aditi is often identified as a cow who provides nourishment. As the cosmic cow, similar to Isis and Hathor, she supplies milk that is a redemptive drink, called *amrita*.

Aditi gave birth to the twelve spirits of the zodiac, called Adityas, meaning "children of Aditi." One of these spirits rules each month, and so Aditi marks time, as her children structure the limits of formerly boundless space. She set her children in place to rule the order of the cycles of nature, and as the sun, she journeys through the year to visit them. One of these spirits is the hero Aryaman, probably Aries, who became the ancestral god of the Aryans. Aditi is said to unbind or unlimit those who petition her, and her role as guardian of cosmic moral order is similar to that of her son, Varuna.

CONTEMPLATION

*The wheel of seasons begins again
as the children of Aditi go forth.*

Eostre

RENEWAL

Eostre (YO-ster) is the Germanic goddess of spring. She is also called Ostara or Eastre, and her name is the origin of the word *Easter*, the name of the only feast day in the Christian calendar that is still tied to the moon. Eostre is a goddess of dawn, rebirth, and new beginnings. Her festival is celebrated on the first day of spring, when she is invoked at dawn with ritual fire, quickening the land, while the full moon symbolically sets behind her. Eostre's return each spring warms the ground, preparing for a new cycle of growth.

One year the goddess was late, and a little girl found a bird near death from the cold. The child turned to Eostre for help. In response a rainbow bridge appeared and Eostre came, clothed in her red robe of vibrant sunlight, melting the snows. Because the creature was wounded beyond repair, Eostre changed it into a snow hare, who then brought gifts of rainbow eggs. Hares and rainbows are sacred to her, as is the full moon, since the ancients saw the image of a hare in its markings.

CONTEMPLATION

Sometimes, old forms must be surrendered gracefully in order for life to be reborn in new and higher forms.

Persephone

REBIRTH

Persephone (per-SEF-oh-nee) is the Greek goddess of spring. Each year at the end of winter, Persephone returned to the surface of the earth for a joyful reunion with her mother, Demeter. In winter, while Persephone lived in the underworld as the Queen of Hades, Demeter's grief caused earth to become cold and barren. When mother and daughter were symbolically reunited every spring, birds sang in the trees and flowers opened again.

Persephone is also known as Kore, and she was Proserpina to the Romans, whose name means "to emerge" in Latin. In some versions of the story, Pluto (Hades), tricked Persephone into eating pomegranate seeds so she would have to stay in the underworld. In other versions she ate the fruit of her own accord. Now Persephone spends four months in Hades and eight months bringing light and warmth to the earth.

CONTEMPLATION

Even during the darkest night of despair,
I know that the dawn always comes.

MARCH 24

Atalanta

INDEPENDENCE

Atalanta (at-ah-LAN-tah), whose name means "balanced," is an Amazon goddess from ancient Greece. When she was born, Atalanta was exposed on a rock and left to die at Parthenia because her father wanted a son. Atalanta was suckled by a she-bear sent by the goddess Artemis to rescue her. Some stories say Atalanta was actually Artemis herself in the form of a bear. Atalanta grew in stature and became a great hunter and warrior. She even killed two centaurs who tried to rape her.

Eventually her father heard of her fame and adventures and wanted her to marry so he could gain recognition from her renown. She was tricked into marriage by agreeing to a footrace, but in the end she married for love. Some stories say she and her mate were later changed into lions who pulled the chariot of the great mother goddess Cybele.

CONTEMPLATION

If I am true to myself, even the most challenging or hurtful experiences can be turned into wisdom and strength.

Nerthus

TRUCE

Nerthus (NUR-thus) is a Norse Teutonic fertility goddess who drove across Denmark in a wagon drawn by cows, blessing the bounty of the land. Abundance followed her, and every place her bare feet touched the earth, something grew. She was a member of the Vanir, the peace-loving gods who were always at odds with the warring Aesir. Mythically, Nerthus may be the mother of the goddess Freya.

Nerthus ruled over Midgrad, the habitation of the Danish gods. Sacrifices were offered to her in a sacred grove on the island of Fyn in a large lake in Denmark. The height of her power was near the time of Ostara, the spring equinox. At the time of her joyous spring festival, peace prevailed and her worshippers did not take up arms or wage war. Nerthus teaches that nothing is so important that we can't take time for gratitude and celebration.

CONTEMPLATION

Today I choose to wage peace,
knowing war comes from a state of fear and lack.

Nike

VICTORY

Nike (NYE-key) is the Greek goddess who personifies victory in all areas of life, including athletics. Because of this, designer Jeff Johnson, hired by footwear entrepreneur Phil Knight, recommended using her name for the well-known company. The triumphant power of the ancient goddess manifested in the most successful shoe company ever.

Proving that size is not a measure of power, Nike was sculpted by the Greeks as a tiny winged figure. She was said to perch on another god's shoulder or peek out from under the robes of a goddess. Exquisite reliefs of Nike grace temples in Greece. Her most famous representation is a headless statue called Nike of Samothrace, on display in the Louvre in Paris. Although she was capable of running and flying at great speeds, Nike was often depicted playing a lyre or flute.

CONTEMPLATION

Many battles are mental, and a quick mind
and clever strategy may win out over brute force.

Reindeer Goddess

DIRECTION

Today's goddess is a Siberian reindeer spirit and guardian of all newborns, especially those of spring. German archaeologists discovered a complete female reindeer skull mounted on a seven-foot ritual pole, which evidently had fallen into an ancient sacrificial lake near Hamburg. Aged antlered females such as this were sacred to ancient tribes and their shamans. Among ruminants such as deer, elder females became the pathfinders and leaders of the pack.

Reindeer and caribou are the only species of Cervidae in which antlers grow on females. According to the Alaska Department of Fish and Game, both male and female reindeer grow antlers each summer. Male reindeer drop their antlers at the beginning of winter, usually late November to mid-December, while female reindeer retain their antlers until after they give birth in spring. (According to historical renditions depicting Santa's reindeer, every one of them had to be female.)

CONTEMPLATION

I trust that the wisdom of my uniquely feminine experiences will enable me to find a true path.

Gendenwitha

PARADOX

Gendenwitha (ghen-den-WITH-ah) is an Iroquois goddess whose name means "she who brings the day." She is seen in the form of Venus as the morning star. Her story is a sad tale of star-crossed love, like Romeo and Juliet's. She loved to dance beneath the starry skies, and a young brave named Sossondowah, who was a great hunter of the spirit elk, fell in love with her. He watched her dance all night, longing to be with her.

He tried to win Gendenwitha with birdsong. In spring he sang like a bluebird, in summer he sang like a blackbird, and in autumn he cried like a hawk and tried to capture Gendenwitha and carry her to the sky. Instead, another goddess, the jealous spirit of Dawn caught the great hunter and forced him to guard her Portal of Morning. She tied him to her doorpost and then changed Gendenwitha into the morning star. Sossondowah still watches Gendenwitha all night, but he can never really be with her. At dawn, as the morning star, and in spite of her grief over not being with her love, she heralds the new day.

CONTEMPLATION

I dance for joy regardless of my pain,
waiting for dawn and the promise of a new day.

Aya

BEGINNINGS

Aya (EYE-yah) is an ancient Chaldean goddess of dawn who was often called the Bride of the Sun and whose light shone on the sea and gave hope to everyone. Much later Aya was merged into the mythology of the goddess Ishtar. Like other goddesses of dawn, Aya is associated with eastern mountains, which are seen as symbolically giving birth to the solar orb each day as it crests the peaks and rises into the sky. Eastern mountains are also imagined as pushing the sun upward into the sky in a birthing process.

Chaldea was a marshy land on the banks of the Euphrates River, where southern Iraq and Kuwait are now. The Chaldeans believed that Aya's mystical union, or sacred marriage, with the sun god caused all vegetation to grow and flourish. She was invoked at all beginnings, when a potent surge of energy was needed to bring the renewing light of dawn.

CONTEMPLATION

*Every day brings the gift of new beginnings
and the strength to begin again.*

Olwen

MASTERY

Olwen (OL-won) is a Welsh goddess of spring and sunlight whose streaming yellow hair flows behind her as she moves. Her name means "white path," and it is believed that she leaves a trail of white clover, or sometimes the trefoil plant, as she passes in the awakening meadows of spring. Her magic causes all the flowers and trees to bloom. She is also called Golden-wheel and White Lady of the Day and is the opposite of Arianrod, who is called the Silverwheel of the starry night.

Olwen's father was a possessive giant who didn't want her to marry, and he set thirteen impossible tasks for her to perform before he would consent. Olwen mastered each task and then married her true love. Some versions of the story say her success in the thirteen tasks brought her father's death, suggesting that he was the annual sun king. The thirteen tasks were a reference to the cycle of thirteen new or full moons in each solar year.

CONTEMPLATION

I can find the inner strength to master seemingly impossible situations, and I trail light and life as I work.

Thorgerd

DEFENSE

Thorgerd (THOR-gurd) is an Icelandic Norse warrior goddess who lives in Thrudheim, the home of the gods. Her name means "Thor's protection," and her qualities might be borrowed from modern epic cartoon characters like the X-Men. She was fiercely protective. When her people were attacked, she became larger than life, and sharp arrows flew from each of her fingers. Each arrow flew straight toward an enemy, and as the swift and deadly projectiles met their target, that enemy was eliminated.

Thorgerd was revered as a mighty patron and protector. She was also invoked for success in fishing and farming because of her uncanny accuracy. Sometimes she was paired with the Norse god Thrud, whose name means "power" or "strength."

CONTEMPLATION

I attack difficult situations head-on and accurately pierce the heart of any problem.

Bellona

DIPLOMACY

Bellona (buh-LOW-nuh) is the Roman goddess of war but also of diplomacy and military authority. Her realm was actually much larger than that of Mars, who became the more famous god of war. Wars were declared in Bellona's temple, but foreign ambassadors and returning generals were also greeted there amid great ceremony.

Bellona is usually depicted in full armor with a torch and a bloody lash. Sometimes her hair is made of serpents, which are symbols of wisdom, signifying that war should not be declared without thoughtful deliberation or attempts at diplomacy. Her name gave us the Latin word for war, *bellum*, and a familiar term, *antebellum*, used especially in the southern United States to describe structures built before the Civil War.

CONTEMPLATION

I choose my battles wisely and always use diplomacy and negotiation first.

PROMISE

Eos (EE-ohs) is the Greek goddess of dawn. Her name is similar to that of Eostre, but Eos is the goddess of every single dawn. She is equivalent to the Roman goddess Aurora. Her sister is Selene, the moon, and her brother is Helios, the sun. Eos had a romance with Astraeus, whose name means "starry," and this union produced four winds: Boreas, the "north wind"; Notus, the "south wind"; Zephyrus, the "west wind"; and Eurus, the "east wind."

Eos was imagined with flaming red hair, clothed in robes the color of golden saffron, and driving a magnificent purple chariot drawn by two horses. In the morning she drove her chariot across the sky, but at other times she was shown riding the winged steed Pegasus. Eos had wings of her own, so when she desired, she flew across the sky carrying a torch, which illuminated the pink clouds of sunrise and set the sky on fire.

CONTEMPLATION

*I greet each dawn with optimism
and a spirit of expectancy.*

APRIL 3

Theia

SIGHT

Theia (THEE-ah) is one of the Titans, the powerful beings who preceded, and gave birth to, the Greek Olympians. Her parents were Gaia and Ouranos, the earth and sky, and her name is generally translated as "goddess." Theia was responsible for giving gold, silver, and gems their brilliance and value. She represents the faculty of sight and the ability to assess situations clearly — the removal of the blindfold of self-deception.

Theia married her brother, Hyperion, who was also a god of light, and she bore Helios, the sun, and Selene, the moon. Her children are known as the "lights" of heaven. Eos, the dawn, is another of her daughters. Theia had an oracular shrine in Thessaly where people came to "see the light" concealed within the darkness of their problems.

CONTEMPLATION

Light enables me to see outer brilliance,
which may glitter but not have intrinsic value.

Inanna

COMPLEXITY

Inanna (ee-NAH-nah) is an ancient Sumerian goddess of love and wine but also battle. Where there's love there's often war, as any couple knows. She was known as the "holy virgin," which at that time meant she was an independent goddess who never married. She is often shown standing on two griffins, female mythical beasts with lion bodies and eagle wings. Six thousand years ago Inanna was associated with the city of Uruk, the largest city in the world then, which was situated east of the Euphrates and west of the Tigris River where Al Muthanna, Iraq, is today. A famous vase found there showed her dressed for a divine marriage.

Like her Babylonian successor Ishtar, Inanna made an annual descent into the underworld. Another fascinating myth tells how she aspired to obtain the Decrees of Civilization, similar to the Tablets of Destiny, in order to increase her power and improve the lot of her people. She traveled in her Boat of Heaven to visit the god Enki at his home in Eridu. After getting Enki intoxicated, Inanna made off with the treasure. Pursuit and battle followed, but Inanna kept the precious tablets.

CONTEMPLATION

My Lady, you are the guardian of all greatness.

— FROM "THE EXALTATION OF INANNA," 2300 BCE, FROM
Inanna, Lady of the Largest Heart,
TRANSLATED BY BETTY DE SHONG MEADER

APRIL 5

Al Uzza

MIGHT

Al Uzza (al OO-zah) is an early desert goddess of pre-Islamic Arabia, and part of a trinity of goddesses that includes Al Lat and Al Menat. Her name means the "powerful one" or "mighty one," and she was worshipped as the morning and evening stars. She was the young maiden aspect of the trinity and was also a mighty warrior shown riding astride a camel. She may have been a djinn, or genie, a desert spirit with magical powers, like the later queen of Sheba. In much later Jewish tradition, she was a rebellious angel who stole magical secrets from the gods and revealed them to Eve.

Prior to the seventh century, Arabia was ruled by powerful queens. Before his conversion, Muhammad honored Al Uzza, but he later betrayed her, destroying her sacred grove of acacia trees south of Mecca. Belief in the "powerful one" survived the desecration of her sacred grove for nearly a thousand years, and even today the star and crescent moon remain as symbols of Islam.

CONTEMPLATION

*I never underestimate the silent might
of feminine strength.*

APRIL 6

Aerten

CHALLENGE

Aerten (AIR-ten) is a Welsh goddess whose name means "firm in battle" and is derived from the Celtic world *aer*, meaning "battle." She had a shrine on the river Dee in Cornwall, Wales, at a place called Glyndyfrdwy. There she was reputed to preside over the outcome of wars between the Celtic clans. According to local legends, three humans were drowned in the river as a sacrifice near her shrine to obtain victory in battle.

Aerten has often been compared to the Greek Fates, which suggests she once had a threefold aspect. Aerten's nature is similar to that of Atroposy, the goddess of fate who cut the thread that determined how long a life would be. She is also similar to the Irish war goddess Morrigan.

CONTEMPLATION

I face my battles with a firm mind,
knowing that most of my struggles are internal.

Nemetona

ENERGY

Nemetona (nem-eh-TOH-nah) is a British goddess honored by the Druids. "She of the sacred grove" is the meaning of her name, which is really an honorific title of the goddess. The sacred grove itself was called a *nemeton*, and at the heart of this grove stood a shrine. Nemetona protected the Druids' sacred outdoor ceremonial sites and engendered a feeling of sanctuary. The origin of her name is also found in the Nemetes, a tribe of Germanic Celts who were the "people of the sacred grove."

Nemetona ruled over warfare as well and was sometimes associated with the god Mars Loucetios, the lightning god. Because of her association with lightning, or fire from heaven, which struck the trees, Nemetona was also connected with sacred trees, especially the oak. She was worshipped at the hot springs in Bath, England, along with the Roman goddess Sulis. Nemetona was pictured as a seated queen with a scepter, and around her stood three hooded figures and a ram.

CONTEMPLATION

*I can create a sacred shrine in my innermost heart
and enter this holy place to pray and gain new energy.*

APRIL 8

Chamunda

FEROCITY

Chamunda (cha-MOON-dah) is seen as a ferocious and avenging goddess. She manifests as an aspect of the Hindu goddess Kali in her role as slayer of the two demons Chanda and Munda, and her name combines the names of these two demons. Chamunda's story relates how the two evil and arrogant generals of demon armies approached the goddess Durga, challenging her to battle. Durga became enraged, and the avenging aspect of the goddess Kali emerged from her forehead, adding her power to Durga's. After her victory, Durga was called Chamunda.

The images of Chamunda as a ferocious war goddess are grim but are not meant to glorify warfare. She is depicted as black with blood red eyes and is accompanied by a jackal. Her tongue hangs out of her wide-open mouth. She is a formidable foe and is armed with a mace and sword. Chamunda carries a noose and wears elephant skin, and when she is engaged in battle she is mounted on a buffalo.

CONTEMPLATION

*I beware the danger of fearsome wrath
and direct my anger into positive channels.*

Goddesses for Every Day

APRIL 9

Khon-Ma

MINDFULNESS

Khon-Ma (cone-MAH) is an ancient goddess of Tibet whose
name means "luck" or "fortune." Tibetan Buddhists say all
the elements are ruled by Old Mother Khon-Ma. She is clothed
in robes of yellow and carries a golden noose, and some
sources say she rides on the back of a large ram.

Certain superstitious practices relate to Khon-Ma, suggesting how ancient she is. Ordinary people believe she has
dominion over all the spirits of earth, some of which are not
friendly and need to be appeased. People hang the skull of a
ram, or pictures of the people who live inside the house, outside the door in order to confuse the spirits and keep everyone
safe. Perhaps such practices are also intended to ward off an
early death and keep the Old Mother from taking her children
back to her womb too soon.

CONTEMPLATION

*I remain ever mindful of the nature of the thoughts I hold,
knowing my thoughts create my world.*

Beiwe

EXPECTATION

Beiwe (BAY-weh) is a goddess of the Saami, the indigenous people of Finland and Lapland. She flies through the sky in a chariot made from reindeer antlers, and her daughter, Beiwe-Neia, a sun goddess, rides along with her. Each spring, as an expression of gratitude for the goddess's return, Finnish people spread butter on their doors at the festival of Beiwe. As the warmth of the sun melts the butter, the people imagine that the goddesses are eating it, since they are bound to be hungry after their long winter's journey.

Beiwe brings the green color of spring and tender green shoots back to the Arctic North each year, providing food for both humans and reindeer. Her grace is invoked to restore mental balance to those who are insane, driven mad by the darkness of her long winter absence. This suggests a recognition of what is now called "seasonal affective disorder," a type of depression that can come from enduring extended darkness. Its counterpart, called summer seasonal affective disorder, is caused by too much light.

CONTEMPLATION

I greet spring in a spirit of joyful expectancy
as the returning light banishes winter's long darkness.

APRIL 11

Joan of Arc

FAITH

Joan of Arc is technically not a goddess, but many goddesses began as human women who were later deified. She is a potent symbol of feminine power and her faith and bravery transformed many lives. From the age of thirteen, Joan, or Jeanne d'Arc, received visions from Saint Margaret of Antioch, Saint Catherine of Alexandria, and Michael the Archangel. Joan became a courageous warrior who gained a kingdom for her king and was then betrayed, becoming a victim in a vicious political struggle.

Joan of Arc was captured and sold to the English for ten thousand francs. She was then tried as a heretic in a corrupt ecclesiastical court and burned alive in 1431. Her case was retried in 1456, and she was acquitted. In a later change of heart on the part of the church, Joan was beatified on April 11, 1905, and officially became a Catholic saint in 1920. Saint Joan is usually depicted in art wearing armor and holding a raised sword.

CONTEMPLATION

Would I be willing to die for my beliefs and inner voices?

APRIL 12

Macha

ACTION

Macha (MAH-caw) is a threefold Celtic goddess who can appear in different guises: Macha the Red Mane, Macha the wife of Nemed, and Macha the wife of Cruinniuc. As Macha the Red Mane, she was seen as the battle aspect of the goddess Morrigan. In a nasty gesture of intimidation, the heads of those slain in battle were stuck upon tall stones called the pillars of Macha, *Mesred machae* in the Celtic language. Macha the Red Mane became the queen of Ireland when she took the throne after her father, one of three rotating kings, died. She is the only queen in the list of High Kings of Ireland.

As wife of Cruinniuc, Macha, like the goddess Rhiannon, was forced into a race while she was pregnant with twins. Cruinniuc boasted that his wife was faster than the king's horses, and the king demanded that Macha prove it. She won the race, but when it was over she cursed the king and the kingdom of Ulster, saying that in its greatest hour of need, their lineage would suffer like a woman in childbirth. Afterward, she died giving birth to the twins.

CONTEMPLATION

I recognize the dangerous power of curses
and take great care with my words.

Neith

ATTENTION

Neith (neet) is the Egyptian goddess of war and hunting, and her worship began far back in predynastic times. Depicted with a shield and crossed bows and arrows, Neith was credited with making all the weapons for warriors. She also stood guard over the bodies of fallen soldiers. In later periods she wore a weaving shuttle on her head and was said to weave the wrappings for mummies as well as the bandages for those injured in battle.

Neith was the protector of Sais, located on the western edge of the Nile Delta. Sais was the capital of Egypt in the seventh century CE, during the Twenty-sixth Dynasty. Herodotus reported that her temple rivaled the Temple of Karnak. A great annual festival called the Feast of Lamps was held in her honor, where many lamps were lit and burned outside all night. Because her cult center was near the delta of the Nile, the crocodile god Sobek was her son. In hymns and prayers, Neith was called Opener of the Ways, and so is the feminine counterpart of the jackal god Anubis.

CONTEMPLATION

*If I focus on what's most important,
the way will be opened for me to move ahead.*

Bendis

CONFLICT

Bendis (BEN-dus) is the Great Goddess of Thrace and the island of Lemnos, an area now contained in southern Bulgaria, northeastern Greece, and part of Turkey. In ancient Thracian culture, it was the women who worked the land and tended the herds. Powerful Bendis was called the fierce Huntress of the Two Spears. Her name means "to tie," and she is pictured grasping the branch of a holy tree that grants access to the underworld.

As early as the time of Plato, her spring festival, called the Bendideia, was celebrated in Peiraeeus in Crete. The event included nighttime torch races on horseback, which Plato mentioned in his *Republic*. The women who worshipped Bendis wore the skins of lions and foxes and performed ceremonies in her honor in the sanctity of sacred groves. One story tells that the women of Lemnos once revolted in her name and killed all the men on the island, but scholars now believe this was an invention of the Athenians to justify their takeover of Lemnos.

CONTEMPLATION

I am woman, hear me roar.

— HELEN REDDY, "I AM WOMAN," 1972

Nemesis

RETRIBUTION

Nemesis (NEM-eh-sis) is a Greek and Persian goddess of both justice and retribution. Her name means "due enactment." The daughter of the goddess Nox, whose name means "night," she relentlessly dispensed punishment to the guilty. Nemesis is pictured in a queenly manner, riding in a chariot drawn by griffins, mythical beasts said to be symbols of retribution. The griffin had the body of a lion, the head of an eagle, and prominent equine ears; female griffins had eagle wings and eaglelike talons in place of the lion's forelegs.

Nemesis is usually pictured winged, wearing a crown decorated with stags, and holding an apple in one hand and a silver wheel in the other. As a "dispenser of dues," she was seen as counteracting the good fortune given by Tyche. She is connected to the idea that all things are balanced on the scales of time, and this aligns with the concept that all debts, and taxes, come due eventually.

CONTEMPLATION

The scales of justice weigh every deed,
so I thoughtfully choose a wise and loving course.

Andraste

INVINCIBILITY

Andraste (on-DRAH-stay) is the warrior goddess of victory of the Icenain tribe of Celts, who once lived on the southeastern coast of England, where Norfolk is today. Her name is thought to mean "the invincible one," or "she who has not fallen." Andraste was invoked by the Celts in Britain on the eve of battle to gain her favor and to divine the outcome of the conflict. The famous Celtic warrior queen Boudicca, or in Latin Boadicea, embodied this goddess in her campaign of retribution against the Romans. After Boudicca's husband died in battle, the Romans pillaged the town, flogged the queen, and raped her two daughters. In 60 CE, Boudicca retaliated and launched the most potent native rebellion since the Romans had first invaded Britain.

The goddess Andraste was worshipped in sacred groves and woodland shrines, and one of her legends relates to a particular grove in Epping Forest in southern Britain. Andraste's symbol is the hare, and the legend says Boudicca released a hare in this grove as part of a rite of propitiation before the famous battle. After another battle, in which she was betrayed by a neighboring chieftain, Boudicca courageously drank poison rather than submit to rape and Roman slavery.

CONTEMPLATION

I will not bow to tyranny and will take a stand
for what's right if battle lines are drawn.

Esharra

DISCERNMENT

Esharra (ah-SHAR-ah) is a Babylonian goddess of green fields and emerging vegetation whose name means "sacred dwelling of the gods." She has another aspect as a warrior goddess who defended the property and land of her followers. In the Babylonian culture of nearly five thousand years ago, women had rights that later took their gender thousands of years to regain.

Esharra appeared as a high priestess in the city of Kish in the famous tale of Sargon's oath, a fictional story based on historical events. The story tells of ancient kingship rituals where contenders were required to pass certain tests. Esharra acted as the initiator in the challenge presented to Sargon to determine if he was worthy to become king. In the legend, compiled from texts and archaeological discoveries, Esharra said to Sargon, "May the light of your soul sustain you in your darkest hour and beyond. Let the testing begin."

CONTEMPLATION

To discover the truth in any situation,
I must learn to ask the right questions.

Eris

DISCORD

Eris (EE-rus) is the Greek goddess of discord and strife. Her mother was the primordial goddess Nyx, whose name means "darkness" or "night," who was one of the first beings to emerge at the beginning of creation. In myth, Eris was frequently not invited to Olympian social affairs, as she tended to stir things up for the sake of excitement. She embodied the idea of uncertainty, upsetting the apple cart to see how the dynamics would be altered. Annoyed by slights, she appeared unannounced at the marriage of King Peleus and the goddess Thetis. Eris threw into the banquet hall one of her golden apples, which she had marked "for the fairest."

A dispute arose among three goddesses over who should have this distinction: Aphrodite, Hera, or Athena. Choosing the winner became the job of Paris, who chose Aphrodite because she promised him Helen. This incident triggered the Trojan War. In 2006, a newly discovered dwarf planet was named after Eris, and, true to her nature, she created quite a ruckus in the astronomical community. The international debate over what defines a planet resulted in the demotion of Pluto to dwarf-planet status.

CONTEMPLATION

Where do I need to challenge the status quo and confront the unexpected?

Dali

ADVENTURE

Dali (DAH-lee), a Russian goddess from the region of Georgia, has dominion over all horned animals and the hunt. These animals are sacred to the goddess, and the people who lived there and hunted them for food respected this fact. They understood the reciprocity of nature and the importance of giving thanks. Dali dwelled in inaccessible regions of wilderness in places of mystery, where she was seldom seen. She wore her long golden hair in practical braids. Hunters were captivated by her strength and ethereal beauty whenever she chose to be seen.

Because she was a goddess of the hunt, Dali sometimes chose to have romantic liaisons with very strong men. She offered herself because she knew she would bear children who would become strong and honorable hunters as a result of these unions.

CONTEMPLATION

I engage my sense of adventure as I enter
the wild and mysterious places within myself.

Medea

CUNNING

Medea (muh-DEE-ah) is a Greek goddess skilled in magic and the art of transformation. The root of her name is the Sanskrit *medha*, which is also the root of *Medusa* and means "wisdom." Wisdom is seen as a feminine quality in India, and the name Medea is still given to girls there. Medea is the daughter of Helios the sun god, and according to some stories, the daughter of the goddess Hekate. Medea had the power to raise the dead to life. She also figured prominently in the famous story of Jason and the Argonauts and the quest for the golden fleece, which was the hide of a powerful winged ram. Her cunning and clever spells put to sleep the dragon who guarded the fleece and enabled the hero Jason to obtain the magic artifact. Later he betrayed her.

Medea rode in a chariot pulled by winged serpents. She is often cast in a negative light in the stories, but her plight is similar to that of many powerful goddesses who were diminished and demonized as the patriarchy took power. There is some poetic justice in the myths, however, as Jason died in rags. Medea, on the other hand, was such a masterful magician that she went directly to the Elysian fields without passing through the underworld.

CONTEMPLATION

I must be very cunning to catch unaware the dragon who guards the portal to my inner worth.

Mahimata

MATERIALIZATION

Mahimata (ma-hee-MA-tah) is an archaic mother goddess of the Hindu religion who is considered to be the cosmic force incarnate. The Rig-Veda, one of the sacred Sanskrit texts of ancient India, describes Mahimata as feminine power. Her name means "mother earth." Mahimata is also seen as the mother of the gods. The text says that "all things exist but become manifest in Her." In the Upanishads, other sacred texts from India, her nature is described as "manifest reality," the all-pervasive cosmic energy present in all things.

The famous epic poem the Mahabharata says she is "the root cause of all things and the eternal upholder of truth." Mahimata is invoked as the supreme power reigning in the cosmos. She rules above all gods and is the principle of cosmic energy incarnate. Mahimata is energy taking shape in the world of appearances.

CONTEMPLATION

I call on the Great Mother, who is the substance of all life, to help me bring my noble desires into manifestation.

TAURUS GODDESSES
The Tree of Life

THE TREE OF LIFE GROWS IN EVERY GARDEN

Taurus is a fixed earth sign and represents the principle of pure substance. Taurus is the matrix that absorbs the impact of the intense energy projected outward by Aries. Energy is action. Matter is reaction. In alchemical symbolism, the matter of Taurus is precipitated from the waters of Pisces, the twelfth sign, by the fire of Aries. The nature of Taurus, traditionally symbolized by the Bull, is characterized by stability and permanence. The spiritual path of Taurus involves cultivating higher values rather than seeking purely material motives. Taurus natives tend to be builders and sustainers and rarely act without reflection.

The goddess sign for Taurus is the Tree of Life. Trees, especially those that bear the fruit of immortality, are connected with the goddess in cultures around the world. She typically lives in a western garden with a serpent who guards the tree.

Gardens located in the symbolic west, the place of the sun's daily death, connote immortality in numerous cultures where the goddess holds the secret to resurrection. The energy that sinks sustaining roots deep into the earth is responsible for the grounding and stabilizing nature of Taurus. Taurus goddesses embody the element of earth, and many are also symbolized by cows or other strong, protective mammals. Qualities of Taurus goddesses are abundance, sustenance, manifestation, security, growth, the establishment of roots, and fertility.

Green Tara

GROWTH

Green Tara (TAR-ah) is a female Buddha and an aspect of the Great Goddess Tara, who encompasses all manifestations of feminine divinity. She is sometimes called the Mother of the Buddhas. Tara appears in a variety of aspects, depending on her color. Her name means "star" or "she who ferries across," and we call on her as we move through the spiritual-growth aspect of our lives. For Buddhists, the Tara Puja, a form of devotion or "praise prayer," is intended to achieve liberation from sorrow. Tara is an approachable deity who can be invoked directly without the intervention of a lama or monk.

Green Tara is Mother Earth in her oldest form. She is the most revered of all the pre-Vedic goddesses of India, the protector of humanity as we cross the sea of existence. Sometimes, just like the Egyptian Isis, she is shown in a celestial boat. Green Tara is often depicted as a sixteen-year-old girl embodying the childlike quality of playfulness.

CONTEMPLATION

I remember to play along the path of my journey and not to take myself so seriously.

Gaia

CREATIVITY

Gaia (GUY-ah) is one of the oldest creation deities. Her shrines were built in mountain caves and in sacred groves of the oldest trees. Much later the Greeks built a temple to Gaia on the side of the white marble mountain of Parnassus at Delphi. She spoke through her priestesses, and for more than three thousand years was consulted by all levels of society. "Deep-breasted" Gaia gave birth to the world and all upon it. She sprang from Chaos and, as a virgin mother, gave birth to Ouranos, the sky. She then bore Ourea, whose name means "mountains," and Pontus, the "sea." Gaia later mated with Ouranos, to give birth to the Titans, six males and six females, the powerful race of divine beings who preceded the Olympians.

Mythically, Gaia's temple was given to her by the great serpent being Python. Even in the subsequent era of the Olympian Pantheon, when Zeus/Jupiter was lord of heaven, the Greeks still swore their most sacred and binding oaths to Gaia because they were still subject to her law.

CONTEMPLATION

*I vow to dig deeply into my latent creative energy,
trusting that I will give birth to something magical.*

Asherah

FERTILITY

Asherah (ASH-er-ah) is an especially ancient fertility goddess who was worshipped in both Egypt and Canaan, the biblical promised land. She is the consort of both Ba'al and Yahweh. A benevolent goddess who gave her love freely, she was also called Mistress of Sexual Rejoicing. In Israel, archaeologists have unearthed thousands of terra-cotta figurines of Asherah, some of which look like pillars or tree trunks, in simple household shrines fashioned to look like small temples. Devotion to her was the domain of women and centered on household shrines and family worship, making life events, such as feeding the family, sacred.

Asherah is usually shown nude, often holding serpents and lilies. She is always associated with trees and sacred groves and may symbolize the Tree of Life itself. Her name stems from a linguistic root that means "straight," and her followers were expected to live upright lives. Sycamores, figs, and mulberry trees were sacred to her. She was driven underground by Jewish orthodoxy, but evidence is emerging that her worship continued in the temple for some time.

CONTEMPLATION

They built worship sites for themselves of sacred stones, high pillars and Asherah poles on every high hill and under every green tree.

— BIBLE, 2 KINGS 17:10

APRIL 25

Ki

MANIFESTATION

Ki (kee) is a Babylonian goddess whose name means "whole earth." The Sumerians considered her the personification of the earth itself. She was the original principle of matter, or manifestation, which was regarded as feminine in nature. Some sources equate her with the goddess Kishar or believe they may be the same. Both are considered to be daughters of the goddess Tiamat. Ki is the earth, and her consort is An, the sky god.

Ki gave birth to all the Anunnaki, a pantheon of high gods who appear in the Sumerian creation epic Enuma Elish. The most prominent of her children was Enlil, god of air. Ki's myths repeat a theme that recurs around the world, in which heaven and earth were once united and then sundered. In Sumerian and Chaldean myth, this union was severed with the birth of Ki's son Enlil, who, as the principle of air, or movement, then flowed between them.

CONTEMPLATION

I remember to breathe consciously, letting the winds of heaven blow through my mind and inspire me toward greater manifestations of wholeness.

APRIL 26

Malkuth

FOUNDATION

Malkuth (mall-COOTH) means "kingdom" and is the name
of the tenth *sephirah*, or sphere, on the Kabbalistic Tree of Life.
Malkuth is symbolically pictured as a young woman who is
crowned and seated on a throne. As the goddess in physical
manifestation, she is, like the goddess Mahimata, the "body" of
the entire manifest universe and the substance of all things.
Malkuth is also associated with Shekinah, the feminine spirit of
the Divine in creation. Malkuth is the "queen" who embodies
the kingdom, and the "spiritual bride" of those who symbolically climb the Tree of Life to attain enlightenment.

The mysteries of Malkuth and the Tree of Life involve the
recognition that life is complex, polarized, and characterized
by duality. There is an enigmatic saying in Kabbalah: "Kether
is in Malkuth, and Malkuth is in Kether." Kether is at the top of
the Tree of Life, and Malkuth is at the roots. The saying suggests that in truth there is no separation, and the earth itself is
understood to be formed of crystallized light.

CONTEMPLATION

I rest my life on a sure foundation of eternal love.

Themis

SECURITY

Themis (THEE-mis) is an ancient pre-Hellenic goddess from the island of Crete. The Amazons, who lived in the Black Sea on a sacred island called Themiscyra, worshipped her in the form of a black stone, just as the devotees of the pre-Islamic goddess Al Menat worshipped a black stone representing their goddess. There was even an ancient stone in the Roman Forum, the Lapis Niger (translated as "Black Stone"), upon which was engraved the sacred law of the goddess. In Iceland, the Great Goddess was adored as a stone called Spamathu.

Themis is the original goddess of prophecy. She was the *themistes*, or "divine voice," who founded the oracle at Delphi (whose name means "womb"), long before Apollo took over. According to legend, when the island of Thera, now called Santorini, was destroyed by a volcanic eruption, Themis, through her oracle, told the survivors to throw the "bones of their mother" behind them as they left her temple. They realized that by "bones," she meant stones. Through the grace of Themis, the "bones" became new human beings.

CONTEMPLATION

I feel secure in the knowledge that death is not final.
The stones of Mother Earth hold ancient memories,
and if I listen closely I hear stories
of countless cycles of new birth.

Goddesses for Every Day

APRIL 28

Zemyna

BOUNTY

Zemyna (zah-MEE-nah) is a Baltic goddess from Lithuania. She is the daughter of the sun goddess Saule and was called Blossomer, Bud Raiser, and Flower Giver in Baltic poems honoring her. All life came from her. Plant life was her domain, particularly spruce, oak, and linden trees. In every yard, one of these trees would be planted in a place of honor and then regarded as a way to climb to heaven.

The top of the tree was considered the most sacred part, as this was closest to heaven. Offerings of food were reverently placed in front of stones near this holy tree or tied to one of the branches. Sometimes these offerings were thrown into a stream of flowing water as gratitude for Zemyna's bounty. Because she was a goddess of spring and rebirth, her blessing was invoked at the birth of every child.

CONTEMPLATION

I see the promise of abundance in every tree.
Today I will offer someone a gift of food
or flowers as a reminder of this grace.

Io

DETERMINATION

Io (EYE-oh) is a goddess from Crete who was worshipped in the form of a white cow. The Greeks identified her with Isis. In early myth, Io was worshipped as "the cow-eyed one." Later, Hera, another ancient deity, was also called cow-eyed. Both references likely refer to the age of Taurus the Bull, four thousand years ago, before the time of the Greeks. Io's magic brought the rain, and rainmaking dances included copying the movement of cattle who had been driven mad by gadflies in the scorching heat.

Io is also famous as one of the moons of Jupiter (the Greeks called Jupiter *Zeus*); astronomers named Jupiter's moons after his numerous mythical dalliances. As was typical in the later patriarchal Greek myths once the goddess had been suppressed, Hera was transformed into a jealous wife, and her earlier and more powerful identity was often disguised, divided, or diluted. Any time Zeus admired someone, Hera, his wife, sought revenge. The apocryphal Hellenic story says that Hera sent a gadfly to torment Io while she was in her cow form. Io then traveled relentlessly until she reached the healing waters of the Nile, where she finally regained peace of mind as well as her human form.

CONTEMPLATION

*I am determined to stand with my truth
and hold my ground, regardless of the
unconscious behavior of others.*

Flora

FLOURISHING

Flora (FLO-rah) is a Roman goddess of spring and blossoming flowers whose name means "flourishing one." She was honored each year at a festival called Floralia, on May Eve, or April 30 in our calendar. This was the time in Europe when cattle were moved from their winter pastures to feast on new green growth in spring fields. Some stories say Flora's name was actually the secret name of Rome.

Her holiday was celebrated from April 28 to May 3 and included, in addition to Floralia, a longer festival of theatric performances and games, called the Ludi Florales, which celebrated the return of spring. This festival was originally open only to patricians, the wealthy elite, but was subsequently opened as well to plebeians, the common people. Later, church fathers became hostile to these celebrations of fertility, which they called "licentious," which means they must have been quite a party.

CONTEMPLATION
I revel in the fragrant joy of spring.

Maia

FLOWERING

Maia (MY-ah) is the Greek goddess (not the Hindu Maya) who embodies the forces of growth and brings the seasonal warming of the earth. Her name is the origin of the English word *May*. Maia was considered eldest of the Pleiades, the seven daughters of Atlas and the Oceanid Pleione, and she is the Great Goddess of the May festival that falls halfway between the spring equinox and the summer solstice. The Celts called this feast Beltane, and the celebration involved the original "wearing of the green" that was later adopted by Saint Patrick's Day revelers. May wine, which later became the blood of the sacrificed savior Jesus when the Catholic Church came into power, was liberally consumed at this festival. On May Day, celebrants honor the renewal and resurrection of earth after the long winter by dancing around a colorful maypole. Catholics honor Mary as Queen of Flowers on this day.

The Greeks knew Maia as the Grandmother of Magic, and some stories say she scorned marriage, preferring to be free, which hints at her ancient, prepatriarchal origins. Maia was the mother of Hermes, also a skilled magician and the messenger of the gods. She gave her son the duty of conducting the souls of the dead to the underworld.

CONTEMPLATION

I celebrate the rites of spring by dancing around a maypole or just blissfully twirling in my pajamas.

Blanche Flor

ALCHEMY

Blanche Flor (blonche flur), meaning "white flower," is a Celtic goddess who represents the maiden aspect of the triple goddess. She is called Dindrane in Arthurian legends and Grail myths, where she is the sister of Perceval, one of the Grail knights. As Blanche Flor she is sometimes his bride. As Dindrane, she is the Grail heroine, who informed her brother of several aspects of her destiny, including a magical ship and the Tree of Life. Dindrane gave her life's blood to heal a woman of leprosy and then instructed that her own body be set afloat in a boat without a crew. This story is similar to the legend of Mary Magdalene, known from the Bible, who cast off in a ship bound for the south of France.

Blanche Flor's body accompanied the Grail knights on their quest to Sarras, the mystical island in the Grail legend. It was at Sarras that Galahad, carrying Blanche Flor's body, looked within the Grail and died with an "odor of sanctity." Like many other goddesses and sacred feminine archetypes, Blanch Flor was later demonized by the church, who accused her of nothing less than coupling with Satan to birth the antichrist.

CONTEMPLATION

Sometimes I may feel adrift, but I affirm that whatever the appearances, I am guided by a sure and steady hand. I know that the alchemy of life turns all to gold in time.

Rafu-Sen

WARMTH

Rafu-Sen (rah-foo-sen) is a Shinto goddess and immortal being who lives high on a sacred mountain in Japan and is said to be the spirit of the plum tree. She represents the cyclical renewal of spring and is envisioned as a lovely maiden with a white, geishalike face. Rafu-Sen is thought to wander through fragrant groves of blossoming plum trees at night. Long, ethereal veils illuminated by the silver light of the full moon trail after her.

One legend tells of a man who was walking through the mountains and became very cold. He entered a wineshop to warm himself. Inside he met a woman with a sweet voice and beautiful countenance with whom he shared several cups of plum wine. He was awakened many hours later by the cold dawn wind and found he had been sleeping under a plum tree. He knew the beautiful goddess Rafu-Sen had graciously saved his life.

CONTEMPLATION

I enjoy the revitalizing warmth of a special drink and take time to renew myself, giving thanks for my blessings.

MAY 4

Taueret

PROTECTION

Taueret (TA-u-ret), whose name means "one who is great," is the ancient Egyptian hippopotamus goddess, known from the archaic period five thousand years ago, when hippos lived in the fertile mud along the Nile. She is also shown as a composite of hippopotamus, crocodile, and lion. All these are fierce creatures who will kill to protect their young and can be very dangerous to humans. Taueret was known, too, as Nebetakhet, an honorific that means "mistress of the horizon." She was portrayed as residing within some of the stars in the far northern sky. The seven stars shown down her back in art are the stars of what we now call the Little Dipper, in the constellation Ursa Minor. The goddess also formed part of the modern constellation of Draco.

Taueret is often depicted as using as an amulet the hieroglyph *Sa*, which means "protection." *Sa* represents a herdsman's rolled-up shelter of papyrus, which provided protection from the harsh desert elements. Sometimes Taueret carried an ankh, representing life, or a torch, which casts light. She was seen as helpful to women in childbirth.

CONTEMPLATION

*I feel a sense of protection and certainty
as I connect my heart to the polar stars that
constantly revolve but never disappear.*

Lakshmi

WEALTH

Lakshmi (LOCK-shmee) is a well-known and beloved Hindu goddess usually equated with wealth. Although most people may believe this refers only to material wealth, her nature is far-reaching and includes the deeper idea of spiritual riches. Lakshmi is also the goddess of Vidya, which means "feminine wisdom," and she is always associated with the lotus. Her name comes from the Sanskrit word *laksya*, meaning "aim" or "goal," and the deeper meaning suggests the ultimate point we strive for in life.

As the consort of Vishnu, and his Shakti, or power, she is Mother of the Universe. Her title Shri connotes the feminine energy of divinity. Lakshmi is honored each year at a major festival called Diswali, celebrated at the time of the rice harvest. It is believed that Lakshmi visits only houses that are clean and where the people are hardworking, so special effort is made to welcome her.

CONTEMPLATION

*What is the aim of my life,
and how am I directing my energies?*

Hathor

HARMONY

Hathor (HA-thor) is one of the most ancient Egyptian goddesses. Her sacred animal is a wild cow, and her magical implement is the sistrum, a type of musical rattle. One image of Hathor is that of a winged cow who gives birth to the universe. In this form, her name is Het Horu in the ancient Egyptian language, which means "house of Horus." Horus is the divine son of the goddess Isis and is Hathor's consort. Hathor's hieroglyph, which appears near her in temple inscriptions, represents a house with a Horus falcon enclosed, which symbolizes the soul's embodiment. Hathor is usually depicted crowned with a solar disk flanked by horns.

When the goddess manifests as the Seven Hathors, who foretold a child's destiny at birth, she resembles the Greek Fates and other goddesses of fortune. Archaic Egypt, like the rest of Africa, was matrilineal, and so the line of succession passed through the queens. Hathor was seen as the mother of all the gods, bringing forth time itself. Egyptian scholars say that, nearly five thousand years ago, in the earliest dynasties, her name was a component of all royal names. A New Year festival was held in her honor at Dendera, which included feasting, music, and dancing accompanied by many sistrums, harps, and drums.

CONTEMPLATION

Today I find a reason to dance for joy
and marvel at the harmony of the universe.

Pomona

ABUNDANCE

Pomona (poh-MOAN-ah) is a Roman goddess of trees, fruit, orchards, and fruit gardens, while her sister goddess Flora has dominion over flowers. Pomona was linked to fertility and the cycle of the seasons and was honored in spring when the fruit trees blossomed. In classical Rome, she was worshipped at a special altar set up in a grove of fruit trees called a *pomonai*, which had been planted outside Rome's gates and dedicated to her.

Pomona was also seen as a goddess of abundance, because, when the fruit that was sacred to her ripened, it literally fell from the trees as a gift. She is usually depicted carrying a cornucopia or sometimes a large platter of fruit. As an amusing anecdote, pomade, a perfumed hair ointment, was once made from apple pulp, which was called pomace.

CONTEMPLATION

*Today I spend time in a blossoming garden
and breathe deeply the scent of a flowering fruit tree.*

Nyame

EMBRACE

Nyame (YAH-meh) is a creator goddess and the supreme deity of the Ashanti people of Ghana in West Africa. The Ashanti people are one of the matrilineal tribes of West Africa and make up the largest tribe in Africa. Sometimes Nyame is seen as a dual figure who is both male and female, but it is the goddess who brought forth humans from water. Nyame is an all-knowing and all-powerful being whose children are lesser gods. One of her children is a rainmaker and another is sunshine. Nyame is invoked to open a new field before planting.

Nyame's permission must be sought before a grave can be dug, since the earth is her body. She lovingly receives her children when they die. Like the Hindu goddess Shakti, she is considered to be the vital force of creation. A graphic symbol that bears her name is called the Gye Nyame, which means "except for God." This symbol is popular in Ghana and reflects the deeply spiritual character of the Ghanaian people and their ongoing link to Nyame.

CONTEMPLATION

Today I gratefully affirm that, "except for goddess," nothing would exist in form.

MAY 9

Pasiphae

BRILLIANCE

Pasiphae (PAH-si-fah) is a Cretan goddess whose name means "she who shines for all." While in the form of a cow, she mated with a sacred white bull and produced the legendary half-human and half-bull creature called the Minotaur, whose name was Asterious, or "star." This myth probably contains a reference to the age of Taurus, the Bull, that occurred four thousand years ago. Pasiphae's children include the ancient Cretan goddess Ariadne, whose name means "very holy," and Phaedra, whose name means "bright." Her other offspring became the line of Minoan kings, although later myths claim that King Minos was her husband and the father of Asterious.

In later Greek myth Pasiphae became the beautiful Phoenician princess Europa, who descended from the cow goddess Io, and it was Zeus who became a beautiful white bull and seduced Europa to produce Minos. These changes in the myths reflect the ascendancy of the patriarchy and the resulting suppression of the goddess. Some scholars also believe an ancient Cretan rite of bull killing that took place every seven years on the island has survived in Spanish bullfights.

CONTEMPLATION

I can be a shining star when I focus on my talents and strengths.

Callisto

INSTINCT

Callisto (cah-LIST-oh) is a pre-Hellenic goddess whose name means "fairest one." Like the later Greek Artemis, who took on her qualities, Callisto is a goddess of the hunt who possessed keen instincts. When she appeared in human form, she was a young woman running through the ancient woods of Arcadia and was the embodiment of the virgin aspect of the Great Goddess.

Zeus, king of the gods, fell in love with her, and she gave birth to Arcas. Some stories say Hera, wife of Zeus, became jealous and changed Callisto into a bear and left her to roam the forest. The bear is one of the most ancient symbols of the Great Goddess, reaching back in time at least seventy thousand years, so it is likely that the goddess appearing as a bear may have been the earlier version of the story. One day Arcas came upon the bear, and Callisto stood on her hind legs to welcome her son. Thinking he was being attacked, Arcas readied his bow, but Zeus turned him into a small bear before he could shoot. Grabbing both bears by their tails, Zeus hurled them into the sky, where they still roam close together around the North Pole, immortalized as the constellations Ursa Major and Ursa Minor, the Great Bear and her cub, the Little Bear.

CONTEMPLATION

*I feel the invisible strength and protection
of the Great Bear as she eternally circles the sky.*

Hegemone

LEADERSHIP

Hegemone (HEH-jem-mo-nee) is a Greek goddess of the soil and growing plants. Her name means "mastery," and she was also called Queen. No myth about her survives, and although what we know of her comes from the Greeks, it is likely that her origins are older. Her name endures in our language in the term *hegemony*, which is defined as leadership, especially of one nation in relation to another, although the implication is really one of dominance. Zeus is usually identified as Hegemone's father. The identity of her mother changes with the story, but she is usually said to be the goddess Eurynome. Hegemone was worshipped at Boeotian Orchomenus — Viotia in modern mainland Greece — along with the Graces, in the form of pieces of meteorites.

In Athens, Hegemone was worshipped as Leader alongside her sister Auxo, whose name means "increase" or "growth." The Spartans preferred two other Graces, named Cleta, whose name is translated as "sound," and Phaena, "brightness." Hegemone is now also one of the irregular, retrograde moons of Jupiter, discovered in 2003 and named in 2005.

CONTEMPLATION

I endeavor to lead by gracious example,
remembering that power doesn't mean "power over."

Cybele

VALUES

Cybele (sa-BELL), called Mountain Mother, is a goddess of sacred caves. She is also known as Augusta, meaning the "great one"; Magna Mater, "great mother"; Alma, "nourishing one"; and Sanctissima, "most holy one." Cybele originated in ancient Anatolia, which is now Turkey. Her crown was a symbolic representation of a city wall, and she drove a chariot drawn by lions and was also associated with bees. She was worshipped on Mount Ida in rites that included ritual baptism in the blood of a sacrificed sacred bull, representing the annual rebirth of her consort, Attis. This indicates that the practice dates from the age of Taurus, the Bull, rather than from the age of Aries, the Ram, when sacrificial lambs were used instead.

Her priests castrated themselves in their worship of the goddess, which, not surprisingly, the Christian church found repugnant. Until 4 CE, a temple dedicated to Cybele stood on a hillside in ancient Rome, near where the Vatican is today. The ruins are still preserved, and the temple site has been maintained.

CONTEMPLATION

I know that my power as a woman is not diminished by outer appearances.

Idunn

SYMBOLS

Idunn (e-DUN) is a Norse goddess of spring whose name means "the renewing one." According to the *Eddas*, a compilation of Scandinavian myths in two volumes, she lived in an orchard in a western garden, where she cultivated and guarded the apples of immortality. The gods required these apples in order to remain youthful; without them, not only the gods but also the whole world would wither. Once the cantankerous trickster Loki duped a giant into abducting Idunn. As the world grew cold, the gods insisted that Loki bring her back, and, disguised in Freya's falcon cloak, Loki snatched her from the angry giant, Pjazi. Her rescue restored immortality to the Aesir, one group of Norse gods.

Idunn also created the runic alphabet called Futhark, an alphabetic script and system of symbols also used for magic and divination. Her consort, Bragi, the god of poetry, became the greatest of all bards because Idunn placed certain magic runes on his tongue.

CONTEMPLATION

If I am wise, I will learn to recognize and interpret the signs and symbols that appear in my life, knowing guidance and direction often come in unexpected ways.

Arundhati

INTEGRITY

Arundhati (ah-ROON-dah-tee), a goddess from India, is one of the Krittika sisters, who are stars in the Pleiades cluster. Their name means "cutters" in Sanskrit, and these sisters are Mothers of the World who judge the acts of sacred kings. Sometimes Arundhati is a goddess of the stars and the darkness of the night sky. In other myths she is the consort of the sage Vasishtha, who was one of the seven Rishis, the seven sages of Hindu cosmology who are thought to have authored the Vedas, sacred texts of India. In myth, the seven sisters of the Pleiades were married to the seven sages represented by the stars of the Great Bear, Ursa Major. Arundhati is always faithful; she bathes in cold mountain streams, never coming too close to the face of the sun, because hot sparks from his fire (*agni* in Sanskrit) might fan the flames of impure desire.

Although the place of the Pleiades in the sky is unremarkable relative to other star groups, there are few cultures that do not have important myths about this asterism. The Pleiades are in the constellation of Taurus, the Bull, and so are close to the ecliptic, the sun's apparent path in the sky, which makes them easy to observe.

CONTEMPLATION

I cleanly cut away all that is false or unworthy of me.

Prakriti

EARTH

In Hindu cosmology, Prakriti (PRA-kree-tee) is the basic feminine material out of which the entire universe is formed. Before anything existed, she joined with Purusha, the primeval male principle, to bring forth the universe. Prakriti is said to be composed of three aspects, or *gunas*: *tamas*, meaning "darkness"; *rajas*, "passion"; and *sattva*, "goodness." She is the shifting nature of these aspects as they move and combine in manifestation.

Prakriti is also one of three aspects of the Great Goddess. Maya, another aspect, is the dancing veil of illusion, and Shakti is the force of life itself. As Mother of Nature, Prakriti is recognized as the mother of Brahmin, the creator aspect of the Hindu trinity of gods. In the healing system of Ayurveda practiced in India, she is also seen as the nature of our health, which is composed of three *doshas*, or elements: Kapha, Pitta, and Vata. How these are balanced and supported determines our well-being.

CONTEMPLATION

The spontaneous creativity of my mind brings forth either beauty or disorder.

MAY 16

Asase Yaa

ETHICS

Asase Yaa (ah-SAY-suh yah) is a goddess of the Ashanti people of western Africa. Called Old Woman Earth, she is a creation goddess who gave birth to all of humanity. She also reclaims her children at death as they return to the earth, which is her womb. Her consort is the sky god. All over Africa, people are expected to care for the earth, to nourish and cherish her, in order to leave a legacy for future generations.

Asase Yaa is also known as the Upholder of Truth. Those whose truth is doubted are asked to touch their lips to some soil, her sacred body, to assure others that they are speaking the truth. Ashanti farmers pray to her when planting, as she gives them the right to cultivate the land. It is believed that her spirit lives in the plowed field, not in churches and temples. Her sacred day is Thursday, and on this day every plow must rest.

CONTEMPLATION

Before I speak, I make sure my words are only truth.

Mut

RETURN

The Egyptian goddess Mut (moot) was known in the Middle Kingdom of Egypt, four thousand years ago, as Mother of the Sun, in Whom He Rises. Mut took the form of a sacred celestial cow and in this role was Queen of Heaven. The hidden god Amun, the invisible god of air, was her consort, and their yearly "marriage" was one of the great annual celebrations. Amun was later combined with the sun god Ra, and he symbolically rode across the sky on Mut's back. He "rose" at Heliopolis, the city of the sun, and Mut was believed to carry him to his divine destination in the sky. This may also signify the shift from the age of Taurus, the Bull, to the age of Aries, the Ram, since Amun was associated with the ram. When Amun rode on the back of Mut, the celestial cow, the focus shifted away from the Apis bulls of the prior period.

Mut's name means "mother," and she was seen as a great world mother who conceived and brought forth all that exists, including the gods. Mut wears the double crown of Upper and Lower Egypt. Khonsu, a moon god, was her son. She is sometimes pictured with the ostrich feather of the goddess Ma'at at her feet. At Luxor, remains exist of a temple with a sacred lake that was dedicated to Mut.

CONTEMPLATION

Time changes things, and I grow older, but every dawn the sun returns. This morning, I rededicate myself to holding my torch high and casting a bright light in the world.

Hou Tu

APPRECIATION

Hou Tu (how too) is a Chinese fertility goddess. As the patroness of earth's abundance, Hou Tu claims the earth as her symbolic element. The emperor of China offered sacrifices to her on a square marble altar in the Forbidden City at each summer solstice. These rituals were intended to invoke Hou Tu's blessings and grace for a plentiful harvest and to bring balance to the earth.

Hou Tu is similar to the goddess Gaia and, in some sense, represents the deification of the earth. Earth has often been personified as a deity, in particular a mother goddess. Hou Tu's domain is all earth magic, and the ceremonies and rituals performed in her honor were believed to bring the people into resonance with their Divine Mother. Without this, the world would become cold and barren.

CONTEMPLATION

How can I express my appreciation for all the gifts the earth provides?

Haltia

ACKNOWLEDGMENT

Haltia (HALL-tee-ah) is a goddess of the Baltic Finns. She is a benevolent earth goddess considered to be an actual part of the structure of the home. Her energy was perceived as forming the house and holding the building together. She lived in the roof beam of every house, and people believed they needed to acknowledge her presence by reverently greeting her every time they crossed the threshold. When Haltia was properly respected and appreciated, she brought blessings and protection to the inhabitants.

Haltia is similar to the Russian Domovoj, who are house spirits like domestic dwarves. She is also considered to be the tutelary genius, a sort of guiding spirit, for each person occupying the house. When people moved from one house to another, they took a log, or some ashes from the fireplace, and reverently placed the offering in their new hearth to welcome Haltia to her new home.

CONTEMPLATION

*I give thanks for the blessing of my home
and honor whatever spirits protect me.*

White Buffalo Calf Woman

CEREMONY

White Buffalo Calf Woman is the daughter of the sun and moon and comes to earth as a *wakan*, a holy woman, in critical times to teach humanity. She is Whope, "falling star goddess," to the Plains Indians, and Ptesan Wi, or "white buffalo calf woman," to the Sioux. She is a sacred being of supernatural origin who appeared out of a mysterious cloud two thousand years ago, blessing the Sioux with a sacred bundle and seven sacred rituals. One of these gifts was the *chununpa*, or Sacred Pipe, the holiest of all their symbols of worship. Although usually called Peace Pipe, the *chununpa* is also used in other ceremonies.

In her story, White Buffalo Calf Woman appeared to two men on a vision quest during a time of famine. She told the Sioux she would return every time the world was in danger. Ptesan Wi said that as long as the people followed the sacred ceremonies and traditions she gave them, they would remain guardians of the land and would never die out.

CONTEMPLATION

I choose a way to honor the sacred in my life and take time to step into this power.

GEMINI GODDESSES
The Bee

COMMUNITY DEPENDS ON POLLINATION
BY EACH MEMBER

Gemini is a mutable air sign that represents the principle of motion. The energy of the third sign is the result of the irresistible force of Aries impinging on the immovable object Taurus. Spinning motion on an axis is the result. Gemini's expression is to adjust and adapt in an ever-widening collection of data and search for meaning. Learning to tame the mind is Gemini's quest. Geminis are curious and social, desiring to make connections and form relationships, and they are rarely still. In traditional astrology, Gemini is represented by the Twins, showing the sign's dual nature.

The goddess sign for Gemini is the Bee, an ancient symbol of royal power and the sacred feminine. Myths of the Queen Bee, and the priestesses who tend her hives and shrines, exist in diverse cultures. Bees fly from flower to flower, drinking nectar, preparing to make honey, and pollinating flowers that bear fruit and yield seeds in a perpetual cycle of renewal. The industrious bee is an appropriate symbol for the pollinating nature of the intellectual air sign, Gemini. Among Gemini goddesses are magicians, clever tricksters, and shape-shifters, as well as those who are gifted with words and language. Gemini goddesses are animated, verbal, intellectual, versatile, and magical.

Melissa

ROYALTY

Melissa (muh-LISS-ah) was the name of the goddess Artemis when she was worshipped as the Queen Bee and honey goddess. *Melissa* means "honeybee" in Greek and was also the title given a high priestess of the goddess Artemis. The plural is *Melissae*, and there is evidence that there were thousands of these priestesses. Beekeeping has a long history in many cultures, and honey has been prized for thousands of years. There is also a shamanic tradition of beekeeping associated with the goddess, since the queen bee is the heart of the hive and her daughters are the workers. At certain times, the queen lays eggs that will become male drones. The queen bee mates in the air with whatever drone manages to get to her first, describing the ancient role of the goddess in choosing her own mate.

Honey was seen as the sacred substance of the goddess, and the honey jar, the *pithos*, was a symbol of the Divine Feminine womb of creation. In Egyptian myth, honeybees were regarded as the tears of Ra the sun god, spontaneously created from the sun and responsible for all vegetation on earth. In myth, Adrastia was a bee priestess and Melissa's sister. Adrastia fed the infant Zeus on honey while Amalthea, the goat, provided him with milk from one of her horns. In Hebrew the name Deborah means "bee."

CONTEMPLATION

Love is the true power at my "center" that holds the space for all the outer activity in my life.

Carmentis

SPEECH

Carmentis (car-MEANT-is) is a Roman goddess said to have created the Latin alphabet, or to have altered the Greek letters for the Romans. She was known for the magical and soothing power of her words. Carmentis was especially revered at her temple in Rome that stood next to the Porta Carmentalis, one of the gates of Rome near the Capitoline Hill, named to honor her. No leather or iron was permitted at this temple, meaning her female devotees would enter barefoot. Likewise, because Carmentis is a patron of birth, no blood sacrifices were permitted.

At one point, the women of Rome revolted when their freedom to ride unescorted in carriages was revoked. Calling upon Carmentis, the women said they would bear no more children. Afterward, their right to ride in the carriages unescorted was restored. Among her areas of responsibility, Carmentis was a protector of women giving birth, and she was honored at the beginning of the new year and asked to bring blessings to new endeavors.

CONTEMPLATION

I am aware of the power of my words
and use my voice consciously, avoiding harm.

Quinoa-Mama

INVOCATION

Quinoa-Mama (KEEN-wah-MAH-mah), a pre-Columbian goddess of grain, was invoked by the Incas of Peru at the beginning of each planting season. The grain quinoa was one of their most important crops and for six thousand years has been a staple food for the people who live in the Andes. The Incas called their crop *chisaya mama*, "mother of all grains," and ritually tossed the first seeds of the season with special golden implements. Quinoa is grown mostly for its edible seeds, but the leaves too are eaten.

Girls and women made special dolls in Quinoa-Mama's honor from the leaves and ground grain of the quinoa plant. They kept the dolls for one whole yearly cycle, until the time of the next planting, when the dolls were ritually burned, invoking an abundant harvest for the next season. This was seen as a surrender of everything from the previous year and a request to bless the new crop.

CONTEMPLATION

All things happen in their own time,
and I learn to release what has passed,
so that something better can grow in its place.

Sara-la-Kali

PILGRIMAGE

Sara-la-Kali (SA-rah-lah-KAH-lee), or Sara the Black, is a spirit being of the Romani, or Roma, people, who are more commonly known as Gypsies. May 24 is the festival of Black Sara, and every year thousands of Gypsies go on pilgrimage to Sainte Sara-la-Kali's crypt. Her shrine is located in the church of Saintes-Maries-de-la-Mer on the Île de la Camargue, France, at the mouth of the Rhône River. The site is also the location of relics dedicated to three Marys: Mary Magdalene, Mary Salome, and Mary Jacobe, who, according to a mysterious legend, were cast adrift in a boat with an enigmatic figure called Black Sara after the crucifixion of Jesus. The numerous statues of Black Virgins in churches in France and elsewhere in Europe are the source of much speculation.

Until 1912, only the Romani were permitted to enter this sacred shrine. In it, one large central candle is lit amid a flaming forest of white candles held by the pilgrims. Sara's origins are a mystery, although scholars now believe the Romani may have come out of India around the ninth century. The ceremony in Saintes-Maries-de-la-Mer, in which the statue of Sara-la-Kali is immersed in the sea, closely parallels annual processions that take place in India, where statues of the Indian goddess Kali are immersed in water.

CONTEMPLATION

Today I take an inner pilgrimage, lighting a white candle in honor of the mysteries of the Divine Feminine.

Charis

GRACE

Charis (CHAR-is) is the embodiment of the principle of grace, and in Greek myth she is the mate of Hephaestus, the black-smith god. Like many ancient goddesses, she appears in a triple aspect, or threefold manner. She takes the form of the three Graces, daughters of Aphrodite by Zeus. Their names are Aglaea, meaning "splendor" or "radiance"; Thalia, "abun-dant" or "rejoicing"; and Euphrosyne, "heart's joy." (A different Thalia is one of the nine Muses.)

The Graces are called Charities in Greek, and they worked together with the nine Muses. While the Muses provided the raw material for creativity, it was the Graces who bestowed inspiration and, as Alexander Pope said in his *Essay on Criticism*, "a grace beyond the reach of art." The Graces were said to represent the rays of the sun, and some scholars believe the word *charis*, or "grace," had the same meaning as the Sanskrit *karuna*. The Greek poet Pindar said, "If anything sweet or delightful warms the heart of any mortal, whether she has beauty, skill or the light of victory, it is the gift of Charis."

CONTEMPLATION

I give thanks for my unique gifts,
through which I bring light and beauty to the world.

Izanami

INVITATION

Izanami (iz-ah-NAH-mee) is a primordial Japanese Shinto goddess of creation. Her name means "she who invites," and she has dominion over death as well as creation. She was an original deity who emerged into existence along with her twin brother, Isanagi, who is also her husband. They possessed a magic spear decorated with jewels, and together they created the first island in the Japanese archipelago, which now contains three thousand islands. They began by standing on the bridge between heaven and earth and churning the sea below with the spear to form an island.

Izanami died giving birth to one of their children and then became queen of the underworld. Her brother-husband pursued her, but she could not leave the darkness, and he could not remain in the land of the dead. Her myth is similar to those of Persephone and Inanna, and it relates to the continual cycle of death and rebirth of the growing things on earth, as well as to the polarity of light and dark.

CONTEMPLATION

What unhealed pain lives in darkness in my life
that I need to face and bring into the light?

The Cherubim

ANGELIC PROTECTION

The cherubim were originally female angels of the highest order who supported the throne of God and were associated with the goddess Asherah. *Cherubim* is the plural of *cherub*, but these powerful beings bear little resemblance to the small, chubby angels who appear on greeting cards. Cherubim are related to the winged bulls of Babylon, also called cherubim, who guarded royal gates. The latter creatures had wings, tails, bull's bodies, and human heads, like the creatures in Ezekiel's biblical vision.

Early images of cherubim depict them as the intimidating guardians of a sacred tree. An ivory plaque in the Louvre, in Paris, shows a single female cherub guarding the Tree of Life. Thousands of years after the plaque was created, when Genesis was recorded, cherubim were viewed as part of the cult of Yahweh, standing guard to prevent human access to the Tree of Life. They also form what is called the "mercy seat" on the Ark of the Covenant.

CONTEMPLATION

I acknowledge the presence of my holy guardian angel and feel grateful for her protection.

Caer Ibormeith

FLIGHT

Caer Ibormeith (care ee-BORE-meeth) is an Irish shape-shifting goddess who spent alternating portions of her life as a swan and as a human girl. Her name means "yew berry." Each year when summer ended, she went with her companions to a lake, where they were all transformed into beautiful swans. Caer Ibormeith surpassed all the other swans in beauty and whiteness. She lived on Lough Dragon, "Dragon's Lake," and always wore a golden necklace whether she was a swan or a girl.

Her mate, called Augus, was a god of poetry. He fell in love with her while she was in human form and then sought her when she became a swan. She finally consented to be his bride if he too would become a swan. Together they flew three times around Lough Dragon and then lived happily ever after, alternating between human and bird form.

CONTEMPLATION

*Where do I need to "shape-shift" in my life
and take on another form or aspect?*

Polik Mana, Butterfly Maiden

LONGEVITY

Butterfly Maiden, or Polik Mana (POE-lick MA-nah) to the Hopi, is a maiden who dances in the spring to bring life-giving rain to the deserts of Arizona and elsewhere on the earth. She is also a woman dancer at initiations for young Hopi girls. The Butterfly Dance takes place in August or September and is filled with beautiful color and gratitude, recalling the beauty of the butterfly as she dances from flower to flower in spring, pollinating the fields and bringing joy.

As many as one hundred pairs of girls and boys dance in the village plaza in late summer before the harvest, giving thanks for what Butterfly Maiden accomplished through her spring dance. The children are accompanied by a chorus of fathers, brothers, and uncles chanting meaningful lyrics. They pray for rain, health, and long life for all creatures as they give thanks for the blessings Butterfly Maiden gave by pollinating fields and flowers.

CONTEMPLATION

My life is a dance of joy,
and happiness extends its duration.

Dione

ORACLE

Dione (dee-OH-nay), an ancient Cretan goddess, was the Titan daughter of Gaia and Ouranos. Her name actually means "goddess." She was the oracular goddess of Dodona in what is now modern Greece. Three old women, or crone prophetesses of Dodona, who were known as Pleiades, or "doves," were her priestesses. The rustling of a beech tree in the wind answered personal questions, and only the aged women were permitted to interpret the answers as the sacred tree spoke to them.

Later sources claim Dione was the first consort of Zeus and also the mother of Aphrodite, suggesting both her antiquity and her exceptional power. She was a goddess of fertility and inspiration. The oracle site was in use well into the Christian era, until the holy tree was spitefully cut down in 391 CE.

CONTEMPLATION

Under the boughs of a sacred tree,
I listen in silence to the voice of inspiration.

Laka

ATTRACTION

Laka (LAH-kah) is a goddess and ancestral spirit of ancient Hawaii whose domain is cultivated vegetation, herbal lore, and wild forests. Her name means "gentleness," and she embodies the power of attraction and invocation. She is thought to have blessed the ancient Hawaiian people with the sacred dance of hula. Every time the traditional dance is performed in Hawaii, an altar is prepared in Laka's honor.

The ritual of placing a lei, or flower necklace, over someone's head is an ancient tradition in Hawaii. *Lei* means "garland" or "wreath" in Hawaiian, and the lei is a symbol of honor and respect. This beautiful flower necklace conveys spiritual meanings of connection, unity, and healing. It has different meanings, depending on the circumstances and time of life of the person receiving it, and its flowers are chosen to convey a specific meaning. Leis are always a gift of love. Some denote celebration and welcome, while others represent grieving. Pregnant women receive open leis. Wildflowers are especially sacred to Laka, and her special lei is made from the maile plant.

CONTEMPLATION

Today I gently sway my hips, honoring the rhythms of life and attracting the gifts of nature's bounty.

Inari

FLEXIBILITY

Inari (in-ARE-ee), a Shinto rice goddess, is one of the most mysterious deities of Japan. She is androgynous and can appear in either female or male form, depending on the situation. Perhaps this symbolizes the versatility and importance of rice to the Japanese culture. Rice is processed and prepared in many ways and is used to make both sweets and wine. The Japanese emperor still performs a rice ceremony as part of his succession to the throne. The festival of Inari is held in spring when the cultivation of rice begins. Inari, as a goddess of blessings, good gifts, and abundance, is similar to the Hindu goddess Lakshmi.

Each year Inari descends from a high mountain to the rice fields to protect the harvest. She is also a shape-shifter. The magical fox, Kitsune, is Inari's messenger, and it is believed that the goddess also takes this form. A pair of foxes usually accompany Inari in artistic representations. Similar to figures in Lakota lore, Inari sometimes appears in the form of a trickster spider to teach a lesson.

CONTEMPLATION

Today I prepare a sacred meal that includes rice,
giving thanks for all the sustenance in my life.

JUNE 2

The Rusalka

PLAY

The Rusalka (roo-SAL-ka) are Russian or Slavic nature spirits, similar to elves and fairies. They are talented shape-shifters and are often described as the souls of women who died by drowning. Sometimes they are cast in a negative light, like the Sirens, but usually they are considered benevolent. They were beautiful and beguiling creatures who possessed eternal youth and were especially known for their beautiful voices. The Rusalka were imagined with long, flowing green hair, and as balancing on tree limbs or bathing in streams.

The Russians celebrated Rusalka Week at the beginning of summer, weaving garlands for the spirits and later tossing these into streams. The people danced and sang all night in the forest. During these celebrations, it was believed the Rusalka emerged from the lakes and streams and danced in the moonlight, blessing the land. Wherever their feet touched the ground, the grass would grow green and thick. Perhaps it is the Rusalka who are forming the mysterious crop circles?

CONTEMPLATION
I take time to dance and play,
as my childlike joy breathes life into all my endeavors.

Renenet

IDENTITY

Renenet (REN-eh-net) is an Egyptian goddess of great power who in ancient times gave newborn babies the gift of their true names, called their Ren. Her name means "she who gives Ren." The name she bestowed was an aspect of the eternal soul, and it was said that a baby had Renenet on its shoulder from the first day. She is depicted in art as a rearing cobra, and it was said that her gaze could either wither her enemies or grant abundance to crops. The parts of her name mean both "nourishment" and "snake."

In her capacity as a snake, Renenet was the wife of Sobek, the crocodile god of Upper Egypt, who represented the life-giving fertility of the Nile flood. She was also mother of Nehebkau, who had domain over the Ka and Ba, other important facets of the soul. An ancient hymn to Renenet from the Egyptian Book of the Dead says, "I will make the Nile swell for you, without there being a year of lack and exhaustion in the whole land, so the plants will be flourishing, bending under their fruit."

CONTEMPLATION

What quality describes the "true name" of my soul?

Nungeena

RESTORATION

Nungeena (noon-JEE-nah) is an Australian mother goddess who saved the world after it was nearly destroyed by hordes of insects. She is seen as a benevolent guardian spirit. The Aborigines say that, in the very earliest part of the Dreamtime, many things were created by the god Baiame. But a jealous evil spirit named Marmoo wished to destroy all these creations and fashioned ugly and destructive insects to consume everything on earth.

Baiame had to find Nungeena to help, so he searched for her where she lived in a beautiful valley by a waterfall. Nungeena had saved and hidden precious seeds in case of drought, and because of her, the world could be replanted. Her myth is a story of the ongoing balance of creation and destruction and the importance of learning prudence and stewardship.

CONTEMPLATION

I will always safeguard a portion of the blessings that come into my life.

JUNE 5

Zoe

ANIMATION

Zoe (ZOH-ee) is a deity of the Gnostic Greeks who is said to possess a fiery breath. Her name means "life," and she is mentioned in the "Hypostasis of the Archons," or "The Reality of the Rulers," part of the Nag Hammadi library, a collection of ancient codices uncovered in an Egyptian hamlet. Zoe is called the "female instructing principle," and she taught "the Adam," or humanity. She was a daughter, or "emanation," of the Great Goddess, whom the Greeks called Sophia. In the old tales it was Zoe who animated the clay Adam after various other gods had tried but failed. Certain other spirits were angry with her success and cursed her.

She laughed at the spirit called Yahweh for having the arrogance to curse her, and threw him into the abyss. Zoe was sometimes called Eve, and in this case Adam was said to call her Mother of All Living. In the "Hypostasis of the Archons," it is the goddess Zoe who guides humanity to the eternal life of spirit.

CONTEMPLATION

The eternal life of spirit breathes life into all my efforts.

Goddesses for Every Day

Vach

SOUND

Vach (vok) is a Hindu goddess called She of the Thousand Forms. Her name means "voice," and she was once a goddess of thunder. Vach is the goddess of the word, language, and both divine and human speech. In the Vedas, sacred literature of ancient India, she is called the Melodious Four-Uddered Cow whose milk sustains all. Her udders are also seen as the four quarters of existence that became the cardinal directions and the four seasons of the year.

Vach is herself the power of sound and vibration, and so her magical vibratory power, like that of the Egyptian frog goddess, Heket, created the world. Since all is frequency, her nature holds the vibratory matrix for all forms that come into manifestation.

CONTEMPLATION

I recognize that the frequency of sound underlies the world of form, so I choose to create sounds of harmony rather than discord.

Etain

TRANSFORMATION

Etain (ET-ain) is an Irish Celtic goddess and a cyclic dweller in the underworld. Her name means "shining one," which links her to the Sidhe, the fairy folk of Ireland. Her myth says she was once a beautiful fairy, and the king of the fairies fell in love with her, angering his wife, who turned Etain into a butterfly. The angry wife then caused a storm to blow Etain far away from her home.

Butterflies are symbols of transformation because they start their lives as caterpillars and then undergo a metamorphosis to become beautiful winged creatures. After numerous exploits, including being born a princess and marrying the high king of Ireland, Etain was found again by the fairy king, who still longed for her. As in a fairy tale, the two lovers flew away disguised as swans and lived happily ever after.

CONTEMPLATION

What needs to be sheltered in a protective chrysalis and transformed into something else entirely?

Nephthys

BOUNDARIES

Nephthys (NEP-this) is an Egyptian goddess whose name means "lady of the temple enclosure," referring to a divine dwelling. She was said to have a fiery breath and to be capable of incinerating the pharaoh's enemies. Her magical spells were necessary to navigate the treacherous realm of the Duat, the region of the sky where the soul journeyed after death. The god Set was her husband, and although in later versions he is cast as the villain in the story of Isis and Osiris, the ancient Egyptians, who saw him as the desert, worshipped him.

Nephthys had a role as a guardian in the transitions of death, which was similar to the role Isis played in transitions of birth. Each evening Nephthys rode in the night-barque (boat) to protect the sun god Ra as he traveled through the twelve hours of night. She was both guide and guardian in the darkness, and the Egyptian Book of the Dead proclaimed that she could give the pharaoh the power to see "that which is hidden by moonlight." She was sister to Isis and helped her when Isis went on her quest to find the pieces of Osiris's body. His brother Set had murdered Osiris, cut apart his body, and buried it in pieces all over Egypt.

CONTEMPLATION

What is hidden by darkness or denial in my life that needs to be acknowledged or to be set aside from my heart?

JUNE 9

Laima

LUCK

Laima (LIE-mah) is a goddess of fate and good fortune from Latvia and Lithuania and is seen as the personification of these ideas. Her name actually means "luck." With her sisters, Karta and Dekla, Laima is part of a trinity of goddesses similar to the Norns and the Fates. She and her sisters travel to where women are giving birth and decree the child's fate. In the 1959 Disney version of *Sleeping Beauty*, they appear as three good fairies, Flora, Fauna, and Merryweather, who arrive to bless a young princess. Similarly, three wise men come to the birthplace of the infant Jesus. Goddesses and archetypes of fate always seem to come in threes.

Much can be averted through prayer, but it is Laima who makes the final decision in matters of destiny. She was originally depicted in the form of a bird, but later she took on human form. Birds remained important to her, however, and many pieces of flint carved in the shape of her sacred birds have been found in the area of Aestii on the southeastern shore of the Baltic Sea. To this day, the people of Latvia still use the expression "Laima willing."

CONTEMPLATION

I believe my luck can be changed through intention and focused will.

JUNE 10

Juno

FINANCES

Juno (JOO-no) is the Roman queen of the gods and one of the most important Roman deities. The month of June is named for her. She was the special protector of the Roman state and served as a counselor to the rulers. In her role as Juno Moneta, she watched over the finances of the empire. She is similar to the Greek Hera and the Etruscan Uni. A guardian goddess of women and the consort of Jupiter, Juno was powerful in her own right and, like her sky god partner, able to wield fiery thunderbolts.

When Gaul attacked Rome, it was said, her sacred geese sounded the alarm and saved the city, mythically linking her with Mother Goose. One of her festivals, celebrated on July 7, was called Nonae Caprotinae, "the Nones of the Wild Fig," and was no doubt held in fields near fig trees accompanied by dancing and joyous revelry.

CONTEMPLATION

*If I learn to be a good steward of my financial resources,
I will be protected during difficult times.*

JUNE 11

Mater Matuta

HAPPINESS

Mater Matuta (mah-tare mah-TOO-tah) is a goddess of ancient Rome whose festival was celebrated on June 11. Her temple was in the Forum Boarium, which served as the cattle market. Mater Matuta is the patron of newborn babies but also protects harbors and those who travel on the sea. She is a goddess of light who is associated with dawn. A restored Ionic temple rededicated to Mater Matuta, decorated with ox skulls and garlands of flowers, still stands today in the midst of modern structures in Rome.

Her June celebration was called the Matralia. This festival was open only to single women or older women who were still in their first marriages. The matrons offered Juno cakes that had been baked in earthenware pots. Women walked in procession, proudly carrying their nieces or nephews and praying for their welfare. This is thought to signify that women should care for their sisters' children as if they were their own.

CONTEMPLATION

Happiness is a quality of mind
that is profoundly influenced by choice.

Heket

REGENERATION

Heket (hay-KET) is an Egyptian goddess of fertility and re-generation. Her icon is the frog. Multitudes of frogs appeared in Egypt at the time of the annual inundation of the Nile and served as harbingers of the flood. Heket was part of the Osirian family, and *hekau*, or "words of power," were said to emerge from her priestesses. Egyptians had to learn these verbal formulas to gain access to various parts of the underworld.

Heket also served as a midwife and protected women in childbirth. She is the female counterpart of the ram-headed creator god Khnum, as she helped to fashion the physical forms of children in the womb. Amulets that looked like small boats (barques, or arks) were named after her. In her role as regenerator, Heket attended the sun god Ra as he was reborn each morning, and she also assisted Isis in bringing Osiris back to life. Like Isis, she was called Great of Magic and could touch lifeless humans with the ankh, restoring life to them.

CONTEMPLATION

I will speak words of power and breathe fresh life into all my projects.

JUNE 13

Metis

COUNSEL

Metis (MEH-tis) is a Greek goddess who is the personification of wisdom. Her name means "prudent counsel," and it was said that Metis knew more than all the gods. As the daughter of Oceanus and Tethys, she was a powerful Titan. Some sources say Metis was the same as Medusa, who is an ancient archetype of feminine wisdom.

In later myth, Metis became Zeus's first wife, which diminished her, since he was an Olympian rather than one of the earlier and mightier Titans. She was responsible for administering the remedy that caused the Titan Kronos to disgorge all of his own children, whom he had swallowed so they wouldn't supplant him. Greek myth says that when Metis was pregnant with Athena, Zeus swallowed her, as he feared his firstborn son or daughter would be more powerful than himself. He believed that, if he swallowed her, he could partake of some of Metis's wisdom, and she would not literally have been murdered by his hand. Although Metis did not survive, nine months later Zeus had a terrible headache, and then their daughter Athena sprang from his forehead. In this way he could also claim to have given birth to wisdom.

CONTEMPLATION

I look deeply within myself to find or receive prudent counsel in all my affairs.

Uksakka

DOORWAYS

Uksakka (uk-SAH-kah) is a goddess of the Saami, the indigenous people of Lapland and Finland. The word *Akka* denotes a goddess or female spirit. Uksakka is a goddess of birth and a midwife who looks after newborn children. Special prayers were said to the goddess during labor, and after the birth the mother would eat a special porridge dedicated to Uksakka, offering thanks for the safe delivery of her baby.

There were three Akka spirits, exemplifying the principle of the triple goddess and inhabiting different parts of the house. Maderakka lived inside the walls, Sarakka lived below the fireplace, and Uksakka guarded the portals, including the one of birth. She also inhabited the space around doorways. Uksakka is thought to be a special guardian of toddlers and a help to mothers when babies start walking and moving around.

CONTEMPLATION

The stages of life are like doorways. I gracefully let go of the past as I learn to navigate new possibilities.

Anima Mundi

BREATH

Anima Mundi (AH-nee-mah MOON-dee) is a Roman divine concept whose name translates to "soul of the world." The name comes from the root word *ane*, which means "to breathe." Anima Mundi was especially revered by the Roman Gnostics. Some philosophers insisted that her pure and ethereal spirit permeated all of nature and existence. The Stoics asserted that Anima Mundi was the only vital force in the universe. Although Plato usually gets credit for this idea, her origins are much more ancient and bear strong similarity to those of goddesses described in certain Eastern doctrines.

Carl Jung revived the ancient terms *anima* and *animus* and said we all possess an anima, a female soul, and an animus, a male soul. In the sixteenth century, the French mystic Guillaume Postel said the soul's male half had been redeemed by Christ, and the female half was unredeemed and awaited a female savior. This was an improvement over an edict issued by the Council of Nantes in 660 CE, which, as Claudia Dreifus reports in her book *Seizing Our Bodies*, declared all women to be "soulless brutes."

CONTEMPLATION

I take a deep breath and give thanks to the heavenly mother who gave birth to all souls in the beginning.

JUNE 16

Canola

MUSIC

Canola (cah-NO-lah) is a particularly ancient Irish goddess who is said to have invented the harp, one of the long-cherished symbols of Ireland. The legend of the harp's creation relates that Canola once walked along the shore of an ocean in the darkness, following the sound of haunting music and trying to learn its source. Becoming exhausted, she finally stopped and was lulled to sleep by the mysterious and melodious noise.

When she awakened at dawn, she realized the enchanting sound had been made by the wind singing through sinew clinging to the dried bones of a whale. Canola was so inspired by the magical music that she created the first harp. The actual origin of the harp as an instrument is unknown, but harps can be found in Celtic carvings, on the walls of Egyptian tombs, and in Viking images.

CONTEMPLATION

Today I make joyous music with whatever I find
— a cigar box banjo or a grand piano.

Ilmatar

SPIRIT

Ilmatar (ILL-mah-tar), a Finnish creator goddess called the Daughter of Air, is thought to have emerged from this element. She is an immensely powerful virgin sky mother who created the universe from seven cosmic eggs. In some stories, Ilmatar was impregnated by the wind and gave birth to the earth and stars and the first human, who was a bard. She also gave birth to the gods of magic and smithing. Sometimes she is identified as the mother of the great magician Ilmainen, who created the sun.

Ilmatar is also mother of the god of music, Vainamoinen. Sometimes Ilmatar is shown as an androgynous being who was the creator of everything. Some of her honorifics are Virgin Daughter of Air, Sky Mother, Water Mother, Creatress Goddess, Daughter of Nature, and Mother of the Waters.

CONTEMPLATION

I take time to ponder what I long to bring into being from the magical substance of my creativity.

Eurynome

SPONTANEITY

Eurynome (yoo-RIH-noh-mee), whose name means "universal one," is a Titan goddess, perhaps the first. The Titans were powerful beings who preceded the Greek Olympians. According to legend, in the beginning Eurynome rose naked from Chaos. She began twirling in a dance that separated the sea from the sky and darkness from light, bringing order out of Chaos. Her spinning created the earth and the stars.

The motion also generated a strong wind that she magnetized. She rolled the wind into the shape of a great serpent and named it Ophion. This wind serpent became her mate, and she transformed herself into a dove who laid a cosmic egg that brought forth all things. In pride and arrogance, the snake later took responsibility for everything, so Eurynome banished the great serpent to an underworld dungeon, where he still causes trouble from time to time.

CONTEMPLATION

Today I enjoy the liberating power of twirling,
imagining that my spinning brings worlds into form.

Penelope

IMMORTALITY

In Greek myth, Penelope (pen-ELL-oh-pee) is the wife of the hero Odysseus, king of Ithaca. She was also cousin to Helen of Troy. In the older stories Penelope is a powerful spring fertility goddess whose role is to choose the annual king. She mated with numerous suitors, including Hermes (Mercury to the Greeks), and gave birth to the god Pan. In his book *The White Goddess*, Robert Graves called Penelope "She Whose Face Is Veiled."

Penelope was famous for her cleverness, and while Odysseus was fighting the Trojan War for twenty years and believed dead, she defied her many suitors by saying she couldn't marry until she finished weaving a funeral cloth for her father-in-law. She promised she would choose among the suitors when the robe was complete. Each day she worked at her loom, and each night she cleverly unraveled what she had woven. In this way she mystically kept Odysseus alive. This became known as Penelope's web, something forever worked on but never completed.

CONTEMPLATION

I cleverly weave the threads of my life into a beautiful,
if impermanent, tapestry.

186   Goddesses for Every Day

CANCER GODDESSES
The Shell

PRECIOUS PEARLS ARE FORMED BY FRICTION

Cancer is a cardinal water sign that marks the summer solstice and adds the powerful quality of emotion to the mental nature of the preceding sign, Gemini. Cancer acts like the womb and holds the energy of the universal-mother principle, providing the vessel from which all forms are born. Cancer energy is highly instinctual, nurturing, and protective, engendering longing to make a home and build emotional connections. Learning to stabilize and steady the emotions is the path of Cancer.

The goddess sign for Cancer is the Clam Shell, symbol of the ocean, from which Cancer's traditional symbol, the Crab, also emerges. Shells, which are containers of life, appear in numerous cultures as images of the goddess. Sometimes it is the cowrie shell, which is widely revered and is suggestive of a woman's sexual anatomy. The goddess Venus mythically emerged from the ocean on a clam shell. Cancer is ruled by the moon, so lunar goddesses are included in this section. Cancer goddesses are nurturing, often creators, and are linked to the ocean, which is the source of all life. They are protective mothers who guard the home, keep the hearth fires burning, and honor their ancestors.

JUNE 20

Frigg

STILLNESS

Frigg is a Norse and Teutonic goddess of love and fertility who can be seen in the atmosphere and clouds. The English word *Friday* comes from "Frigg's Day." Her palace is known as Fensalir, which means "sea hall." She was sometimes known as the White Lady of Midsummer, or summer solstice, but was more often known as a quiet deity of wisdom. Her story comes down to us from the *Eddas*, a compilation of Scandinavian myths in two volumes. Frigg was the most revered of the Norse goddesses and the only one who sat on a throne beside Odin.

Beautiful Frigg is tall and stately. She is depicted in either snow white or dark clothing and wears heron feathers in her headdress. A ring of keys, symbols of hidden treasure or secret wisdom, hangs from her girdle. Sadly, most people have only heard her name in the derogatory slang expression *friggin*, which is a demeaning reference to her generous and loving spirit.

CONTEMPLATION

Regardless of outer circumstances,
I can enter the stillness within and find wisdom.

Cancer Goddesses

JUNE 21

Anuket

SWELL

Anuket (on-new-ket) is the Egyptian goddess of the Nile. In ancient Egypt, the Dog Star, Sirius, brightest star in the sky, rose at the time of the summer solstice.

Due to precession, the slow backward motion of the stars relative to earth, Sirius now rises before the sun closer to the end of July. This annual event heralded the Egyptian new year and announced the annual flooding of the Nile. Anuket was originally a water goddess from Sudan, and she was very popular in Nubia. Her name means "embracer," suggesting the nourishing action of the floodwaters fertilizing the arid land. Her temple was built on the island of Sehel near Aswan, in the southern part of Egypt.

Anuket is depicted wearing a crown of reeds and ostrich feathers. Her sacred animal was the fast-moving gazelle, which races like the swiftly flowing waters of the flooding river. When the flood began each year, so too did Anuket's Festival of Inundation, where she was worshipped as Nourisher of the Fields. People threw coins, gold, jewelry, and other precious items into the river, expressing their gratitude for the life-giving waters.

CONTEMPLATION

I embrace the cycles of life and the shifting swells and troughs of my emotions.

Hestia

HEARTH

Hestia (HEST-yah) is the firstborn Olympian, older even than Zeus, and was the daughter of Kronos and Rhea. Her name figures in an ancient Greek expression, "Start with Hestia," meaning "Begin at the beginning." She is the symbol of the hearth fire, living in the center of the flame. Her name in Greek means "hearth" and is thought to originate from the earlier Sanskrit word *vas*, which means "shining." The Greek philosopher Pythagoras said, "The fire of Hestia is the center of the earth," and the Roman statesman Cicero described her as the "guardian of innermost things."

Thousands of years ago the hearth was a simple circle of stones, and hearths formed the first altars. A portion of what was burned in the hearth was seen as a sacrifice, and the smoke that rose to heaven was seen as a prayer, a consciously created connection between those who sent their offering upward and the Divine. It's no coincidence that the two words *heart* and *hearth* are nearly identical. The symbolic hearth of Delphi was both the spiritual heart of ancient Greece and the center of the world. If the sacred hearth fire went out, it could be rekindled only by the sun, or by rubbing two sticks together.

CONTEMPLATION

Home is where the heart is,
and I kindle a sacred fire in my hearth.

Cancer Goddesses

Aine

KINDLING

Aine (AW-nee) is an Irish goddess of sovereignty whose name means "bright spark." She was worshipped in ancient times at the summer solstice, when people lit torches made in her honor. Farmers and others who worked in the fields celebrated her feast by waving their fiery torches over the crops and cattle in the fields. They performed this ritual as a means of protection and replenishment for the growing season, invoking Aine's blessing. The people circled her sacred hill and abiding place, Cnoc Aine, near Munster in southern Ireland, carrying the torches in a counterclockwise procession, and then walked home in a solemn manner.

Aine was thought to be Queen of the Fairies and so had great life-giving and healing power. Her bright spark is equated with the strength of the sun at the summer solstice, bringing maximum light to the earth each year. Sometimes she appeared over an enchanted lake in the form of a whirling fairy wind, and sometimes she took the form of a red mare that no one could outrun.

CONTEMPLATION

Tonight I light a torch, or build a bonfire, bringing the energy of renewing fire to kindle the flame of inspiration.

JUNE 24

Satet

TEARS

Satet (saw-TET) is an Egyptian goddess who was thought to release the Nile flood each year at the summer solstice. Upper Egypt, at the southern source of the Nile, was called Ta-Satet, or land of Satet. The goddess was also called the Queen of the South. Her main temple was on the island of Sehel, about two miles south of the present-day city of Aswan in southern Egypt. Along with Khnum and Anuket, Satet formed a triad, which was worshipped at a temple on Elephantine Island. Satet is depicted in art as a woman with a star on her head and carrying water jars. The star is no doubt Sirius, which rose before the sun each year at this time, announcing the annual flooding of the Nile.

The yearly inundation was known as the "Night of the Teardrop." Each year, the great goddess Isis shed one magical tear, which would be caught by Satet in her jar and then poured into the river to begin the inundation. Satet also used her magical and purified waters to cleanse the dead as part of the embalming ritual.

CONTEMPLATION

If I shed a tear today,
I know it is a blessing of purification and renewal.

Cancer Goddesses

Coyolxauhqui

REVELATION

Coyolxauhqui (coy-yo-LOCKS-kee) is an Aztec moon goddess. According to her myth, she became aware that her mother, the earth, called Coatilcue, was magically pregnant with a new god. Coyolxauhqui became jealous and tried to convince her brothers, the stars, to kill their mother. Although still in the womb, the unborn sun perceived the threat and warned his mother. When the powerful sun and war god emerged from the womb of the earth, he was ready for battle. He cut his sister to pieces before she could commit her treachery.

And so it is, her legend says, that every month the moon is cut into pieces in the sky in a reenactment of the battle between the siblings. The constant interplay between the sun and moon, and light and dark, is symbolized in this tale, which like many Aztec symbols is filled with violence and conflict. A now-famous stone sculpture of this goddess was discovered by engineers laying cables in Mexico City in 1978. Subsequent excavations showed that it stood at the foot of a major Aztec temple.

CONTEMPLATION

*I learn to dance in harmony
with the ever-shifting balance of light and dark.*

Woyengi

CONSEQUENCES

Woyengi (wo-YEN-ghee) is a creation goddess of the Ijaw people of Nigeria. Her name means "great mother," and she came down to earth on a magnificent bolt of lightning. When she landed, the only things she found were a table, a chair, and a flat stone resting on mud. Woyengi scooped up the mud and made numerous little mud dolls, and then breathed life into each one. This story has a familiar ring, but the Genesis story came much later.

The little dolls got to choose which gender they would be. Later, some of them complained that they wanted to make another choice, but Woyengi said they had to learn the deeper nature of the form they had chosen. Her myth tells of the consequence of choice. The moral of her story is that we must learn to accept the experiences of life and not feel resentful toward others. We make the best choice we can and live with the result or make a new plan.

CONTEMPLATION

I accept the consequences of my choices and actions.
I can always choose again.

Mari

SOURCE

Mari (MAH-ree), like the Egyptian Isis and the Hindu Devi, is an overarching Great Mother goddess. She is the source of all life and has come down to us in many forms and with many different names, including Mariamne in Greek, Miriam in Hebrew, and the familiar Mary. *Ma-Ri*, which means "to bear a child," is from the ancient Sumerian. The biblical Mari-El combined goddess with male god, and the Egyptian Meri-Ra was seen as the union of water and the fire of the sun. All the versions of her name are related to the ocean and water. The city named Mari, situated on the central Euphrates River, was sacked by the Babylonian king Hammurabi in 1800 BCE.

Mari is usually depicted in a blue robe wearing a necklace of pearls, both symbolizing the ocean and her most-revered title, Star of the Sea. She is also known as Queen of Heaven. There was a goddess of ancient Crete named Mari, as well as a Hindu goddess with the same name who was worshipped in wells. The word *marriage* comes from the Latin word *maritare*, which means "union under her auspices."

CONTEMPLATION

I hear Mari's ancient voice in the ocean waves
and in the whisper of a shell held to my ear.

Hina

FEMININITY

Hina (HEE-nah) is a great goddess, or Akua in Hawaiian, who seems to be the eldest of the indigenous Hawaiian pantheon. She is known all over Polynesia and the Pacific, and in one tale it is Hina who created the Hawaiian Islands, by pulling them from the ocean. She blesses the gathering of seafood, as she created all life in the reefs and the creatures are her gifts to the people. Her name means to "blow in a straight course," like fair winds on the ocean. Hina is also associated with healing and the making of tapa, a fiber fashioned from the inner bark of the mulberry plant and used to make both cloth and bedding in old Hawaii.

Hina is a goddess of the moon, the ocean, and healing. Because she is a lunar goddess, she rules over all phases of life, from conception to death. She is always connected to the colors silver and white, and her sacred food is the coconut. She is the essence of feminine energy, and part of her name, *hine*, is used as a suffix to indicate anything feminine.

CONTEMPLATION

*Today I reach deep and pull a beautiful creation
from the waters of my consciousness.*

Latmikaik

DEPTH

Latmikaik (lat-MEE-kak) is a sea goddess of the Palau Islands in Micronesia. Palau, an archipelago of 340 islands, is located between Guam, the Philippines, and Papua New Guinea. Latmikaik is both a cocreator and coruler of the world. In one story, she was the first creature who came into being, and she took the form of a giant clam, a symbol of fertility to the islanders. She gave birth to countless fish as a result of the turbulent waters in the sea.

Latmikaik's human children emerged in the mythical first world of creation and are the ancestors of the Palau Islanders of today. Her fish children once built a tower that reached all the way to heaven. The people of the islands still believe that fish spawn when the waters are rough and cloudy enough to protect them from fishermen. Latmikaik may live at the bottom of the ocean, but she is now also distinguished astronomically by being one of the coronas of the planet Venus.

CONTEMPLATION

*My dreams partake of the depths of the ocean
and reach to the heights of heaven.*

Papatuamuku

POLARITY

Papatuamuku (pah-pah-two-ah-MOO-ku) is a Maori goddess worshipped by the indigenous Polynesian people of New Zealand, who have struggled to maintain their cultural identity against the forces of European colonization and Christianity. The word *Maori* means "ordinary" in their language and distinguishes humans from the gods. Papatuamuku, sometimes called simply Papa, is a powerful goddess of creation who, together with her consort, Rangi, gave birth to the seventy gods of the Maori.

Papa and Rangi are primordial parents locked in an eternal embrace of creation. She is Earth Mother and he is Sky Father. Their original embrace was so intense that not even light could penetrate. Darkness was everywhere. The other gods became jealous and annoyed, and fearful that the continual darkness would deprive them of life, and so they plotted to destroy the lovers. One of the children finally separated his parents, and light and space were born. Although the lovers are now separated, the water cycle of the earth keeps them in everlasting contact as rain falls from the sky and evaporates back into the clouds.

CONTEMPLATION

Where am I clinging so tightly
that there is no room for growth?

Rhea

FLOW

Rhea (RAY-ah) is an ancient mother goddess and queen of the Titans, who lived in the golden age that preceded the Greek Olympians. She is the daughter of Gaia, the earth, and Ouranos, the sky, and she is Demeter's mother. Her name means "flow," in the sense of menstruation and the waters of birth. Rhea is also considered to be the great mountain mother of Mount Ida in Crete. One of her symbols is the swan because it is a gentle creature but also a formidable guardian and opponent.

In later Greek myth, Kronos (or Cronus) was her brother, and he became her consort, which diminished her status. The Romans knew her as Magna Mater, meaning "great mother." In Cretan ancient myths, she had no consort. In fact, Rhea was Mother Time herself, who ruled alone, and it was she who wielded the sickle of the moon that was later appropriated by Father Time. Like Cybele, Rhea was pictured on a chariot drawn by two lions, which hints at her antiquity. Rampant lions often flanked her statue at the entrance of ancient cities.

CONTEMPLATION

*I glide through this day as serenely
as a majestic swan on a still lake.*

Goddesses for Every Day

Nu Wa

CHILDREN

Nu Wa (noo wah), called Lady Dragon, is a Chinese creation goddess who sculpted humanity from mud long before the story appeared in the biblical book of Genesis. Nu Wa was the first female figure to appear in Chinese legends. She is depicted as a beautiful woman from the waist up, and below the waist she is composed solely of the tail of a dragon. One Chinese legend tells of a dragon emerging from the Yellow River with ideograms on her back. In the beginning, earth and sky were separated and Nu Wa was on earth. Earth was filled with beautiful trees, flowers, and different animals, but Nu Wa was lonely and desired companionship.

One day, Nu Wa saw her reflection and decided to create a mud doll in her own likeness. Using the yellow mud from the Huango-Ho River, she sculpted a figure that resembled her but had ordinary legs instead of a dragon's tail. She blew her fiery breath into her creation, giving the figure life. She was so entertained by her companion that she created countless figures. Nu Wa was careful to make humans male and female, able to create their own children, as they were not immortal like her.

CONTEMPLATION

I work consciously with the raw material of my life,
sculpting something beautiful.

Cancer Goddesses

Yemaya

TIDES

Yemaya (yah-MY-ah) is one of the Orishas who make up the Yoruban pantheon of divine beings who embody aspects of nature and the spirit world. The belief system of the Yoruba people of West Africa is thousands of years old, and it spread to the New World by means of the slave trade. There the people preserved their beliefs by syncretizing their deities with Catholic saints, creating Santeria, the "Way of the Saints." Yemaya has been equated with Mary, in her role of Star of the Sea.

Goddess of the oceans and motherhood, Yemaya is said to be the mother of many other Orishas. In Brazil, on New Year's Eve, her worshippers erect elaborate altars on the beach, which they cover with food and candles. They believe Yemaya receives their offerings and takes their gifts into herself by means of the morning tides. She has many aspects, and one is that of a fierce warrior being, called Yemaya Okute.

CONTEMPLATION

Today I make my life an offering of beauty,
knowing that the tide washes away all things.

Libertas

LIBERTY

Libertas (LI-bur-tas) is the Roman goddess of liberty, immortalized in a statue in New York Harbor. Libertas was always shown wearing a pileus, a felt cap that was given to freed slaves. She also wore a laurel wreath and carried a spear. Libertas embodies the idea of personal freedom as well as the collective freedom of a nation. She was Britannia to the British, and Marianne to the French. Her image appeared on the Roman denarius coin, a day's wages for a laborer, and temples in her honor stood on two of Rome's ancient hills.

The full name of the statue that stands in New York Harbor, a gift from France in 1886, is *Liberty Enlightening the World*. Our statue wears a crown with seven points, rather than the pileus cap, and she holds a book that represents freedom through knowledge. Liberty carries a torch to illuminate the minds and hearts of humanity. A poetry contest held to raise money for the statue's pedestal was won by Emma Lazarus. Along with the prize, she received the honor of seeing her sonnet, "The New Colossus," appear on the statue's base.

CONTEMPLATION

A woman with a torch, whose flame
is the imprisoned lightning,
and her name, Mother of Exiles.

— EXCERPT FROM EMMA LAZARUS, "THE NEW COLOSSUS"

Cancer Goddesses

Oshun

ANCESTORS

Oshun (OH-shun), a goddess of the Yoruba people of West Africa, is one of their seven great Orishas, or spirit beings. The Yoruba were hard hit by the slave trade, and those who were enslaved took their beliefs with them to Brazil, Cuba, Haiti, and the southern United States. Oshun's domain is the freshwater of rivers. In his book *Living Santeria*, anthropologist Michael Atwood Mason says, "The elders declare that 'Oshun is the owner of the river.'" She is a goddess of shifting currents and renewal who is thought to live in the movement of running river waters, and she loves the color yellow and the number five.

In Oshun's myth, the other gods sent her on a quest to the blacksmith Orisha, who had grown tired of creating and allowed the world to become bleak. She persuaded him to continue creating and later became the messenger between the realm of the Divine and the ordinary world of humans. Like the Roman Venus, she loves beauty. Her altars, which contain offerings of items in groups of five, must always be beautiful. Oshun is invoked to bring renewal and the blessing of lifegiving waters to dry and barren land.

CONTEMPLATION

If I still the outer noise in my world, I can hear the voices of my ancestors whispering messages of wise counsel.

Goddesses for Every Day

Leucothea

RECOVERY

Leucothea (loo-coh-THEE-ah), whose name means "white goddess," was a Greek sea goddess. Her nature comes from the image of whitecaps on the ocean or the foam of the tides. Author Robert Graves further immortalized the White Goddess in his book by the same name. In Laconia, she had a sanctuary with a dream oracle. In her earlier human form, as Ino, she is said to have cared for the god Dionysus when he was an infant, hinting at her much earlier role and at her power in festivals of fertility.

In Greek myth, Leucothea threw herself and her infant son into the sea to escape Hera's wrath. Naturally, the child belonged to the perpetually dallying Zeus. However, Dionysus would not let her die, and he transformed her into the White Goddess of the waves; her son became the sea god Palaemon, a patron of one of the Panhellenic games. In a later story, Leucothea rescued the hero Odysseus from drowning.

CONTEMPLATION

I call on the white waves to keep me afloat
and not let me drown in the tides of my emotions.

Kaguya Hime

TREASURE

Kaguya Hime (kah-GOO-yah HEE-may) is a Japanese goddess of the moon. She appears as a tiny baby girl in a shining
bamboo plant, or as a wondrous, tiny singing woman. Her legend tells of a kind old man who, while walking in a bamboo
forest, found a radiant bamboo plant. When he cut open the
marvelous stalk, he found a baby girl inside. He and his wife
raised her, as they had no children. They named her Kaguya
Hime, and even the emperor desired to court her.

While she lived with the old couple, whenever the old man
cut bamboo in the forest he found money inside. But as time
passed, Kaguya Hime became very sad living on earth. She
told her parents that her true home was on the moon, and that
one day angels would come to take her there. Before she finally returned to her home on the moon, she blessed the emperor with eternal life. Granting immortality was always the
provenance of the goddess.

CONTEMPLATION

What shining vision of prosperity lives in my heart?

Ajysyt

BIRTH

Ajysyt (EYE-yah-sit) is a mother goddess of the Turkic Yakut people of Siberia, who live near the Lena River. Her name means "birth giver," and she is also called Mother of Cradles. She lives atop a mountain in a house with seven stories, where she writes each person's fate in a golden book. Ajysyt guides each soul on its journey from heaven to earth when it is time for it to be born in a human body. She is present at every birth, and women invoke her to relieve the pains of childbirth.

Scholars believe that Siberia may be the origin of shamanism and of the word *shamanism* itself. There is considerable evidence indicating that the earliest shamans were women who knew the magic of birth and death and stood guard at these portals.

CONTEMPLATION

What do I long to birth and breathe life into?

Kami-Fuchi

GATEKEEPER

Kami-Fuchi (KAH-mey-FOO-chee) is a hearth goddess of the Ainu people. The Ainu, who prefer to call themselves Utari, are the indigenous people of the islands we now call Japan. They are ethnically distinct from the Japanese. Kami-Fuchi's full name means "rising fire sparks woman," and she is thought to actually live in the hearth. She is the most important *kamui*, or spirit being, of Ainu mythology and serves as a gatekeeper between the world of humans and the spirit world.

The hearth was seen as the center of the home and also as a portal where people could communicate with their ancestors. The Ainu word for ancestor translates to "those who dwell in the hearth." Kami-Fuchi is a guardian of the home and presides over domestic affairs. Her presence is so important that she never leaves the house. Those who do not honor her with proper maintenance of the home will incur her wrath.

CONTEMPLATION

My home is a sacred sanctuary, and I am the guardian of all that dwells within. It's up to me to tend the fire.

Devi

WOMB

The name Devi (DEV-ee) is also the Sanskrit word for "great mother" and was merged into many Indo-European names. This goddess's name is synonymous with the concept of goddess and also means "the divinity." Devi is cosmic force, and she is the creator, annihilator, and re-creator of the universe, which she holds in her womb. She appears in many forms and with many names, as goddesses with different attributes. The Hindus say Devi gives birth to both force and form, and that without her, nothing would come into being. In her right hand she holds joy and sorrow, and in her left hand life and death.

She is Ma, the gentle and approachable mother. As Jaganmata, or Mother of the Universe, she assumes cosmic proportions, destroying evil and creating and dissolving worlds. In Southeast Asia, Devi is known by thousands of different names and worshipped in ways that reflect local customs and legends about her nature.

CONTEMPLATION

I embody the creative essence of the Divine Mother,
whose womb brings worlds into manifestation.

JULY 11

Kaltes

GENTLENESS

Kaltes (CALL-tiss) is a goddess of the Uguric people of Siberia. She is a moon goddess who watches over birth and is sometimes a shape-shifter like the moon. Rabbits and hares are sacred to her, because the Uguric people, like many cultures, see the shape of a hare in the markings on the moon. (Hares are larger than rabbits and lead solitary lives, while rabbits live in colonies.) Usually Kaltes's nature is as gentle and solitary as her sacred hare. She sometimes has a fearsome aspect, in that she can determine someone's destiny. In earliest times, killing and eating a rabbit or hare was taboo. It was believed that eating a rabbit was like eating your grandmother.

This consumption taboo was lifted at the Celtic festival Beltane, and at the Anglo-Saxon festival of Ostara, at which ritual hare-hunts would take place. Hares often hide in cornfields till the last reaping, and the last sheaf is often called "the hare." Cutting the last sheaf is called "cutting the hare's tail." In some places reapers would throw their sickles at the symbolic rabbit in the field.

CONTEMPLATION

I cultivate the gentleness of a rabbit
and beat a prudent retreat when appropriate.

Coventina

CONNECTION

Coventina (coh-ven-TEE-nah) is a British Celtic goddess of water and springs who was greatly revered by her followers. She is pictured on a leaf floating on water while holding a goblet or urn from which she pours the river, since she is its source. She looks supremely confident. Relics have been recovered from the site of her holy well in Northumberland, England, where her worship, like that of other water goddesses, focused on the spot where spring water bubbled up from the earth and fed a pool. Water was seen as a gift from the goddess.

An excavated shrine along Hadrian's Wall uncovered as many as sixteen thousand coins. Making a wish and dropping a coin into a well in gratitude is an ancient custom. Sacred wells were places of healing and sometimes also the locations of oracles and sites of inspiration. Coventina seemed to have an even more overarching quality as a divine protector and provider.

CONTEMPLATION

My heart is linked to the underground stream that flows securely through every age.

Meskhenet

TESTIMONY

Meskhenet (MESH-kuh-net) is an Egyptian goddess of child-birth. She is called Protectress of the Birthing-Place and is the creator of each child's Ka, a mysterious aspect of the eternal soul. Like other goddesses of fate, Meskhenet had a role in the destiny of children. Women in Egypt gave birth by squatting over birth bricks, thought to be magical objects. Images of these bricks are still visible today on the walls of Egyptian temples. Meskhenet was considered responsible for this birthing, and she is depicted as a birth brick with the head of a woman, or as a woman wearing a headdress made from the uterus of a sacred cow, an emblem of Isis and Hathor.

Meskhenet appears in the Book of the Dead, and in the famous "weighing of the heart" she is shown very close to the scale, as the heart of the deceased is weighed against the feather of Ma'at, goddess of justice. Ma'at's feather represented truth and right relationship to all things. If the deceased's heart was heavier than Ma'at's feather, he or she could not enter the afterlife. Meskhenet testified to the character of the deceased and was thought to assist in a symbolic rebirth in the afterlife.

CONTEMPLATION

I cultivate joy and right relationship to all things,
so that my heart is as light as a feather.

Ngame

REPETITION

Ngame (nee-GAW-may) is a lunar creator goddess of the Akan people of Nigeria. She creates all things by shooting life into new beings through the power of her crescent-shaped bow and life-giving arrows. As the moon, she is also seen as the mother of the sun and, like the Egyptian Nut, she gives birth to her child anew every morning at dawn.

The goddess works in magical and mysterious ways. In a true story that seems more like fiction, the goddess Ngame provided inspiration to and served as a muse for scholar Robert Graves, who felt compelled to write what became the enduring classic *The White Goddess*. A temple was later built for Ngame in Nigeria by members of the Fellowship of Isis from Clonegal Castle in Ireland. A large number of the fellowship's members live in Nigeria.

CONTEMPLATION

*How you come to terms with the Goddess
is no concern of mine.*

— ROBERT GRAVES, *The White Goddess*

Chang-O

FORETHOUGHT

Chang-O is a Chinese goddess of the moon. Unlike most lunar deities, who embody the moon, Chang-O instead makes her home there. In her story her husband was awarded a pill of immortality, which he was warned to approach with respect. He was told to prepare for immortality by praying and fasting for a year. He hid the pill, but Chang-O discovered it, and curiosity drove her to swallow it. She floated to the moon, where she must stay until she can cut down the tree of immortality, located there, and make another pill for her husband. A hare is her constant companion. Once a month, her husband, who went to live on the sun, comes to visit her at the time of the full moon.

The annual moon-cake festival in China, one of the most important festivals for Chinese communities around the world, is celebrated in her honor. On this day, the legend says, the moon is biggest and brightest, magnificently radiating the reflected brilliance of the sun.

CONTEMPLATION

Today I stop and think through the consequences of my actions.

JULY 16

Cihuacoatl

BACKBONE

Cihuacoatl (see-wah-co-AH-til), whose name means "serpent woman" (*Cihua* translates as "woman," and *coatl* as "serpent"), is an Aztec goddess and the mythical mother of humanity in the fifth world of Aztec cosmology. The Aztec believe four worlds have preceded this one. Cihuacoatl ground up bones from the previous four ages and combined this mixture with the blood of the god Quetzalcoatl, whose name means "feathered serpent."

Cihuacoatl had dominion over midwives and the sweat baths where midwives worked to purify those who came for sacred ceremonies. She is a crone goddess, usually depicted as a skull-faced old woman carrying the shield and spears of a warrior. She also is shown wearing a cloak and holding a rattle and a serpent. Childbirth was compared to war, and women who died giving birth were honored like valiant warriors who had died in battle.

CONTEMPLATION

*I stand straight, honoring the cycles of blood
and the valiant courage of women giving birth.*

Mother Goose

MOTHERHOOD

Mother Goose is the familiar character from children's nursery rhymes, such as the one quoted at the end of this entry, but her origins are ancient. Egyptians recognized the Nile Goose, called the Great Chatterer, who laid the cosmic golden egg from which the sun god Ra emerged. Birds appear as symbols and companions of goddesses across cultures and reaching far back in time. Neolithic figures of a bird goddess have been found that are nine thousand years old.

Likewise, winged goddesses appear in diverse places and cultures, and in this global role the Great Goddess has been called Lady of the Beasts. All the animals are her subjects and under her care. Swans and geese are solar birds, meaning they are among those who announce the dawn. Even the humble Christmas goose symbolizes the annual death of the sun at winter solstice. The powerful creator goddess is a far cry from the diminished, albeit endearing, character of Mother Goose with her whimsical rhymes.

CONTEMPLATION

There was an old woman lived under a hill;
And if she's not gone, she lives there still.

— LINDA YEATMAN, *A Treasury of Mother Goose Rhymes*

Haumea

RE-CREATION

Haumea (how-MAY-uh) is a great Hawaiian goddess who taught women the mysteries of childbirth. She is thought to inhabit the Makalei tree, a Tree of Life on the island of Oahu whose mystical branches and deep roots yield infinite amounts of food. Like a cornucopia, the tree symbolically provides many staples to the Hawaiian people, such as coconut, bamboo, taro root, breadfruit, and sugarcane. Haumea is a crone archetype in a trinity of Hawaiian goddesses that includes Hina and Pele.

Haumea had the power to change her form, as her nature was constantly renewing. Although she grew old, she was continually transformed into a young woman, representing the cycles of women's lives and the theme of the constant renewal of life. She is the mother of many children, each of whom emerged from a different part of her body, symbolizing that she is a profoundly nourishing source of life. When she shakes a sacred branch of the Makalei tree over water, she attracts abundant fish.

CONTEMPLATION

A woman's life is rounded by cycles of renewal, rebirth, and resurrection. I choose to move in the flow of whatever cycle I find myself.

Cancer Goddesses

Wawalag Sisters

TABOO

The Wawalag (wah-wah-log) Sisters are powerful spirit beings of the Aborigine people of Australia. Their myth tells of the trials and strengths of motherhood, as well as the dangers of disobeying taboos. The two sisters embarked on a long journey, or walkabout. One sister carried an infant in her arms; the other carried a baby in her belly. As they journeyed on their walkabout, they pointed at objects with their hunting spears and named them.

They came at last to where the Great Rainbow Serpent, Yulungur, lived in water deep in a cave. The myth is complex, and filled with deep significance concerning tribal taboos and rites of initiation. The serpent smelled the blood of birth and swallowed the sisters for trespassing. Later, feeling remorseful, he spat them out. This cycle continued endlessly, and each place where the sisters emerged from the giant snake became sacred. The Aborigines of that part of northern Australian still perform dances every year to ward off the snake and to encourage fertility.

CONTEMPLATION

*I pay attention to custom and tradition
so I don't offend the spirits of water and land.*

Selene

CYCLES

Selene (SAH-leen) is a Greek goddess of the full moon. In classical times she was the daughter of Thea and Hyperion. Helios, the sun god, and Eos, the goddess of dawn, were her siblings. In some stories Helios is her spouse, and as he completes his daily rounds, she begins her nightly sojourn. As beautiful as the light of a full moon, Selene was depicted with wings, and sometimes she was shown riding on a bull. More often, she rode across the night sky in a silver chariot drawn by two white steeds.

Although she is known to have had many love affairs, Selene had a long-lasting relationship with a handsome younger man named Endymion, with whom she had fifty daughters. When she was invisible in the sky at the time of the new moon, it was said that she visited him in Asia Minor.

CONTEMPLATION

I approach my daily tasks in a spirit of service and generosity.

Ilithyia

FECUNDITY

Ilithyia (il-LITH-ee-ah) is a Cretan goddess who acts in the role of divine midwife. Women in childbirth prayed to her as a "liberator" who freed the infant from the womb. She is a maiden goddess who is pictured carrying a torch that symbolizes the act of bringing babies from darkness into light. Writing in the second century CE, the Greek author Pausanias, in his work titled "Pausanias' Description of Greece," called Ilithyia the "Clever Spinner." This identifies her with fate and makes her older than Kronos the Titan. Her much later Roman counterpart is Lucina, an aspect of the goddess Juno, who was called She Who Brings the Light.

Ilithyia was born in a cave. On the island of Crete, even in classical times, sacred caves — symbols of the womb — were dedicated to her. A church dedicated to Mary as Virgin of Fecundity was built on an old site that honored Aphrodite Ilithyia, who was called Mother of Fecundity. Ilithyia's name was used like a surname or honorific for many other goddesses as well, including Isis, Diana, and Artemis.

CONTEMPLATION

I breathe through whatever pains of labor
accompany my creative efforts.

Mary Magdalene

REPUTATION

The human woman we call Mary Magdalene has taken on much larger proportions in terms of what she represents in the collective psyche of humanity. In the New Testament of the Bible, she is Mary of Magdala and is described as one of the most important women in the ministry of Jesus. In Aramaic, *magdala* means "elevated, great, or magnificent." Therefore, some scholars attribute a symbolic rather than a literal meaning to her name. Mary Magdalene is perhaps the most maligned and misrepresented figure in history. In a sense, she represents the devaluing and minimizing of all womankind by the ruling patriarchy. Ironically, she is now a Catholic saint and is revered worldwide on her feast day, July 22.

We may never know her true story, but after the texts of the Nag Hammadi library were discovered in Egypt in 1945, we learned that, in the early days of Christianity, Mary Magdalene was a powerful figure in the group we now call Gnostics. She is described in Gnostic gospels as the most devoted of the early companions of Jesus the Nazarene. In a gospel named after her, she is identified as the apostle to whom Jesus revealed his most profound teachings.

CONTEMPLATION

There are three crowns: the crown of learning,
the crown of priesthood, and the crown of kingship,
but the crown of a good name must be upon each.

— TALMUD, MISHNAH PIRKEI AVOT, 4:17

Cancer Goddesses

LEO GODDESSES
The Cobra

WITH POWER COMES GREAT RESPONSIBILITY

Leo is a fixed fire sign that brings about the process of individuation. Leo energy is expressed as creative and proud, loyal, and loving; Leo natives are eager to display prowess. Leos see themselves as the creative center of their circle of influence, and they must cultivate the quality of personal spiritual dominion and not willfully rule over others. Leos radiate light and warmth and must learn the loving detachment that springs from an understanding heart. The symbol of Leo is traditionally the Lion, the "king of the beasts." Leo represents the principle of dominion.

The goddess sign for Leo is the Cobra, and she is arguably the queen of serpents. Around the world, serpents and dragons are connected with the wisdom of the sacred feminine. Many cultures have also imagined the apparent motion of the sun, the ruling planet of Leo, crossing the sky as a serpent. Dragons are creatures of fire, and in myth cobras are seen as "spitting fire" at their enemies. The image of the cobra goddess named Wadjet, symbol of divine rulership, was worn on the brow of all Egyptian pharaohs. Leo goddesses include radiant solar goddesses and great cats from different cultures, and also those who represent the creative principle of fire in the form of dragons or serpents. Leo goddesses represent nobility, the principle of light, and the fire of the sun. Some of these goddesses are daughters of the sun.

JULY 23

Wadjet

DOMINION

Wadjet (WAH-jet), who was called the Green One, is the cobra goddess of the ancient city of Buto in the Nile Delta of Egypt. She is a fierce, fire-spitting serpent who was equated with the royal *ureaus*, the rearing cobra symbol of royalty and mastery that was part of the pharaoh's crown. Wadjet became the Eye of Ra, or the right eye of the sun. Her name means "papyrus colored," which is a reference to the color of a cobra's skin. Wadjet was the protector of Lower Egypt, where the Nile empties into the Mediterranean. Her name is the word for "cobra" and also the word for "eye."

Sometimes Wadjet is pictured as lion headed and crowned with a sun disk and the *ureaus*. Her counterpart was Nekhbet, the vulture goddess who was the protector of Upper Egypt. Together they were the Two Ladies of the Pharaoh, and the king was said to rule by their grace. Wadjet helped Isis watch over the infant Horus and arranged the reeds to conceal the mother and child when they were pursued with murderous intent by the boy's uncle Set. Wadjet bestowed the crown of Lower Egypt on each new ruler. Her scepter was a long papyrus stem with a cobra twined around it. This is thought to be the first symbol of its kind, and it existed before the biblical Moses raised the serpent in the wilderness.

CONTEMPLATION

Dominion in any situation is achieved by first seeing the truth. Then I can claim the wisdom of a serpent and the strength of a lioness.

Leo Goddesses

Saule

LOYALTY

Saule (SAU-lay) is the great goddess of the Lithuanian and Latvian peoples, who lived in the Baltic area. She was called Balta Saulite, meaning "little white sun." Saule, also called Queen of Heaven and Earth, was envisioned as the sun and was the goddess of amber. She ruled over all parts of life, and at death she welcomed the souls of her children into her garden of apple trees in the west.

In contrast to Selene and Helios, Saule was loyal and hardworking. She left home early each morning to drive her chariot with copper wheels across the sky. It is said her horses never tired, and every day at sunset she bathed them in the sea. Her husband, Meness, the moon, was fickle, staying home all day. Sometimes he appeared and sometimes he didn't, so his moon chariot was not always visible at night. Saule was especially honored by her worshippers on the summer solstice, when she rose crowned with braids made of blossoms from red ferns.

CONTEMPLATION

In all my promises and relationships,
I vow to be as loyal as sunrise.

Pele

TEMPER

Pele (PAY-lay), whose name means "molten lava," is a goddess of fire and lightning who lives in the volcanic crater of Mount Kilauea in Hawaii. She is alive and well in our time and is still a potent deity to the Hawaiian people. It is fascinating to note that the route of her mythic journey to find a home follows the progression of volcanic activity as recorded in geologic time. Every time she landed on an island, it was flooded by her sister Hina, who created a huge tidal wave to keep Pele from settling. In this way, the islands were created. Pele finally found rest in Hawaii.

Humans have never been sacrificed to Pele; only red berries were offered in ancient times. She is respected and feared, if not actually worshipped, as her nature is powerful and unpredictable. Her wrath, which she expresses as volcanic eruptions, is often attributed to her legendary jealousy, which flares in unexpected ways. Some say the red-robed figure of Pele can still be seen dancing on the rim of the volcanic crater.

CONTEMPLATION

You've never seen fire until you've seen Pele blow.

— TORI AMOS, "MUHAMMAD MY FRIEND," *Boys for Pele*

Lalita

BLISS

Lalita (lah-LEE-tah) is a Hindu goddess whose name means "she who plays." All of creation and dissolution is thought to be the play of this goddess. Because one of her forms is a red flower, she is called the Red Goddess. In Tantra, a yantra is a two-dimensional drawing that is thought to be the expression of a deity in linear form. The yantra of Lalita is the Shri Yantra, or "holy" yantra, which is the physical representation of the famous OM mantra, or sound.

Lalita is pictured holding a noose, a goad, a bow, and five flowered arrows. The noose represents attachment, and the goad is repulsion. The bow, made of sugarcane, is the mind, and the five arrows are the senses. It is said that when consciousness perceives the true nature of these symbols, the outward directed arrows become living rods instead of dry sticks. *Lalita* is also an epithet for the goddess Parvati, who is the consort of Shiva. Lalita loves *puja*, or devotion.

CONTEMPLATION

My joy can be seen as a celebration of the goddess and feminine power, and my laughter a sacred sound of praise.

Bast

NOBILITY

Bast (bahst), or Bastet, is an Egyptian cat goddess who was a solar symbol and who later became associated with the moon. While seated on a throne, she is known as Bastet. When the pharaoh prayed to reach the sky, he declared that Bast was his mother and nurse. Her image and nature are more like those of the Egyptian sand cat, which is believed to be the ancestor of the domestic cat. Bast is pictured as a cat, or as a woman with the head of a cat. Cats were sacred to her, and to harm one was considered a major sin. Cats were revered by the ancient Egyptians for their cleanliness and nobility, and because they controlled the rodent population and, as a result, reduced the spread of disease.

Bast's cult center, Bubastis, was once the capital of Egypt, and the Greek historian Herodotus described it as a place of splendor and glory rivaled only by temples to Ra and Horus. Bast was honored in Upper Egypt, while her more aggressive counterpart, Sekhmet, was worshipped in Lower Egypt. Her festival was like Mardi Gras, accompanied by much singing, dancing, and drinking. Temples in Egypt still have honored cats who manage the rodents.

CONTEMPLATION

I call upon the noble nature of the feline within myself,
knowing that true strength and power
are not a matter of brute force.

JULY 28

Mahuika

SPARKS

Mahuika (mah-WHEE-kah) is a Maori goddess of fire. She lived in the underworld, where she held the secret of making fire. The moral of her myth is how precious the gift of fire has been to humanity. In her story, the "spark of Mahuika" refers to fire. As is typical in myth, the tale changes in the telling, but Mahuika had five children who were the fiery fingers of her hand.

Long ago, all the light had gone out in the world, and the trickster god Maui was pleased, as he liked the darkness. He plotted to steal all the fire so the world would remain dark. At the end of the story, after he had managed to steal all but one of her fingers, Mahuika escaped into a kaikomako tree with her last finger. To this day the Maori of New Zealand say the sleeping child of Mahuika can be awakened by rubbing together the dry wood from this sacred tree.

CONTEMPLATION

Whether I light a candle or a campfire,
I give thanks for the precious gift of fire,
the gift of a goddess whose spark lives on.

Goddesses for Every Day

Qadesh

ECSTASY

Qadesh (ka-DESH) is a Middle Eastern goddess of sacred ecstasy and sexual pleasure. Scholars believe she was originally a Syrian goddess whose name meant "holy one." She was called Mother of Compassion, and she had dominion over sacred sexuality and women's mysteries, which were performed with reverence. Qadesh was depicted riding naked on a lion, which hints at her antiquity. Like Asherah, she holds serpents and lotuses. Qadesh was adopted around 1600 BCE, during the historical period called New Kingdom Egypt (the Eighteenth Dynasty to the Twentieth), and was incorporated into a triad with the fertility god Min and the war god Reshep.

The act of procreation was seen as divine generation, and the *hieros gamos*, "holy marriage," a union of humanity and the Divine, was reenacted in Qadesh's temples. "Holy women" who served as temple *qadeshes*, or representatives of the goddess, dispensed these sacred mysteries. The honoring of sacred sexuality in this manner was later condemned by the Hebrews.

CONTEMPLATION

Sacred sexual union is an expression of ecstasy.

Hae-Soon

RADIANCE

Hae-Soon (hi-soon) is a Korean sun goddess. She was one of three sisters who lived in the mountains with their mother. In a story similar to that of Little Red Riding Hood, the mother was eaten by a female tiger, and the tiger, pretending to be the mother, then threatened the sisters. The girls were not deceived, and they climbed a tall tree to escape. But the tiger followed. The sisters prayed, and a magical chain of gold descended from heaven. The girls were able to climb the chain and escape into the sky. One sister became a star, one became the moon, and the third sister, Hae-Soon, became the sun.

As Hae-Soon set off on her daily journey, people came out to look. She was very shy and blushed brightly with embarrassment, causing the people to look away and protect their eyes from her radiance. Feeling more confident since the people couldn't see her, she proceeded on her rounds. The light of the sun goddess brightens the day but is too brilliant for people to look upon directly.

CONTEMPLATION

Even though I may doubt myself,
I let my unique radiance brighten the world.

JULY 31

Gayatri

POETRY

Gayatri (GUY-ah-tree) Devi is a Hindu goddess whose name means "singer." She is an incarnation of the goddess Saraswati and is the wife of Brahma and mother of the four Vedas. Gayatri has five heads that look in every direction and eight arms, which hold a lotus, ax, whip, conch, bowl, mace, bracelets, and crown.

Gayatri is thought to be a hymn made visible, and her hymn is a poem that is among the most revered Hindu chants, the Gayatri mantra. Found in the Rig-Veda, this hymn is vastly ancient, and it praises the principles of light and consciousness. Brahmin priests memorize the words to this hymn and sing it to the "savior sun" each morning before sunrise. Yoga practitioners perform a series of asanas, or postures, called the salute to the sun, that is also related to Gayatri's mantra.

CONTEMPLATION

Oh God! Thou art the Giver of Life,
Remover of pain and sorrow,
The Bestower of happiness,
Oh! Creator of the Universe,
May we receive thy supreme sin-destroying light,
May Thou guide our intellect in the right direction.

— GAYATRI MANTRA, FROM THE RIG-VEDA (III, 62, 10)

Leo Goddesses

233

Surya-Bai

KARMA

Surya-Bai (SIR-yah-bye) is a complex Hindu goddess who is the daughter of the sun. When her name is rendered as *Surya-Savitiri*, she is said to represent the sun at the winter solstice. In some legends she has twin spouses who are gods of light, and in others she is the wife of Soma, or sometimes Chandra, the moon. Like other solar deities, Surya-Bai is described as riding across the sky in a chariot. Her chariot is pulled by two Asvins, "wonder workers," who are the twin gods of day. Together these three represent morning, noon, and night.

Sanskrit writings reveal a legend of deep love related to the mango tree. While married to the king of the land, Surya-Bai transformed herself into a golden lotus to avoid persecution by an evil sorceress. The sorceress became angry when the king fell in love with the beautiful lotus, and she burnt the flower to ashes. But good overcame evil when a magnificent mango tree sprang from the ashes and Surya-Bai stepped out of a ripe mango that had fallen to the ground. When the king recognized her as his long-lost wife, the two rejoiced.

CONTEMPLATION

*Even though my life may seem to lie in ruins at times,
I know that I can rise from the ashes like the phoenix,
as the scales of Karma balance all.*

Goddesses for Every Day

AUGUST 2

Sekhmet

FIRE

Sekhmet (SEK-met) is an Egyptian goddess envisioned as a fierce lioness or as a woman with the head of a lioness. She is crowned by the solar disk, and the hot desert winds are her breath. One image of Sekhmet is as the Eye of Ra, which is represented by the fire-spitting *ureaus*, the rearing cobra symbol. Her name is translated as "mighty one" or "one who is powerful." Sekhmet was also given such daunting titles as One before Whom Evil Trembles and Lady of Slaughter. She protected the pharaoh by stalking the land, destroying his enemies with arrows of fire. Sekhmet's body took on the bright glare of the midday sun, and so she, like Tefnut, was also called Lady of Flame.

Accomplished in magic and sorcery, Sekhmet used her power constructively in healing. Tame lions were kept in temples dedicated to Sekhmet at Leontopolis. She is like the alchemical Red Lion, representing the height of creative power, and she holds the magic of alchemical fire, which burns away impurities. Sekhmet is also a powerful protector, like a lioness defending her cubs.

CONTEMPLATION

I consciously direct the energy of purifying fire.

Leo Goddesses

Taillte

CLARITY

Taillte (TAL-tu) is an Irish goddess of the month of August and midsummer, the halfway point between the summer solstice and autumn equinox. A town in County Meath, Ireland, was named after her. As a human figure, Taillte was the daughter of the last Celtic high king of Ireland. She later became a goddess and was said to be the foster mother and nurse of Lugh, the god of light.

Taillte lived on the magical Hill of Tara. From the crest of her domain, she oversaw the clearing of a vast forest on the plain of Breg, where her castle was built. Her annual festival began at midsummer and lasted through August, featuring fairs, markets, and athletic events. The Tailltean Games, which ran from 1829 BCE to 1170 CE, were celebrated as a sort of Irish Olympics.

CONTEMPLATION

What needs to be cleared from my life
so that I can create and flourish?

Shakti

POWER

Shakti (SHAHK-tee), who is mystically the same as Parvati and Durga, is the most powerful manifestation of the Divine Feminine in the Hindu tradition. Her name means "to be able," and she is the essence, or power, of divinity, which takes form and moves all things. She is said to be indistinguishable from the one who beholds her, expressing a great mystery. Every god had to have his Shakti in order to move or act. She is worshipped by millions in India, who perceive her as more important than her consort, Lord Shiva, for without her, Shiva is impotent.

Shakti is also a balancing energy, restoring equilibrium to situations that have become out of balance. She is thought to bring all good things to those who follow the path of devotion and virtue. Kundalini Shakti is a manifestation of this fiery goddess and is said to reside at the base of the spine like a coiled serpent of potential, waiting to be awakened. When the goddess Kundalini Shakti awakes, she uncoils and her power unfurls up the spine. Eventually, her power enlivens the higher spiritual centers, called *chakras* in Sanskrit, bringing enlightenment.

CONTEMPLATION

*Coils of unleashed and unlimited power
lie at the root of my being.*

Leo Goddesses

Budhi Pallien

WILDNESS

Budhi Pallien (BOO-dee PAL-ee-en) is a fierce goddess of the Assamese people of northern India. This region, part of the Seven Sisters States in northeastern India, is famous for Assam tea, jungles, and abundant wildlife. The native language derives directly from Sanskrit, and the culture claims some of the oldest existing pieces of literature. Budhi Pallien roams the jungles in the form of a great tigress, protecting her territory. Although tiger preserves exist in the area, wild tigers are still being killed and are in grave danger of extinction.

Budhi Pallien is a shape-shifter and can transform herself from human to feline form. Sometimes she travels with a companion tiger, moving through the jungle and looking out for the creatures she guards. She possesses a great deal of natural wisdom and is able to communicate with the animals and send messages or signals to people when she is in human form. Humanity certainly needs to heed her message about caring for the wild places and the creatures who live there.

CONTEMPLATION

I have the strength and power of a great cat,
and I ponder deeply before I strike.

AUGUST 6

Durga

DIVINE AID

Durga (DUR-gah) is one of the manifestations of the Hindu goddess Devi and was called into being to destroy a group of evil demons threatening to take over the world. In an epic battle, she killed the demon Mahish and all his lieutenants. Durga, whose name in Sanskrit means "invincible," is depicted mounted on a giant yellow tiger, heading into battle. Her skin is the same yellow color as her tiger's hair.

Demonic forces are said to be destructive and quick acting, while divine forces are constructive in nature and work more slowly and thoroughly. When these forces are out of balance, all the deities unite to become one force, which is the goddess Durga. Since she is such a powerful protector, women also invoke Durga on the sixth day after childbirth, asking for a much-needed day of rest.

CONTEMPLATION

I battle the forces of destruction in my life, which include the demons of poverty, illness, and negative behavior.

Tiamat

GENERATION

Tiamat (TEA-ah-mot) is the great Babylonian dragon woman of "bitter waters," or the salty sea, as opposed to the fresh river water represented by her mate. She existed alone in the primordial abyss before creation and was called Ummu-Hubur, she who formed all things out of "the Deep" of her nature. Tiamat is a central figure in the Babylonian creation epic Enuma Elish, and it was she who possessed the Tablets of Destiny. Tiamat had different names according to the Chaldeans and Assyrians and was seen as a beneficent creator.

Later, in a chilling act of matricide, she was murdered by her son, Marduk, which suggests the emergence of the patriarchy, since the earlier stories tell a different tale. In this other version of the myth, he turned half of her body into the sky and the other half into the sea. Some equate the giant constellation of Draco with Tiamat. In the Hebrew scriptures, Tiamat became Thom, the "Deep." Intriguingly, the Hebrew name Miriam and the biblical name Mary also mean "bitter waters."

CONTEMPLATION

The Eternal Parent, wrapped in her ever-invisible robes,
had slumbered once again for seven eternities.

— HELENA BLAVATSKY, *The Secret Doctrine*

AUGUST 8

Python

GUIDANCE

Python (PIE-thun) is an ancient Greek goddess in the form of a great dragon. She was born to Hera without the aid of Zeus, indicating that she is particularly ancient. Mythically, dragons are creatures that breathe fire. In the earliest stories, Python is called Delphyne, and her famous oracular shrine stood at Delphi, named after dolphins (*delphis* in Greek). Delphi was built on the slopes of Mount Parnassus and was sacred first to Gaia. At Delphi only her priestesses, called the Pythia, were allowed to prophesy. The Pythia descended into an oracular chamber, sat on a tripod stool, and chewed mind-altering laurel leaves to enhance clairvoyance.

Later the priests of Apollo hijacked Delphi, and in myth Apollo killed the dragon, Python, who guarded the site. However, even when Apollo's priests were in control, the prophecies were still uttered by the Pythia.

CONTEMPLATION

I still my mind and look deep within
for the guidance I need.

Wuriupranili

BENEVOLENCE

Wuriupranili (WUR-ya-pran-IH-lee) is a goddess of the Australian Aborigines. She is called Sun Woman, and she travels across the sky carrying a flaming torch of bark that is the physical form of the sun. Wuriupranili paints the glorious colors of dawn and sunset from the powdered ochre paint she wears. She spreads the paint all over her body, and as she travels across the sky on her daily journey, dust from the paint colors the sky in beautiful streaks.

At the end of the day, when Wuriupranili reaches the western ocean, she touches the torch to the waves to extinguish its fire. Then she uses the glowing embers to guide her through the dark underworld on the night side of earth, so that she can start over at dawn, blessing the world with her light.

CONTEMPLATION

I give thanks for the glorious colors of dawn and sunset,
which fill my heart with joy.

Akewa

INDIVIDUALITY

Akewa (ah-CAY-wah) is the sun goddess of the Toba people of Argentina, who live in an area called Gran Chaco. Akewa was once a being of radiant beauty who illuminated the sky, and she lived with her sisters, who were also beautiful beings of light. They became curious and descended to earth to investigate the male creatures who lived there. Sadly, the men of earth captured the radiant beings. Only Akewa escaped, as she was late in arriving. The Toba believe that all the women of earth are the sisters of Akewa, the sun.

Akewa still journeys across the sky each day, bringing light to the earth and reminding women of their true radiance and nature. Every now and then, she is swallowed by a great jaguar, which causes a solar eclipse. But Akewa doesn't disappear for long, as she is too hot and the jaguar spits her out. In astronomy, Akewa is now a dorsum, or ridge, on the planet Venus.

CONTEMPLATION

My true nature is the brilliance
of my inner radiance and heat.

Hebat

LIGHT

Hebat (hee-baht) is a sun goddess of the Hurrians who was widely venerated throughout the ancient Near East. Like other goddesses of the area, she was depicted standing on a lion, which was her sacred animal. The Hurrians lived in Mesopotamia forty-five hundred years ago and greatly influenced the later Hittites. Hebat was Queen of Heaven and also Mistress of Earth, and was invoked to ensure fertility. In the latter role, Hebat was called Mother of All Living. She was also said to have created the land of cedars in Lebanon.

Hebat's divine consort was the storm god Teshub. She was a goddess of battle as well and was invoked for military victory. Some linguistic scholars believe that Hebat became the Hebrew Chavvah, pronounced "ha-wah," who appears in Genesis as Eve.

CONTEMPLATION

The power of creation and generation is the domain of the goddess. New life is victory over annihilation.

Anat

GUARDIAN

Anat (ah-NOT) is an ancient goddess who was worshipped in Canaan, Chaldea, Sumer, Babylon, and Egypt as Lady of Heaven and Mistress of All Gods. She was mother of the seven Anunnaki, the "great gods" who appear in the Babylonian creation myth Enuma Elish. At the height of her popularity in Egypt, Ramses II chose her as his personal guardian in battle and named one of his daughters after her. Like other powerful goddesses of light, Anat was the female counterpart of the storm god Reshef.

In texts found in the ancient city of Ugarit, which is now part of Syria, Anat is the daughter of the high god El and sister of Ba'al. Although she could be a bloodthirsty goddess of war, she had a benevolent quality that related to fertility. It seems her warlike behavior was limited to coming to the aid of her brother, Ba'al, in his battles. Despite her legendary sexuality, she was a perpetual virgin, as was the biblical Mary. Anat was the northern Semitic name for *Allat*, meaning "goddess," and Anat may have been a composite of Asherah, Astarte, and Ishtar.

CONTEMPLATION

*I ask for the powerful protection of the goddess
if I am required to resolve a conflict.*

Amaterasu

RECOGNITION

Amaterasu (ah-mah-tare-AH-soo), a Japanese sun goddess whose full name is Amaterasu Omikami, shines in heaven and also blesses weaving and agriculture. Her countenance is brilliant, and this goddess of fire illuminates the earth with radiant light. Her brother is a jealous storm god who committed an act of violence toward women and Amaterasu's beautiful garden. Afterward, Amaterasu hid in a cave grieving.

Eight hundred deities gathered outside the cave to coax her out, because the world was growing dark without her. The goddess Uzume performed an outrageous and bawdy dance, using the magical mirror crafted by the goddess Uzume called Yata no Kagami, or Eight-Hand Mirror, which made them all laugh. Finally, overcome by curiosity, Amaterasu emerged and, for the first time, saw her own radiance reflected in the mirror. Awed by her own brilliance, she returned to the world, and all life was renewed. She is depicted with a serpent on her arm and holding her brother's broken sword, which she shattered into three pieces.

CONTEMPLATION

*I recognize that the world needs my special light,
and I joyfully let it shine.*

Hsi-Ho

TODAY

Hsi-Ho (shy-ho) is a Chinese sun goddess whose title is Lady of Ten Suns. In ancient times the Chinese week had ten days, with a different "sun" to correspond to each. There were also twelve moons in the calendar. Hsi-Ho gave birth to all the suns, and she controlled the time each was allotted in its sequential role of lighting the day. A great tree stood in the Valley of the Lake, which was home to the suns. Each morning Hsi-Ho bathed the ten suns in the eastern lake. Then she placed the one whose turn it was to illuminate that particular day in a chariot drawn by dragons to prepare for the journey across the sky. The others waited their turn in the branches of the tree.

Hsi-Ho is also mother to Venus, the morning star, and it is a Chinese custom to light a candle on New Year's Day and give thanks to the particular star under which one was born. The quality of the flame portends what the year may have in store.

CONTEMPLATION

*Just for today I will focus on this day's gifts
in the journey of my life.*

Sphinx

ENIGMA

The Great Sphinx of Egypt is a recumbent lion who faces due east and watches every sunrise and full moon rise. The moon rises due east, opposite the sun, only when it is in the full phase. Because all the lion deities in Egypt were female, it is my belief that the original form of this Guardian of Giza was a great lioness. There is considerable geological evidence that the Sphinx is much older than convention holds, although this is controversial. The word *sphinx* is of Greek origin and comes from a word that means "to draw tight" or "to bind together." A stele nearly three thousand years old, dating from the time of the pharaoh Tutmosis IV, stands between the paws of the Sphinx. An inscription on this stele gives the giant statue the three names of the sun, at morning, noon, and night: Re Khefer, Re Horacty, and Re Atum.

The Greeks borrowed many things from their Egyptian predecessors, and Greek sphinxes too were always female, suggesting an earlier tradition. Sphinxes were seen as guardians, especially of arcane knowledge. Egyptian sphinxes were benevolent protectors, but in Greek myths these lion-bodied creatures could be vengeful, posing difficult riddles to those who dared to pass their borders. An incorrect answer could prove fatal, so it was wise to be prepared.

CONTEMPLATION

The secret wisdom of the Sphinx:
To know, to will, to dare, and to be silent.

AUGUST 16

Yhi

RHYTHM

Yhi (yee) is a goddess of light and creation who lives in the Dreamtime of the Australian Aborigines, whose culture may be the oldest continuous culture on earth. The Dreamtime is imagined as an infinite spiral of possibilities out of which all things emerge. It also establishes law and culture in Aborigine society.

Yhi slept, like the "Eternal Parent slumbering for seven eternities" mentioned by Helena Blavatsky in *The Secret Doctrine*, until a whistle awakened her. As Yhi opened her eyes, earth was filled with light. As she moved, stretched, and walked, flowers and other plants appeared on the surface of the land. Everywhere she looked, the light from her eyes created the creatures and vegetation of our planet. When she finished, she returned to the sky and closed her eyes, and there was darkness. Everyone on earth feared the darkness would last forever, until the first sunrise, when they saw her radiant face.

CONTEMPLATION

Everywhere I glance,
I consciously radiate the warmth of love.

Leo Goddesses

249

AUGUST 17

Sunna

POSITIVITY

Sunna (SOON-ah) is a Scandinavian goddess whose title is Mistress Sun. In Norse mythology the sun is feminine, and in a land where winter has almost no daylight, the sun and her light are welcomed with joy. Sunna carries the sun across the sky each day in her chariot pulled by horses. She is pursued by the mythical wolf beast, Skoll, who will eventually catch her at the time of Ragnarok, the "Twilight of the Gods." The end of our universe will then result. Every now and then, he gets close enough to take a bite of her, causing an eclipse.

Sunna's worshippers carved deep stone circles in the landscape, perhaps representing the circular path of the sun during the year. The *Eddas*, the Norse mythic texts, say that Sunna will one day bear a bright daughter to succeed her. Then the universe will be born anew in another cycle, and the daughter will outshine the mother. Sol was the name of Sunna's mother from an earlier cycle of manifestation.

CONTEMPLATION

My positive state of mind draws blessings into my life.

Goddesses for Every Day

Tabiti

CENTER

Tabiti (tah-BEE-tee) is the Scythian goddess of fire who also ruled the realm of animals. The Scythians, a nomadic horse people of Iranian origin, determined their wealth by the size of their herds. Tabiti was often ritually married to the king or tribal chief. Women were seen as controllers of life and death in this culture. Tabiti was also a supreme goddess who represented the upper level of the universe and the symbolic concept of center.

Her symbol appears in the middle of a beautiful gold mirror found in a burial ground in the Ukraine. (Many cultures regarded mirrors as magical instruments or portals to other dimensions.) These early eastern Europeans swore their allegiance to Tabiti, a goddess seen as part of the earth and as witness to everything. She was part of eastern European culture before the Scythian nomads arrived and was at first represented by a goddess bearing a child. Tabiti was later adopted by the Scythians and depicted as half serpent, with a raven on one side and a canine on the other.

CONTEMPLATION

I see only beauty reflected in the mirror of my soul.

Belisama

LUMINOSITY

Belisama (buh-LEE-sah-ma) is a Celtic sun goddess from Britain and Gaul. Her name means "bright light" and comes from the Celtic roots *belo*, "bright," and *samo*, "summer." She represents the brightness of summer and is a goddess of fire, including sunlight, moonlight, and the fires that forge metal for weapons and crafts. Statues of her depict her with serpents, so she is also a goddess of wisdom and healing and is similar to both Minerva and Athena.

Like other Celtic goddesses, even though she is a goddess of fire she takes physical form as a river. Her worship was widespread, and some scholars believe she was also the goddess of the river Mersey in northern England. This opinion is based on a geographic reference made by the Alexandrian astronomer Ptolemy, but in Roman times it was the river Ribble, also in northern England, that was called Belisama.

CONTEMPLATION

When I give of my gifts in a genuine and joyous way,
I become a luminous presence, spreading light in my world.

Coatilcue

REALITY

Coatilcue (co-AH-till-quay) is the Aztec Mother Goddess who gave birth to all things, including light in the form of the sun, moon, and stars. One of her children is the famous Aztec deity Quetzalcoatl, whose name means "feathered serpent." Her name means "she of the serpent skirt" in the Nahuatl language, and she is pictured wearing a skirt of slithering serpents and a necklace made of skulls, hands, and human hearts. She is similar to the Hindu Kali. As Lady of the Serpent, Coatilcue is a patron to Aztec women in childbirth, since women who died giving birth were honored like warriors.

Coatilcue lives on the mountain Coatepec, or Serpent Mound, and she holds the power of life and death. She is usually seen in her form as the devouring mother, to whose womb all her children return after physical death. Coatilcue became pregnant with another of her children, the sun and war god, when she placed into her chest a ball of white feathers that had fallen from the sky.

CONTEMPLATION

*Dark terrors of the night disappear
in the clear light of day.*

Shapash

INCANDESCENCE

Shapash (SHAY-pash) is the goddess of the sun who was worshipped at sunrise, noon, and sunset by the people of ancient Ugarit, part of modern-day Syria. She was called Luminary of the Deities, Torch of the Gods, and Pale Shamash. From her perspective in the sky, she saw all that transpired on earth. Since she was all-seeing, she was frequently dispatched on errands by the god El or the goddess Anat, acting as their messenger or herald. Shapash's light also guided and protected the souls of the dead on their journey through the darkness of the underworld.

Shapash assisted Anat in her mythical search for the body of the god Ba'al when he was believed dead. She retrieved him from Sheol, the underworld, where Mavet, the god of death, reigned, and returned him to Anat. Shapash is also a deity of justice who often mediated disputes for other gods. She was seen as a bringer of light, the upholder of law and order, and a prophetic oracle. She could also magically cure snakebites. Snake venom poisoning the body was compared to a darkness or mist, which her healing light dispelled.

CONTEMPLATION

*Where does the sun's healing light
need to shine in my life?*

Unelanuhi

CLEVERNESS

Unelanuhi (UNA-la-new-hee) is the Cherokee sun goddess. Her name means "apportioner," and she was responsible for dividing time into units, such as the sections of the day. In the beginning the earth was dark, and Grandmother Spider spun a great web and pulled bright Unelanuhi into the sky to bring light to the world after others had tried and failed.

Her story tells that Unelanuhi had a mysterious lover who visited her only at night. Like the Greek Psyche, who also had a mysterious lover, Unelanuhi conspired to learn his identity. One night she spread ashes on his face. When daylight came, she recognized her brother the moon. The face we see on the moon is the one Unelanuhi formed with the ashes. Now she and her brother meet only once a month in the dark of the new moon. The rest of the time they chase each other across the sky.

CONTEMPLATION

Some things are better left in silence and in secret.

VIRGO GODDESSES
The Sheaf of Wheat

ALL THINGS BEAR FRUIT
ACCORDING TO THEIR NATURE

*V*irgo is the energy of mutable earth and brings the principle of differentiated matter into forms that can become highly specialized. During this phase of the zodiac, plans can be carried out in detail. Virgos have a highly developed sense of discrimination; they tend to be technical in nature and can be overly critical. Virgo natives are well suited to analyzing facts and figures but are generally also oriented toward service. Virgos often struggle with an impossible quest for perfection that can lead to a sense of inferiority. Virgo is the Virgin in traditional astrology. In times past, the word *virgin* referred to a young girl or an unattached woman and wasn't meant to connote sexual inexperience.

The goddess sign for Virgo is the Sheaf of Wheat, symbolically held in the hand of the goddess of the constellation of Virgo. With rare exceptions, the earth is seen as a goddess who sustains her children by means of the annual cycle of fertility and the renewal of the land. The body of the goddess feeds and nourishes her children, and many ancient goddesses embodied the perpetual motion of the agricultural year. Virgo goddesses include ancient goddesses of grain, agriculture, and the harvest, whose myths are characterized by the nature of the earth, fruits of the field, and seasonal cycles. Images of these goddesses often include vast fields of waving grain, overflowing cornucopias, and generous platters of fruits.

Virgo

HARVEST

Virgo (VUR-go) is a representation of many great goddesses of antiquity and signifies the cycle of fertility and the harvest. She is depicted holding a sheaf of grain, usually wheat. In the constellation of Virgo, the sheaf of grain is represented by Spica, the brightest star. Virgo, the Virgin, is the only female figure among the zodiac constellations and, other than Gemini, the Twins, the only human figure. The sun passes through this part of the sky in mid-September, so in a sense she announces the harvest.

In more ancient times, both the goddess and the constellation of Virgo were known as Astraea, the Starry One. Astraea was a goddess of justice and was identified with this constellation because of its proximity to the adjacent scales of Libra, which may have been part of the Virgo constellation thousands of years ago. She ruled the world with her wise ways until humanity became so callous that she returned to the skies, disgusted. Virgo has been equated with many other grain goddesses of antiquity who are related to the seasonal cycles.

CONTEMPLATION
*I will reap the harvest according
to the seeds I have sown.*

Virgo Goddesses

Helen

ROOTS

Helen is an ancient, pre-Hellenic goddess whose myths and stories are complex. Her name means "bright one," and she was most often a goddess of the harvest. She was also sometimes depicted with a magical necklace of stars. One of the oldest temples dedicated to her was situated high on a hill at Therapne, east of what was once Sparta, in the south of mainland Greece. As Helen Dendritus, she was Helen of the Trees, and this connects her with the Hebrew goddess Asherah.

Although she is best known for her connection to Troy and the famous battle, that story was altered over time, and her kidnapping by Paris was a later invention of the Greeks. One of her names was Sparta, and she was queen of this city in her own right. Spartans continued to worship Helen well into the Greek period. Helen's most famous daughter was the precocious Hermione, the Pillar Queen, who became a novice priestess at the age of nine. *Hermione* was certainly an excellent choice of names for the heroine of the Harry Potter series, bringing a goddess into a modern myth.

CONTEMPLATION

I stand tall and straight
and know I am enough.

Fatima

HUMILITY

Fatima (fah-TEE-mah) was the daughter of the prophet Muhammad, founder of Islam, but her human origins have been eclipsed over time, and her story now carries mythic overtones that reach back to pre-Islamic Arabian goddesses. Fatima is the ancestral mother of the imams of the Shi'i Muslims. Members of a Muslim dynasty who trace their descent from Fatima are known as the Fatimid. Among Shi'i Muslims, she has become more of a saint than a human woman. In fact, her myth is at the center of the division between the Sunni and Shi'i Muslims.

Fatima is also called Al Zahra, which means the "radiant one," and, like Mary, she is called Queen of Heaven. Mary is mentioned thirty times in the Quran. According to Father Thomas Carleton, in an essay published on The-Rosary.net, after Fatima's death Muhammad said, "Thou shalt be the most blessed of all women in paradise, after Mary." Fatima is said to commune with angels, and they are said to be at her service. Even the archangel Gabriel is said to sing her praises. Muslim women still celebrate her at an all-female feast, where they say special prayers to her. The power of her myth and the reverence accorded to her are tied to the goddesses who preceded Islam in Arabia: Al Uzza, Al Lat, and Al Menat.

CONTEMPLATION

To be humble is not to be meek,
but rather to quietly and confidently hold my true power.

Goddesses for Every Day

Sabulana

RESTITUTION

Sabulana (sah-boo-LAH-nah) is a savior heroine of the Mach-akeni people of Africa. The people had dishonored the goddess by neglecting to praise her and make offerings. As a result, the goddess withdrew and the bounty of the earth dried up, leaving everyone in great danger of starvation.

Sabulana traveled alone to a sacred ancestral grove, where she danced and sang to the spirits of the ancestors. Her voice was so stirring, and her heart so pure, that the ancestors interceded for her. When she returned, she was honored as chief, and she instructed the people in how to pay homage to the goddess again. The heart of the goddess was filled with compassion, and once again the gardens bloomed and wild game became plentiful. Her courageous acts of restitution to the goddess rescued her people from starvation, and afterward, Sabulana herself was seen as a goddess.

CONTEMPLATION

How have I neglected to honor, praise,
and express gratitude for my blessings?

Uti Hiata, Corn Mother

REVERENCE

Uti Hiata (OO-tee high-AH-tah) is the corn goddess of the Pawnee Indians of the Great Plains. Myths and legends of Corn Mother exist in many lands around the world. She taught the Pawnee the secrets of agriculture and the magic of life and death. Corn Mother is a symbol of the Great Goddess, who gives of the substance of her body and her life to provide food for her children. Corn or maize grows, dies, and returns to the earth each year in a continual cycle of renewal and replenishment.

By honoring these cycles and giving thanks in a spirit of reverence, humanity maintains its bond with Corn Mother and ensures that the blessings will continue. Otherwise, our arrogance might cause the land to become barren. A mountain on the planet Venus, formed by volcanic action, has been named the Uti Hiata Mons.

CONTEMPLATION

The gods are jealous. If you forget
to give smoke they will be angry.

— "HOW CORN CAME TO EARTH," NATIVE AMERICAN LORE,
COLLECTED BY STONEE PRODUCKTIONS

AUGUST 29

Tellus Mater

DILIGENCE

Tellus Mater (TELL-oos MAH-tur) is a Roman goddess whose name means "mother earth." She represents the fertility of the earth and the ability of all beings to reproduce and to populate the planet. She was also invoked for protection against earthquakes. Tellus Mater, who is similar to Ceres, the Roman grain goddess, was responsible for the productivity of farmland. She was said to carefully watch over every single seed from the time it was planted until was fully grown.

A temple built in her honor more than two thousand years ago stood in the Forum Pacis, the forum of peace, in ancient Rome. When couples married, Tellus Mater was invoked during the ceremony to ensure fertility and plentiful reproduction. Oaths were sworn to her as the personification of the earth, who sees all and therefore could judge the veracity of the promise.

CONTEMPLATION

*I vow to lovingly tend the garden
of my life with careful attention.*

Mati Syra Zemlya

ANTIQUITY

Mati Syra Zemlya (MAH-tee SIR-ah zem-ILL-ah) is an especially ancient earth goddess of the Russian and Slavic people. Her name, which means "moist mother earth," is actually a description of her nature. Mati Syra Zemlya is one of the oldest figures in mythology. Her worship may date back as far as thirty thousand years, and she was revered well into the twentieth century despite Christian influence.

People were not permitted to strike the earth with implements before March 25, as the goddess was believed to be pregnant before this time. Her ceremonies were always held outside, and they related to earth's fertility and an abundant harvest. In the month of August, Mati Syra Zemlya was honored in harvest rituals in which women entered the fields at dawn and blessed the earth with hemp oil. As they poured the oil on the land in a sacred ceremony, they faced each of the four cardinal directions in turn.

CONTEMPLATION

I gratefully acknowledge the blessings I
receive from Mother Earth and always
return a portion of the bounty.

Nuzuchi

CARING

Nuzuchi (new-ZOO-key) is a Japanese vegetation goddess who rules over grassy plains and trees and is said to be the renewing spirit of the prairies. She was born after the emergence of the first eight islands of the Japanese archipelago, which now consists of more than three thousand islands. Nuzuchi was invoked as a protector of fields, and especially of herbs and healing plants. Growing things are perceived as holy and are honored, and acts of reverence and care for plants are believed to be important to ensure the cyclical regeneration of life.

In Japan, where there are beautiful old-growth forests, great trees are revered, and peasants once surrounded the trees' trunks with sacred cords. The Japanese once believed trees had souls, known as the Ko-dama, and that their souls endowed the trees with the power of speech. This took the form of rustling leaves, which carried a message.

CONTEMPLATION

Listen to the voices of the trees. What
magical secrets of healing do they whisper?

Eve

LIFE

The story of the Eve we know from the Judeo-Christian Bible, who is blamed for humanity's fall and banishment from the Garden of Eden, contradicts her earlier mythic origins as a goddess. The name Eve comes from the Hebrew word pronounced *hawah*, which means "life" and "to breathe." Scholars believe Eve was derived from Kheba, an earlier goddess of the Hurrians, a culture who lived in Mesopotamia five thousand years ago. According to the Amarna Tablets, which date from around 1400 BCE, Kheba was worshipped more than four thousand years ago, during the late Bronze Age. Hawah was also another name of Asherah, a great mother goddess of pre-biblical times.

The earlier goddesses were associated with serpents, which shows their relationship to both wisdom and immortality. In the Gnostic texts, which were later called heretical by the Catholic Church, Eve is an aspect of Sophia and the embodiment of the supreme principle of feminine wisdom. In this capacity, she was the creator of the Word, *Logos* in Greek. The Gnostics viewed women and men as equal. The discovery of the texts of the Nag Hammadi library in Egypt in 1945 has shed much light on the rich and diverse beliefs of those who lived in the Middle East two thousand years ago.

CONTEMPLATION

*Knowing life is eternal, and justice always prevails,
I trust that women will transcend the so-called sins of Eve.*

Uke Mochi

NOURISHMENT

Uke Mochi (OOH-key MOH-chee) is a Japanese Shinto goddess of food and rice, and her name means "goddess who possesses food." Her legend tells the story of a visit from the evil moon god Tsuki-yomi, the brother of the sun goddess Amaterasu. Uke Mochi offered him food that emerged from her body. In his translation of the Kojiki, a collection of Japanese sacred texts, Basil Chamberlain relates that, when she faced the ocean, fishes came from her mouth, "things broad of fin and narrow of fin." She then turned to face the forest, and game animals emerged from her body, "things rough of hair" and things "soft of hair." Then Uke Mochi turned toward a rice paddy, and she coughed up a large bowl of rice.

Uke Mochi offered all this as a feast to the moon god on one hundred serving tables. The moon god was disgusted by her "impure food," and so he drew his sword and killed her. Even so, her body continued to produce bountiful amounts of nourishment. Amaterasu was saddened by her brother's vicious actions and took everything that came forth from Uke Mochi's body and planted the objects like seeds in order to feed humanity.

CONTEMPLATION

*What can I bring forth today from the
essence of my being to nourish others?*

Pachamama

GRATITUDE

Pachamama's (PAH-cha-MAH-mah) name is usually translated as "mother earth." She is a goddess of creation and fertility to the Chincha people, the indigenous people of Peru. Her consort is Inti. The people believe she created the massive Andes Mountains and taught women the magic of planting and harvesting corn. Before every meeting or festival, the people toast the goddess with *chicha*, a traditional fermented drink made of a specific kind of yellow maize. Because she is such a "good mother," this toasting takes place frequently.

Indians who have outwardly converted to Christianity still honor Pachamama through devotion to Mother Mary. Women sing and speak to benevolent Pachamama as they garden or tend the corn, because she still oversees planting and harvesting. Her legend says that, after she blessed the people with her gifts, she became a dragon and went to live inside the mountains. They still pray to her, asking her not to rumble the mountains and cause earthquakes.

CONTEMPLATION

I raise a toast of gratitude for the bountiful blessings of Mother Earth.

Ninlil

TOLERANCE

Ninlil (nin-LILL) is a Sumerian virgin goddess whose name means "lady of the open field" and also "mistress of the winds." She is a goddess of fertility and was said to have lived in Nippur long before the creation of mere mortals. Nippur, southeast of Baghdad, was one of the oldest Sumerian cities, dating to more than seven thousand years ago. Because she was seen as the earth itself, one of her roles was bestowing kingship. After she had designated a king, that ruler would become her symbolic consort. This symbolic union was seen as ensuring an abundant harvest.

Her myth involves much duplicity on the part of her brother-consort, Enlil, who repeatedly disguised himself in order to ravish her. They had several children from these unwelcome encounters. Once he overcame her in the form of water while she was bathing in a stream. He was banished to the underworld for this, but Ninlil had already conceived, so she followed him to confront him. The myths strongly suggest an astronomical component, as one of their children is the moon.

CONTEMPLATION

*What am I willing to tolerate for
the sake of the greater good?*

Yolkai Estasan

SHARING

Yolkai Estasan (YOLK-eye es-TAH-sun) is a Navajo creator goddess who appears as White Shell Woman in the myths of the Navajo, Zuni, and Apache. This ancient goddess is the source of all life and the ancestor of the Sun Father. She was made from rainbow-colored abalone shell and ruled both the oceans and the fiery sunrise.

Her honoring ceremony includes a young girl running toward the east two times on the first day and three times on the second day. The girl's main duty, however, is to grind corn for a huge ceremonial cake called *alkaan*, which is baked in the ground. The bowl of batter is blessed with cornmeal and covered with husks. A cross made of two husks is oriented to the four cardinal directions and placed in the center. The bowl of batter is then buried in the ground, and a fire is built on top and tended all night. The *alkaan* is then consumed in a spirit of sacred communion, and special prayers are said for the harvest.

CONTEMPLATION

Today I can bake a special cake and share it with friends, honoring earth's blessings.

Mayauel

COMFORT

Mayauel (my-ah-WELL) is an Aztec fertility goddess of the Nahua people of Mexico. She became the first maguey, which is the Spanish name for any of several types of agave plant. Mayauel was originally a gentle girl who had been kidnapped by an evil goddess who lived in the sky. The hero-god Quetzalcoatl rescued her, and they took flight, hiding in the branches of a tree. But the evil goddess found the girl and tore her body into small pieces.

Quetzalcoatl reverently buried her, and the tears of his grief watered the ground. The grave was blessed by gods and goddesses, and all the pieces of Mayauel sprouted into the first sacred agave plants. The hallucinogenic properties of agave brought Quetzalcoatl comfort during his mourning. The Aztecs prepared a sacred drink from the plants that they used in rituals. In another story, the nature of the plant was revealed to a special couple when a plant was split in two by lightning. We know this plant as the source of tequila, which has engendered many other kinds of not-so-sacred rituals.

CONTEMPLATION
Where do I find comfort when I am in pain?

Virgo Goddesses

Selu, Corn Woman

MERCY

Selu (SAY-loo) is known as Corn Woman to the Cherokee, and she represents the feminine principle. Her story is similar to that of the goddess Mayauel. Selu and her husband, Kenatu, who represents the masculine principle, adopted a wild boy they found in the woods. He turned out to be a bad influence on their son. One day the boys followed their mother to discover the origin of the corn she fed the family. As they spied on her, she pulled an ear of corn from her rib. The wild boy said she was an evil witch and they should kill her.

Resigned to her fate, Selu told them that, if they must kill her, they should cut her body into seven pieces, place them in a field, and sprinkle her blood on the field. They did not do as she told them, and instead placed her head on a pole and buried the other pieces. The next day, corn stalks with golden hair grew from her head. Their mother told them in whispers that, if tended reverently, this corn would be food for the Cherokee people. Selu found fulfillment through her sacrificial death as she became an eternal help to the Cherokee people.

CONTEMPLATION

*What can I offer as a gift that I
create from the substance of my true self?*

Mary

DIVINITY

Mary, the virgin and mother icon of Christianity, is an ancient archetype. Her origin can be found in the earlier Sumerian goddess Mari. Mary's name comes from the Hebrew *Miriam*, which means "bitter waters," as in the salty sea. Whoever she may have been historically, her story is the same as those of virgin mothers of divine sons from many traditions. Like those goddesses, she holds the power of a goddess, or an independent woman, who gives birth in a miraculous manner. The Catholic Church celebrates the feast of Mary's birth on September 8.

Worship of Mary is widespread and includes the worship of her apparition in various places around world. The Catholic Church erected basilicas on seventeen of these locations. Veneration of Mary around the world has increased in recent times, suggesting a deep and unmet need in humanity to revere the sacred feminine. Sometimes profound healing is born from the bitterest of experiences.

CONTEMPLATION

*A great sign appeared in the sky, a woman
clothed with the sun, with the moon under her feet,
and on her head a crown of twelve stars.*

— BIBLE, REVELATION 12:1

Virgo Goddesses

Qocha Mama

COMPROMISE

Qocha Mama (COH-cha MAH-mah) is the Blue Corn Maiden of the Hopi. Corn is considered to be the "mother" and is a metaphor for life itself. The cycles of planting and harvest are at the center of Hopi ceremonies, where the sun's movement through the seasons relates to the directions. Corn is the most important substance to the Hopi, so seed corn, the life of the mother, is kept for two years in case of drought. Corn is harvested after the *katsinas* go back to their home in the peaks of the San Francisco mountains each year. The *katsinas* are spirit beings thought to reside in all people, animals, and plants. They appear each year at the summer solstice, which begins the yearly ceremonial cycle.

Each color of corn has a special significance, and the Corn Maidens have a central place in myth and ritual. Blue Corn Maiden is thought to be the prettiest of the corn sisters and occupies the direction of north. Her story includes a mythical kidnapping by Winter Katsina, who loved her, and a subsequent rescue by Summer Katsina so she could go back to the people and grow corn. The problem was solved by a familiar mythic compromise, in which she spends half the year with each of them. In this way the earth is green and growing half the year, and cold and barren while Qocha Mama lives with Winter Katsina.

CONTEMPLATION

The fine art of compromise
can usually prevent a battle.

SEPTEMBER 10

Nokomis

SUBSTANCE

Nokomis (no-KOH-miss) is a North American Algonquin Indian goddess whose name means "grandmother." She is a sacred earth mother who nurtures all living things. Nokomis gave birth to all creatures and also created food for humanity. She was the first to tap maple trees for their sweet syrup. The Indians understood that food came from the very substance of the goddess as a blessing, and they honored the yearly cycle of life and death. The Iroquois call her Eithinoha, which means "our mother" in their language.

Nokomis had a daughter who was the spirit of corn, and the legend about the two of them, which includes an annual disappearance and reappearance, is similar to that of Demeter and Persephone. In this way, the growing cycles of earth wax and wane in a continuous cycle. One legend tells how Nokomis fell to earth and became Wenohan, the wife of the famous hero Hiawatha.

CONTEMPLATION

What creative act flows from me that will be a gift to everyone in my life?

Modron

TRANQUILITY

Modron (MODE-ron), a Welsh Celtic goddess whose name means "divine mother," is a goddess of peace and children. Like other Celtic goddesses, she is also a river goddess and is sometimes described as having a triple aspect, like the Roman Matronae or the Greek Fates. And like other Celtic goddesses of the changing times of the year, she teaches that all things, whether joyful or sorrowful, are transitory and will pass. Her son is the famous Mabon, who was kidnapped when he was only three days old and, like a Welsh Jonah, was finally rescued from inside a large salmon. Mabon is also the name of the autumn equinox festival in the Celtic wheel of the year, representing a balance of light and dark.

Sometimes Modron is mated with Urien, who is a god of the underworld. Later in her story she is also linked with the similar character Morgan Le Fay in the Arthurian legend. Here, Modron lives on the island of Avalon with her eight sisters (who are like the Greek Muses) and works as a healer. In more recent times Modron became a creature in the popular electronic game Dungeons & Dragons.

CONTEMPLATION

*Can I finally lay to rest an old pain
and allow healing to take place?*

Chicomecoatl

SURVIVAL

Chicomecoatl (chi-co-may-co-AH-til) is an Aztec goddess whose name means "seven serpents." Her name is also a day in the Aztec calendar, and she is usually shown holding ears of maize, sometimes called Indian corn. She is also seen with a water flower, a type of lily, and holding a sun shield. Chicomecoatl is a goddess of plenty and fertility who presides over vegetation, especially maize, which was central to Aztec culture. Some believe she was worshipped by those who preceded the Aztecs and had gentler ways (the Aztecs believed the gods needed to be appeased through human sacrifice).

Every September, altars in homes were decorated with corn plants and seeds that had been blessed in the temples. At some point during the month, a young Aztec girl, who represented the goddess herself, was ritually sacrificed in atonement. The priests beheaded the girl, and then her blood was poured over a statue of the goddess.

CONTEMPLATION

*What would I be willing to do
to survive or to save my tribe?*

Al Lat

GREATNESS

Al Lat (ah lot) is an Arabian goddess of great antiquity who preceded Islam. Her name is a shortened form of *Al Ilahat*, as described by the Greek historian Herodotus, who equated Al Lat with the Greek Aphrodite. In fact her name means "goddess" and is the feminine equivalent of the masculine Allah, which means "god." She was a fertility goddess of the earth and all its fruits and was part of a trinity from pre-Islamic Arabia that includes Al Menat and Al Uzza.

Her symbol is the waxing crescent moon, sometimes shown with the sun disk on top. This symbol was often inscribed on incense burners, and the crescent moon with the star of Al Uzza is still found on flags in Arab countries. Those who worshipped her credited Al Lat with inventing the saddle, which allowed the Arabs to range far on the camel, the ship of the desert. Her counterpart Al Uzza, the Mighty, was often shown riding on a camel in her role as a war goddess.

CONTEMPLATION

*By the salt, by the fire, and by
Al Lat, who is greatest of all.*

—— ANCIENT ARABIAN OATH, FROM
Encyclopedia of Religion and Ethics,
EDITED BY JAMES HASTINGS

Goddesses for Every Day

Zaramama

NURTURING

Zaramama (ZAH-rah-mah-mah), whose name means "grain mother," is a Peruvian fertility goddess. The Incas believed she appeared in fields of maize in the form of plants that took strange shapes. They saw her in plants that had multiple ears, or two plants that were joined together. As a special honor to Zaramama, the Incas sometimes made dolls from these unusual plants and dressed them like human women in robes and shawls with silver clasps.

At other times Zaramama was thought to appear in earthly form as corn stalks that were hung on willow trees in her honor. The people danced around the trees and burned the stalks as an offering to her, invoking her blessing in order to ensure an abundant harvest.

CONTEMPLATION

I give thanks for the special qualities
and unique character of the plants
that share my home. I nurture them and they nurture me.

Amritika

AMBROSIA

Amritika (ahm-reh-TEEK-ah) is the Hindu goddess associated with *amrita*, which in Sanskrit means "that which is immortal." *Amrita* is the elixir of life, or waters of immortality, the drink of the gods that renders them immortal. Amritika pours *amrita* and represents the nature of the Divine Feminine in the process of spiritual transformation. Amritika can also dispense the nectar of the gods as a love potion or hallucinogen, depending on the circumstances.

Sometimes this priceless substance is said to be the fruit of a certain tree, but in Yoga philosophy *amrita* is said to flow from the pineal gland and down the throat when one is in a state of deep meditation. Soma was a similar substance, and its mythology is related, but soma came from a plant. In Greek myth the drink of immortality was called ambrosia, the red wine of Hera, and was responsible for keeping the Greek gods immortal.

CONTEMPLATION

*What needs to be transformed in my life,
and where will I find the power to transform it?*

Hera

HONOR

Hera (HEAR-ah) is an ancient sky goddess from Crete. She is the Queen of Heaven, whose once-great stature was eroded and vilified upon the ascendance of her philandering husband from the Greek era, Zeus. Hera means "our lady," and was probably not the original name of this early goddess. In later myth Hera became queen of the Olympians when she married Zeus against her will. Originally, she was the daughter of the Titans Rhea and Kronos, and her worship preceded that of her latecomer husband. Some scholars believe that the escapades of Zeus mythically represent the overtaking of the goddess by the patriarchy.

In Hera's magic western garden of immortality, the goddess grew her sacred fruits, the apple and pomegranate. Hera also dispensed ambrosia, the magical elixir that was the gods' source of immortality. In later myth she possessed an apple tree in Hesperides, the western paradise, which was guarded by serpents. The gardens of goddesses are often described as situated in the west, where the sun sets, making them symbols of immortality.

CONTEMPLATION

Can I hold my head high,
even in situations where I have not chosen that path?

Sophia

WISDOM

Sophia (soh-FEE-ah) means "wisdom" in Greek, and to the Gnostics of two millennia ago, Sophia was the Holy Spirit and the third person of the Trinity. She is considered by the Gnostics to be the creator of the physical universe, while the earth and its inhabitants were created by the Hebrew god, Yahweh. Certain Gnostic texts call the Holy Spirit "God the Mother." In Gnostic tradition, Sophia, like the goddess Zoe, later cast Yahweh into the darkness of the abyss. In the "Sophia of Jesus Christ," a scroll from the Nag Hammadi library, her myth relates a "fall from oneness and a return to Light." Other traditions describe a similar process to explain the unfolding process of creation and evolution.

Sophia as the Wisdom of God, or Chockmah in Hebrew, appears in the Bible in Proverbs, Psalms, the apocryphal Wisdom of Solomon, and the New Testament. Chockmah, along with the goddess Shekinah, expresses the feminine side of God in Judaism. In Greek Orthodox tradition, September 17 is the feast day of Saint Sophia, who had three daughters: Pistis, "faith"; Elpis, "hope"; and Agape, "love." All three daughters were tortured and martyred for their faith.

CONTEMPLATION

Incline your ear to Wisdom, and
apply your heart to Understanding.

— BIBLE, PROVERBS 2:2

SEPTEMBER 18

Pyrrha

PERFECTION

Pyrrha (PEER-ah) is a Greek goddess who was the daughter of Pandora. She was the first human woman, and she later married Deucalion. Their story is the Greek version of Noah and the Ark, and in fact, legends of devastating floods appear in the stories of many cultures. At a time when Zeus decided to destroy humanity in a flood, ending the Bronze Age, Pyrrha and her husband were deemed worthy to survive. In fact, Pyrrha was described as "perfect."

Apollodorus relates, in *The Library of Greek Mythology*, that the couple built a boat, and, after floating for nine days and nights, they came to rest on the sacred mountain of Parnassus. The couple were the only survivors of the flood, so they asked a boon of the goddess Themis. They beseeched her to repopulate the world. She told them to "throw the bones of their mother." Pyrrha understood that this meant the stones of Gaia, the earth. Every stone Pyrrha threw became a baby girl, and those Deucalion threw became boys. The Greek word *oud* means both "stone" and "people."

CONTEMPLATION

Stones and crystals carry memories of the earth and can store ancient wisdom.

Etugen

CLEANSING

Etugen (ET-too-jen), also known as Itugen, is an ancient Mongolian earth goddess. Her name is derived from Otuken, the holy mountain and legendary holy city of the Tuje people of Mongolia. The Mongols represent her as a young woman riding on a gray bull. Etugen watches over the health of our planet, and when she believes that earth needs to be purified because of the actions of humans, she causes earthquakes. She shakes herself to slough off the impurities. Sometimes Etugen is also seen as a group of feminine elemental spirits.

Polish anthropologist Maria Antonina Czaplicka spent years doing fieldwork in Siberia in the late 1800s. Her research revealed that different tribes, including the Mongol, Yakut, Altaian, Turgout, and Kirgisl, used almost identical-sounding words to signify a female shaman: *utagan*, *udagan*, *ubakan*, *utygan*, and *utugun*. For a male shaman, they used very different words. Some scholars believe that shamanism was originally the domain of women and passed to men only later. The old word for shaman also sounds like *Etugen*, the Mongol name for this earth goddess. The Siberian earth goddess also has affinities with the Bear constellations, and in one Tartar dialect *utagan* means "bear."

CONTEMPLATION

*I shake up my world, freely letting
go of stuck and toxic energy.*

Annapurna

EUCHARIST

Annapurna (ah-nah-PUR-nah) is a Hindu goddess whose Sanskrit name means "filled" (*purna*) with "food" (*anna*) and is understood to also mean "everlasting food." She was Anna Perenna to the Romans and was seen as the home and support of all the gods. Annapurna provides the sustenance of daily bread and the harvest. She is envisioned as a great breast full of nourishment and is often depicted seated, feeding a child. Symbolically, when food is prepared as a sacrament, it nourishes the soul to fulfill its destiny.

Annapurna is sometimes regarded as an incarnation of Parvati, the consort of Shiva. A common image in Indian temple art shows Shiva with a begging bowl beseeching Annapurna for food that will give him Shakti, or energy, to achieve enlightenment. The goddess makes her home on Annapurna mountain in the Himalayas, from which many streams flow to water the fields below. The mountain's highest peak is more than twenty-six thousand feet tall.

CONTEMPLATION

*I celebrate food as ceremony
and consciously consume what will
feed my body and my soul.*

Demeter

INTROSPECTION

Demeter (da-MEE-ter) is a Greek goddess of vegetation, grain, and the harvest. She was Ceres to the Romans, the origin of our word *cereal*, and was known by other names in different cultures. In a timeless tale of the cyclical death and rebirth of the agricultural year, Demeter and her daughter, Persephone, were separated each fall as Persephone traveled to the darkness of the underworld to be with her husband, Hades, who had originally kidnapped her. During this four-month period, Demeter's grief made the world cold and barren; mother and daughter were reunited each spring and their joy made the world bloom again.

According to some myths, Demeter began the secret rites of initiation held at Eleusis in ancient Greece by teaching Triptolemus, demigod of agriculture, the secret of cultivating corn. Scholars believe the rites, which flourished during the Mycenaean period (circa 1600–1100 BCE), were celebrated annually in a mystical enactment of the yearly cycle by means of a communion with corn, bread, and wine, bringing participants into resonance with the Mother Goddess. In her earliest stories she is one goddess with a triple aspect — maiden, mother, and crone — and the cycles of the year reflect the stages of manifestation of the goddess's life.

CONTEMPLATION

As the wheat grows from the tiny coiled seed, everything has its season. I consciously honor the ever-shifting and repeating cycles.

LIBRA GODDESSES
The Dove

PEACE BEGINS WITHIN

Libra is a cardinal air sign that begins at the autumn equinox. Libra embodies balance and the principle of equilibrium, which results from the interaction of Leo and Virgo, a marriage of spirit and matter. Libra energy is characterized by harmony, and Libra natives are inclined toward cooperation, compromise, and partnership. But trying to be all things to all people brings potential challenges. Libras seek the mirror of relationship and the accompanying lessons but can have difficulty standing up for themselves. Sometimes they try to maintain peace at any price, resulting instead in conflict.

The goddess sign for Libra is the Dove, an ancient emblem of the goddess Venus, the traditional ruler of Libra. Birds are connected with the sacred feminine around the world and viewed as messengers to heaven. In Hermetic tradition — the wisdom teachings thought to have originated in Egypt — the language of the birds, or the green language, is the province of the goddess. White doves are ancient symbols of peace and purity; even the ancient Egyptians revered them. Doves, with their billing and cooing, are also symbols of love. They have no mating season, so they can mate all year. Libra goddesses embody the idea of love, peace, beauty, art, and elegance. Although Libra seeks peace and harmony, conflict is inherent in relationships, so this dual air sign includes goddesses who can appear as fierce birds of war. Libra is also the sign of marriage, so these goddesses learn to balance the challenges that relationships present.

Venus

VENERATION

The Roman goddess Venus emerged from the earlier Greek Aphrodite, and doves were one of her sacred symbols. Our word *veneration* comes from her name. Venus was chiefly a goddess of love, and in fact, she gave birth to the god Amor after her liaison with Mars. The archetype of this goddess has come down through the ages under many names: Ishtar, Inanna, Astarte, to mention just a few. Aphrodite is a goddess of generation and regeneration through sexuality, which was seen as the sacred renewal of life. The planet Venus appears in eight-year cycles, appearing and disappearing as the morning star and evening star, a cycle seen by many cultures as one of renewal.

Venus was a less complex deity than Aphrodite, dealing more with gardens and groves and other growing things of earth. Natural stone altars beneath large trees were sacred to Venus and were attended by virgins of both genders. The duke of Venice, a city named for the goddess, symbolically married her by throwing a gold wedding ring into the sea.

CONTEMPLATION

External beauty is fleeting.
Inner beauty lasts forever.

SEPTEMBER 23

Turan

ASSERTION

Turan (TOUR-ahn) is an Etruscan goddess of love and fertility. Her name comes from the Etruscan word *turan*, which means "to rule," and there appears to be a quality of confidence and assertiveness about her. Turan was the patron goddess of the city of Velch near the coast of central Italy in the area that is now Tuscany. She appeared on Etruscan art, especially mirrors and vases, and was often shown with doves or swans. Sometimes she was portrayed as a young girl with wings. Similar to Aphrodite and Venus, she was a goddess who blessed sexuality and the resulting fertility of the land. Turan is often shown with the moon goddess Zirna, who is depicted with a half-moon hanging from her neck.

The mysterious Etruscans preceded the Romans, thriving, as early as 1200 BCE, in what later became Italy. Linguists can now interpret their unique language, left in tomb inscriptions, but the meaning of many words is still unknown. Like other cultures, the Etruscans were defeated and taken over by the Romans. Turan managed to survive in the folklore of Tuscany and is still known as Turanna, who is like a benevolent fairy godmother.

CONTEMPLATION

*I have a strong sense of self
and stand up for what I believe.*

Ishtar

RECIPROCITY

Ishtar (EESH-tar) is a Babylonian goddess represented by the planet we call Venus. Her symbol is the eight-point star, representing the eight-year cycle of Venus as morning star and evening star. Ishtar is related to the earlier Sumerian goddess Inanna. Carvings on boundary stones in the British Museum show symbols of the sun, moon, and Venus, the star of Ishtar. She is the daughter of Sin, the moon, and the sister of Shamash, the sun. Ishtar is mythically related to Aphrodite and Astarte.

Although her nature is complex and includes death and war, Ishtar was predominantly known as a goddess of love and compassion. She was called Courtesan of the Gods and gave her love freely, and her generous sexuality was believed to be linked to earth's fertility. As a result, she was the most popular goddess in Babylon and Assyria. Ishtar made an annual descent into the underworld, which was symbolically related to the growing cycles on earth and to the cyclical disappearances of Venus as morning and evening stars. At each of seven gates, Ishtar was required to give up one article of clothing.

CONTEMPLATION

*I give my love unconditionally, knowing
it nourishes and blesses the earth.*

Freya

NEGOTIATION

Freya (FRAY-ah) is a Norse goddess and daughter of the gods Njord and Nerthus. Our word *Friday* comes from her name. In myth Freya was born to mitigate a conflict between two different groups of Norse gods: the earlier and peaceful Vanir and the subsequent, warring Aesir. As leader of the Valkyries, she also has the attribute of the destroying crone who brings the darkness. She receives half of the dead who come to the Great Hall, while the god Odin receives the other half.

One of her most potent attributes was that she could take the shape of a falcon, or wear a magnificent cloak made of falcon feathers, which enabled her to fly at will. She also soared across the sky in a chariot drawn by gray cats. Amber was sacred to her, as the gem formed from the tears she wept for her missing husband, Od, who was likely Odin. Some stories report that Freya was wanton and promiscuous, while others insist that this was vicious slander spread by the mischievous trickster god Loki, who desired her himself. Freya labored each winter solstice to bring forth Baldur the sun king.

CONTEMPLATION

The quality of decision is like
the well-timed swoop of a falcon,
which enables it to strike its victim.

— SUN TZU, *The Art of War*

Pax

PEACE

Pax (pahx) is the Roman goddess of peace, and she is the origin of the term *Pax Romana*. The term is Latin for "Roman Peace" and refers to the long period of relative peace and minimal expansion by military force experienced by the Roman Empire between 27 BCE and 180 CE. The goddess Pax is the daughter of Zeus and Themis and the equivalent of the Greek Eirene, who was one of the Horae, keepers of the seasons and guardians of the gates of heaven.

Caesar Augustus, who is thought to have longed for peace, elevated the Roman worship of Pax, transforming it from an abstract principle of peace to an actual goddess. During his reign, Pax and Eirene were common names for girls. Pax was depicted as a young woman with a scepter, cornucopia, and olive branches, traditional symbols of a peace offering.

CONTEMPLATION

Dona nobis pacem. Grant us peace.

— LATIN PRAYER FROM THE "AGNUS DEI"
SECTION OF THE ROMAN CATHOLIC MASS

Isis

MAGIC

Isis (EYE-sis) is the Greek name for the great Egyptian goddess of magic. Her name in the ancient Egyptian language is Auset, meaning "seat" or "throne," which is her hiero-glyphic symbol. She was also called She of Ten Thousand Names. Among those names were Mut-Neter, Mother of the Gods, Maker of Sunrise, Lady of Heaven, Queen of the South, and Lady of the North Wind. Her symbol was the star Sept, which we call Sirius. The reappearance of Sirius, rising before the sun at the summer solstice, signaled the annual Nile flood.

Isis was also Queen of Magic. Through her knowledge, and while in the form of a falcon, she revived her dead hus-band, Osiris, long enough to conceive their divine son, Horus. She was especially skilled in the magic of *hekau*, the uttering of words of power. The Egyptians believed that certain words were like magic formulas and had to be spoken with special tones and at specific times.

CONTEMPLATION

I am All That Has Been,
That Is, and That Will Be.
No mortal has yet been able to
lift the veil that covers Me.

— INSCRIPTION ADDRESSED TO ISIS
ON AN EGYPTIAN TEMPLE DEDICATED TO THE GODDESS NEITH
IN THE NILE DELTA, AS RECORDED BY PLUTARCH

Goddesses for Every Day

DESIRE

Semiramus (sem-ee-RAY-mus) is an Assyrian goddess of love and war who is credited with building Babylon and creating the famous Hanging Gardens, one of the seven wonders of the ancient world. Mythically, Semiramus is the daughter of the mermaid goddess Atargatis and the merman god Oannes, who had the body of a man combined with the tail of a fish. The dove of Ishtar fed her as an infant, and legend says Semiramus became a dove at one point, linking her to the worship of Ishtar. A statue of Semiramus with a golden dove above her head stood at her temple at Mabbog in the north of what is now Syria.

As a human woman who was later elevated to the status of goddess, Semiramus is usually connected to the historical figure Sammuramat, who was once queen of Babylon and Assyria. Sammuramat is reputed to have conquered the Eastern world by leading military campaigns against Persia, Egypt, Libya, and Ethiopia. Some sources say she castrated the males in her household, suggesting that her priests were eunuchs. Semiramus has often appeared as a warrior-queen in stories, including Dante's *Divine Comedy*, and numerous edifices have been named for her.

CONTEMPLATION

*Desire is the fuel of life but is meant to be
purified and directed along constructive channels.*

Star Woman

APPEARANCE

Star Woman is a goddess of the people of the South African bush. She is a beautiful star, actually the planet Venus, who visits earth periodically and carries off an ordinary male to be her lover. The chosen mate is usually old, ugly, and disadvantaged, but by virtue of his liaison with Star Woman he is transformed into the equivalent of a young and handsome prince. There seems to be a deeper message contained in this myth, about beauty residing in the eye of the beholder.

Similar myths appear around the world, telling the story of the appearance of Venus as the morning star and her disappearance and reappearance as the evening star. In the famous *Song of Hiawatha*, by Longfellow, it is the "Sacred Star of Evening" who is revered. The Pawnee Indians perform a ritual at a specific time of year, when two special stars are twinkling in the Milky Way. They believe this represents a ritual mating of the morning and evening stars, which brought the world into being.

CONTEMPLATION

*What blessing of enduring beauty
do I long to call down from the stars?*

Kishijoten

ACCOMPLISHMENT

Kishijoten (kee-she-JO-ten) is a Shinto goddess of beauty, song, dance, opera, luck, and fortune. She is the patron of the arts, perhaps like the Greek Muses. Shinto is the native religion of Japan and is generally translated as the "Way of the Gods," but it did not have a name until it became necessary to distinguish it from Buddhism. As a bestower of blessings, Kishijoten is similar to the Hindu goddess Lakshmi. Sister to the warrior god Bishamon, Kishijoten is one of the seven deities of good fortune, and she possesses a special jewel that brings good luck.

Kishijoten was a protector of the geishas, which translates to "persons of art." The geisha tradition emerged in feudal Japan when ordinary women were not permitted in business situations. Geishas were highly trained to entertain men, and over time, the geisha tradition developed into a highly respected occupation that involved rigorous training and preparation.

CONTEMPLATION

*Do I long to create something of
beauty, a poem, a song, or a dance?*

Fides

FIDELITY

Fides (FEE-days) is a Roman goddess of faith and trust. Her name means "good faith" in Latin, as in making an honest oath or declaring a sacred trust or vow. Our word *fidelity* is drawn from her name. She was responsible for overseeing oaths and verbal contracts and was invoked to ensure loyalty. Her nature forms the basis of all human relationships, ensuring that they will be established in honesty and experienced in fidelity. Her counterpart in Greek mythology is Pistis, who is the *daimona*, or spirit, of trust, honesty, and good faith. Pistis is one of the good spirits who escaped Pandora's box and fled back to heaven, abandoning humankind.

Fides is depicted wearing a white veil and a crown made from an olive branch. Her priests wore white robes. Her temple was situated in the capital, where all official treaties with foreign states were kept under the protection of this goddess. Her festival day was celebrated on October 1. Fides was venerated with the honorific title of Fides Publica Populi Romani, which means "loyalty toward the Roman State."

CONTEMPLATION

When I give my word, I do so in
good faith and with total integrity.

OCTOBER 2

Radha

BELOVED

Radha (RAH-dah) is a Hindu goddess who was the most beloved of the god Krishna. The story of their love affair is the subject of exquisite Indian art and poetry. Radha is sometimes depicted as a breathtakingly beautiful young girl bathing in a river, and her devotees honor the sanctity of the feminine in both essence and form. Radha was a *gopi*, or goatherd, one of several with whom Krishna played as a boy. She secretly longed for the young god while he played his flute and flirted shamelessly with the other girls.

Radha symbolizes the human soul moving through eternity and seeking union with the Divine. The relationship of Radha and Krishna is seen as the highest form of devotion and represents the ideal love between the lover and the beloved. When Krishna went off to vanquish enemies, Radha waited. When Radha as the goddess makes love with the god, they bring worlds into form. When humans join together in this spirit, they create the next generation.

CONTEMPLATION

The cosmic fire that burns in my heart for the beloved is the sacred fuel that brings worlds into form.

OCTOBER 3

Ishikoredome

SELF-AWARENESS

Ishikoredome (ish-ee-koh-ray-DOH-me) is a Japanese Shinto goddess responsible for stonecutting and for aiding artisans. In the story of Amaterasu, after the sun goddess retreated to a cave with her light, it was Ishikoredome who crafted an exquisite mirror in which Amaterasu could see her beautiful reflection. This mirror had religious significance as a symbol of the soul's purity. Japanese folklore says that the mirror and a sword were given to Amaterasu's grandson and then passed to the Imperial House of Japan. The name of this famous mirror is Yata no Kagami, which translates as "eight-hand mirror." The sacred mirror, believed to be endowed with magical properties, is now part of the Imperial Regalia of Japan and is housed in Ise Shrine in Mie prefecture in Japan in a sanctuary built for Ishikoredome.

Mirrors were powerful symbols to the Japanese, and their nonreflecting sides were often decorated with animal totems such as dragons, tigers, serpents, and the phoenix. Mirrors were thought to be gateways, or portals, into the unseen and to have special powers for divination. They might represent knowledge or enchantment, like the magic mirror in the story of Snow White. In the story of Amaterasu, the goddess Uzume performed a risqué dance with this magic mirror and made everyone laugh, stimulating Amaterasu's curiosity.

CONTEMPLATION

*When I look deeply into my own eyes in
a mirror, what is the truth I see reflected?*

Goddesses for Every Day

OCTOBER 4

Urvasi

ELEGANCE

Urvasi (oor-VAH-see) is a Hindu goddess who brings success in love. She is an Apsara, a beautiful celestial maiden, and her name means "widely extending." The Apsaras often bless people during important passages in their lives. Urvasi's most prevalent myth tells the story of a meditating sage. Indra, king of the gods, did not want the sage to acquire divine powers (a story similar to that of the Tower of Babel), so he sent two beautiful nymphs to distract him. In an unruffled response, the sage placed a flower on his thigh, *ur* in Sanskrit, and created Urvasi. Her beauty far transcended that of Indra's nymphs.

After the sage created Urvasi, she occupied a place of honor in Indra's court, but like Aphrodite, she created chaos in heaven, since all the gods desired her. Urvasi is mentioned in the Rig-Veda, sacred literature from India, in which she is famous for a love affair with a human king named Pururava. In this role she embodied intellectual beauty and the unfolding of spirituality in the human condition. The swan is her sacred animal.

CONTEMPLATION

I let my inner beauty unfold and come forth,
like blooming rose petals opening.

Guinevere

SELF-KNOWLEDGE

Guinevere (GWEN-eh-veer), who is also known as Gwenhyw-far, is an ancient form of the triple goddess who made her way into the Arthurian legend. By the medieval period, Guinevere was always cast in the role of unfaithful wife to Arthur because of her relationship with Lancelot. In the Arthurian legend her unfaithfulness, not unlike that of the biblical Eve, caused the decline of the kingdom. Hidden in this story is the long takeover of the Divine Feminine by the historical emergence of patriarchy.

Guinevere symbolized the throne of England in the same way that Isis was the throne of Egypt. As a result, in myth she was continually abducted by would-be rulers who needed her to legitimize their sovereignty. However, Celtic queens had as much power as, perhaps more than, the kings, because they bestowed kingship. The queens were permitted to have multiple relationships. In her earlier origins as the White One, Guinevere was, as with the goddess Athena, associated with the owl.

CONTEMPLATION

I must first know my own nature
in order to be true to myself.

OCTOBER 6

Astraea

BALANCE

Astraea (ah-STRAY-ah), also called Star Maiden, was the Libyan goddess of holy law who held the scales of justice that weighed the claims of opposing parties in disputes. She is similar to the Egyptian Ma'at, as Astraea also weighed the souls of mortals, determining whether they would go to the Elysian fields and eternal bliss or to the underworld to seek redemption. In Greek myth, she was the daughter of Zeus and the goddess Themis, who was the original goddess of prophecy and mythically endowed her daughter with farsightedness.

Astraea was said to be the last of the immortals to live among humans at the end of the golden age, offering hope as the turning wheel of the ages moved into darker times. She later abandoned earth, as it became too painful. She ascended into the sky to hold the scales of justice that are now part of the constellation of Libra. Long ago they were the claws of the Scorpion and, before that, part of Virgo.

CONTEMPLATION

What is the measure of my life, and how will
I judge myself when, at the end, I look back?

Branwen

ALLIANCE

Branwen (BRAN-wun) is a Welsh goddess whose name means "white raven." She is the daughter of the sea god Llyr and is a goddess of beauty and love. She is considered to be one of the three matriarchs of Britain, along with Rhiannon and Ceridwen. She is also the maiden aspect of the triple goddess. In stories, Branwen is renowned for her black-haired and fair-skinned beauty and is sometimes called Venus of the Northern Sea.

Her beauty attracted the king of Ireland, and her brothers arranged a marriage, which, for a short time, united Wales and Ireland. But once the Irish lord took her home, he treated her like a slave. Branwen could take the form of a white raven, so, during her captivity, she trained a starling to speak and sent a message home. She feared her own escape would cause her husband to search for her and retaliate. Her family came to her rescue and launched an attack, but few of them survived the war. During her captivity Branwen bore children. Her son, the male heir, was also killed in the conflict, and she later died of grief. Perhaps this tale points to the danger of taking away a woman's power and her ability to choose. It's said that, on her last visit to earth, Branwen left her Bow of Destiny at her southern shrine.

CONTEMPLATION

Who shall I align myself with in order to receive a needed message about change?

Kayna

TRUST

Kayna (KAY-nah), sometimes called Cain, is a Celtic goddess who had the power to foretell the death of kings. She is the daughter of Branwen, and it seemed appropriate to place them next to each other. October 8 is Kayna's feast day. She is the patron saint of Glasgow, Scotland, and is another goddess of the principle of sovereignty. She is depicted dressed in gray with long tresses reaching to her knees. She has also been mythically linked to the goddess Ceridwen.

Her name comes from *cain*, which means "beautiful" in Old Welsh, and it is cognate to that of the later Saint Keyne, pronounced the same. Kayna was born in Wales, and a famous holy well in Cornwall is named after her. In surviving folk tradition, the first of a married couple to drink from the well will rule the marriage. In an amusing anecdote about relationships, a new husband rushed from the church to be first at the well, only to learn later that his new bride had brought a bottle of the well water to the church. It pays to plan ahead.

CONTEMPLATION

I always drink deeply of the waters of life,
and do not fear the resulting emotions.

Ma'at

JUDGMENT

Ma'at (MOO-aht), one of the great goddesses of ancient Egypt, embodies the principle of right relationship to all things. Her name means "truth." In the Hall of Two Truths, which exists in the Egyptian afterlife, the heart of the recently deceased is weighed in the pan of a balance scale against Ma'at's ostrich feather. If the heart is judged to be heavy, or impure, it is consumed by a complex creature named Amit, and the soul is doomed to remain in the Duat, the Egyptian underworld, where the sun god Ra makes his perilous journey from west to east every night. If the heart is light, balancing with the feather of truth, the soul is eligible to enter paradise, after passing more tests, of course.

Ma'at is the daughter of Ra and regulates his daily path through the sky. She represents the principles of order and harmony in the universe, without which everything would descend into chaos. Her icon, which appears on her head, is a white ostrich feather. The ostrich is known for its keen and far-seeing vision. Like Isis, Ma'at is often portrayed with the enormous spread wings of a sparrow hawk, which is a type of falcon.

CONTEMPLATION

I weigh my words before I speak, knowing the power they send forth into the world.

Eagle Woman

SELF-ESTEEM

Eagle Woman is an American Indian goddess. Everywhere on earth, birds are symbolically connected to the goddess. They are seen as messengers to the gods, since their wings take them toward heaven. As the lion is the leader of the animals, so the eagle is leader of the birds. The eagle has been venerated by nearly every tribe of Indians, and its feathers are always prized. The eagle flies higher than any other bird and is said to be the first creature to greet the rising sun. The eagle, like the ostrich, represents keen sight as well as vision from the heights.

Although the eagle is generally associated with masculine energy and is connected to warriors, power has no gender. Eagle Woman is a potent symbol of this archetypal power in feminine form. To wear or hold an eagle feather is to have contact with the Great Spirit and to honor creation in the highest way. To possess an eagle feather is a great honor, which comes with great responsibility.

CONTEMPLATION

*When I speak, my voice is strong and proud,
carrying the voices of all my ancestors.*

OCTOBER 11

Daphne

WIT

The goddess Daphne (DAFF-nee), or "laurel" in Greek, is a priestess of Gaia. In some stories she was one of the Pythia at the oracle of Delphi, and in others she acted as high priestess in secret rituals that celebrated the feminine nature of the earth. Men were forbidden to attend these ceremonies. But naturally, human nature overcame this taboo, and according to legend, a curious male named Leukippos attired himself as a woman and entered the sacred grove. Apollo the sun god, who sees all, revealed the interloper's treachery. Afterward, at Apollo's suggestion, the ceremonies were performed in the nude, or while "sky clad."

Unfortunately, Apollo had his own agenda and tried to rape Daphne, revealing in myth the historical takeover of the shrine of the goddess at Delphi. Daphne appealed to Gaia, who turned her into a laurel tree just in the nick of time. The evergreen laurel has mind-altering properties, and the leaves were chewed by priestesses at Delphi to induce an ecstatic trance. In later myth Apollo wore a laurel crown as a source of inspiration. Laurel crowns were given to the best poets, and we still use the word *laureate* as a term of high honor.

CONTEMPLATION

Gaining the moral high ground in a situation is sometimes a matter of using my wits and acting swiftly.

Goddesses for Every Day

OCTOBER 12

Pajau Yan

TRANSITION

Pajau Yan (PAH-jow yon) is a goddess of the Cham people of Vietnam. Five hundred years ago, with the rise of the Khmer empire, the Cham fled from the kingdom of Champa, in central Vietnam, to the south-central coast. Although most are now Muslim, the ancient Cham were Hindu. The Cham were heavily influenced by India, and they still practice some of their earlier beliefs. Pajau Yan is a benevolent goddess of beauty, goodness, and healing. She is especially attentive to women's concerns.

Pajau Yan has the power to raise the dead but was punished for this ability and exiled to the moon. She now gives beautiful flowers to the newly deceased to ease their transition and bring them pleasure. When an eclipse of the moon occurs, casting the lunar orb into shadow, Pajau Yan is said to be honoring the sun. Three major religious festivals honor the dead in Vietnam, and departed ancestors are visited at their grave sites with gifts of flowers, incense, and votive papers, so the role of this goddess is still culturally significant.

CONTEMPLATION

Today I buy fresh flowers to adorn my home,
and I inhale their intoxicating fragrance,
knowing they will not remain beautiful for long.

Hi' iaka

SACRED DANCE

Hi' iaka (hee EYE-ah-kah) is a Hawaiian goddess who is the daughter of Haumea and the sister of Pele. She is the patron goddess of Hawaii and of hula, the sacred dance of Hawaii. Hi' iaka lives in a sacred grove, where she spends her time dancing with the spirits of the tropical rain forest. Her story says she was originally conceived in Tahiti and then carried by the goddess Pele, in the form of an egg, to the Hawaiian Islands. She is the goddess of the islands, cliffs, and caves and is praised in music and dance at festivals.

In one of her legends, she went as a messenger to Pele's lover, only to learn that the young chief had died of longing for Pele. Hi' iaka revived him, but the tempestuous Pele was filled with jealousy and sent a fire to destroy the sacred grove. At that point, disgusted with her sister, Hi' iaka took the young man for herself in spite. It is the loving fire of Hi' iaka that breathes fire into Hawaiian volcanoes.

CONTEMPLATION

I dance and sway, moving for pure joy.

Erzulie

DUALITY

Erzulie (er-ZOO-lee) is a goddess from West Africa and Haiti who is part of the pantheon of beliefs called Vodun. We refer to it as Voodoo, and this system is still actively practiced. Erzulie is the *loa*, or goddess, of love and beauty. She is complex with a double nature, revealing the extremes of feminine power. As Erzulie Freda, she is portrayed as a wealthy white woman who loves flowers and dancing and lives in luxury. But as Erzulie Dantor she is a scarred black woman who is seen in a fierce warrior aspect, protecting a young child and showing the strength that is hers.

Erzulie embodies the beauty in nature as well as elemental forces and the struggle to survive. Her symbol is the heart, and she is a patron of gays and lesbians. Erzulie differentiates the plane of reality occupied by humans from that of other aspects of creation and is thought to embody artistic ability. Those who were taken as slaves concealed their beliefs within Christian symbolism, and so Erzulie has elements attributed to the blessed Virgin Mary.

CONTEMPLATION

Beauty is elusive, and a matter of opinion,
but the ferocity of a mother's protection is a sight to behold.

OCTOBER 15

Morrigan

SOVEREIGNTY

Morrigan (MORE-ee-gun) is one of the Tuatha De Danann, the "Tribe of the Goddess Danu." She originated in the megalithic cult of Mothers, who appeared in triple form or threefold aspect. As a raven or a hooded crow, she was a war bird, emerging from a fairy mound to perch on a standing stone and caw her warnings. She held the element of fate, as she chose those who would die in battle. In human form she was a giantess. Sometimes she was thought of as a phantom queen ruling over the world of ghosts, especially those of people who had died in battle.

Morrigan was skilled in magic. She always performed a rite of divination before battle to perceive the outcome and cast charms to strengthen those she favored. Her power in warfare was wielded through magic and chanting rather than force. Like other ancient goddesses, she offered the gift of sovereignty to kings. She was the nemesis of the Irish hero Cuchulain, as he refused her offer of love because of her appearance. He did not recognize the deeper truth that kings ruled only by virtue of the goddess's power, and so his choice rendered him helpless at a crucial point, bringing about his downfall.

CONTEMPLATION

*I seek the wise counsel of an older woman
and honor the voice of experience.*

OCTOBER 16

The Harpies

WINDS OF CHANGE

The Harpies, like many other goddesses, had a triple aspect. The three sisters were named Celaeno, meaning "dark"; Aello, "storm swift"; and Ocypete, "swift wing." Some stories portrayed a fourth sister, Podarge, "fleet foot." Their home was a sacred cave in Mount Dicte on Crete. *Harpy* is the singular form, and when alone, the Harpy was often called the Virgin Eagle. The modern Harpy eagle, the largest American eagle and one of the most powerful birds of prey in the world, lives in isolated virgin forests. Although the literal meaning of the name is "whirlwind," the Harpies were often depicted as vultures with the faces of women. The goddess archetype of the Harpy is probably mythically related to that of the Gorgon Medusa, who is another ancient custodian of feminine power.

Like other powerful goddesses who became demons, the Harpies were once life-giving deities. With Zephyrus, the west wind, as the father, the Harpy Fleet Foot gave birth to the horses of Achilles. The Harpies were also called Pluckers, as in those who pluck the strings of the harp, and they are sometimes pictured this way. They conducted souls of the dead to the afterlife, and, demonstrating one of the ways symbols remain in our consciousness, we still imagine angels plucking harps in heaven. The Greek poet Hesiod described the Harpies as "lovely-haired," but, sadly, they are now seen as demons.

CONTEMPLATION
Change is in the wind.
I set my sails to move in a new direction.

Libra Goddesses

315

Nekhbet

INFINITY

Nekhbet (NECK-but) is a predynastic Egyptian goddess who takes the form of a white vulture. She is seen as a griffin vulture, which is a symbol of the goddess and royalty. Her title is White Crown, and she is one of the Two Ladies by whose grace the pharaoh ruled; the other was the goddess Wadjet. Vultures are powerful birds known to be good mothers, and like eagles they soar high in the sky, bringing them close to heaven. Nekhbet also protected the pharaoh and was seen to hover above the king in times of battle.

The earliest reference to this goddess was made more than five thousand years ago. The oldest oracle site in Egypt was a shrine to Nekhbet at her city, Nekheb, the original "City of the Dead." In art, Nekhbet wears the crown of Upper Egypt, while her counterpart, Wadjet, the cobra goddess, wears the crown of Lower Egypt. Nekhbet holds a staff that is a long-stemmed lotus with a serpent twined around it, and she is pictured carrying the *shen*, a knotted rope, the Egyptian symbol of infinity, in one of her talons. Her consort is Hapy, god of the Nile.

CONTEMPLATION

*I live for today, but my heart
knows that my soul is eternal.*

The Kathirat

CHARM

The Kathirat (KAH-thu-rat), or Kotharat, are wise goddesses from Ugarit, an ancient Syrian port city on the coast of the Mediterranean. These goddesses sometimes appeared in the form of swallows and were thought to embody the correct order in which everything should be accomplished. In one story they are called Swallowlike Daughters of the Crescent Moon. The Kathirat are generally seven in number and are similar to the Greek Graces. They are present in stories in which couples are hoping to conceive a child, and they help make wedding ceremonies more auspicious.

The Kathirat were responsible for setting the bride-price for every woman, including the powerful goddess Ishtar, and they often oversaw the proceedings of weddings and births. They possessed many gifts, such as song and dance and what we might call charm and the social graces. All the facets of grace were seen to be feminine qualities.

CONTEMPLATION

Grace under fire is the essence of charm.
I take a deep breath and know that all is in order.

Changing Woman

RITUAL

Changing Woman, or Asdzan Nadleehe in the Navajo language, is a powerful sky goddess among the Dine, as they call themselves. After her birth, Changing Woman grew from infancy to adulthood in four days, which symbolically links her to her counterpart, the goddess White Shell Woman. Changing Woman created the original four clans of the Dine from the substance of her body, and she represents the changing nature of life on earth. She embodies the maturation process from girlhood to womanhood, and also the nature of life itself. Her home is in the western ocean, and as the wheel of the year turns, Changing Woman endlessly transforms from maiden, to mother, and then to crone.

The Blessingway, the ceremony and foundation of Navajo life, is the story of Changing Woman. The ritual relates all the teachings and history a person requires in order to walk in balance on the earth. In Navajo legend, Changing Woman participated in the creation of humanity and later gave birth to the warrior twins Monster Slayer and Born for Water, who are epic heroes.

CONTEMPLATION

Different though we may be,
we are all of one spirit.

Astarte

CONTRADICTION

Astarte (ah-STAR-tay) is a goddess of ancient Phoenicia, which once thrived in the Middle East. She had a shrine at Byblos (in the part of the world that is now Lebanon) that dates back to the Stone Age. According to legend, she descended from the sky in the form of a fiery star. She is equivalent to the Babylonian goddess Ishtar and to Aphrodite of Greece and was worshipped in Egypt during the Eighteenth Dynasty, thirty-five hundred years ago. Astarte was seen as an overarching deity who both gave life and took it away. She was beautiful and fierce, and, while displaying the second aspect, she was called Mistress of Horses and Chariots. Any goddess this powerful was typically later transformed into a demon by the Catholic Church.

She was associated with the planet Venus, and as the morning star, she was a warrior clothed in fire. When she appeared as the evening star, she kindled the flames of desire. Every year on December 25, the ancient Syrians celebrated her giving birth to a new solar king, who would rule for one year as a symbol of the sun's annual journey. Astarte is sometimes pictured standing naked on the back of a lioness.

CONTEMPLATION

I accept the contradictions within myself,
the anger and the love,
and I learn to act appropriately in every situation.

OCTOBER 21

Xochiquetzal

IMPERMANENCE

Xochiquetzal (so-chi-KETZ-al) is the Aztec goddess of love and beauty, and her name means "flower feather." In a group of gods who are usually fierce and often bloody, this gentle goddess is a welcome relief. She is one of the day deities of the Aztec calendar, and her day name is Xochitl. Her day was set aside to create something beautiful, reminding us that external beauty is transitory. A feast was held in her honor every eight years, linking her to the cycle of Venus. Those participating in this festival wore masks decorated with animals or flowers.

Xochiquetzal was the patron of artisans and the goddess of plants and flowers. She wore a headdress made from her namesake, the beautiful bright green quetzal bird. She is usually shown accompanied by a butterfly, who, of course, helps pollinate the flowers, which are sacred to her.

CONTEMPLATION

I set aside time today to create something beautiful that is true to my heart.

Airmid

NATURE

Airmid (AIR-mud) is a goddess of the Tuatha De Danann, the Celtic people of the goddess Danu. She is a goddess of healing who has deep knowledge of growing things and is said to have tended a sacred and magical spring that had the power to restore life. People who had been mortally wounded or had died of disease were cast into the well and emerged miraculously restored. As a result, Airmid was said to have knowledge of the healing power of water and to understand the magic of sound vibration. Her talents mixed the elements of earth and water.

One of her myths tells how, after Airmid buried her beloved brother, 365 healing herbs began to grow on his grave, one for every nerve in the body, and one for every day of the year. (Their calendar did not include leap year.) In this way, she gained knowledge of all the herbs in the world. Her father was jealous of her wisdom and supposedly deliberately confused the lore of the herbs for other healers, but this inner wisdom remained with Airmid.

CONTEMPLATION

Flowers and other growing things provide
beauty and healing power in my life.

SCORPIO GODDESSES
The Spider

EVERY STRAND IN THE WEB OF LIFE IS CONNECTED

Scorpio is a fixed water sign that represents the idea of dynamic power. This potent energy of desire can be used in construction or destruction, death or resurrection, and is characterized by great intensity. Scorpios deal with issues of power — temptation relating to the use of power, exercising discipline, and an urge for emotional control. Scorpios are reserved, and more happens to them internally than is expressed on the surface. This is a path of transforming the desire nature, of tempering a purely physical desire to reproduce and pursuing a spiritual aspiration. Therefore, cultivating an orientation toward service will release the coiled energy in a positive manner.

Scorpio is the eighth sign, traditionally represented by the Scorpion. Scorpio represents the life force and how that energy is expressed, so this sign is connected to sexuality as well as healing. The Spider is the goddess sign for Scorpio, as she is the great weaver who spins creation, and the literal web of life, from her own life force. In Scorpio the substance of life is spun out of the spider's belly, creating the potential for something to manifest. But it is in Capricorn, the sign of form, that the threads take shape and are woven into the tapestries of our lives.

Scorpion and spider goddesses are included here, as well as goddesses who embody passion, sexuality, and healing. Serpent goddesses, when they act as healing agents, appear here, representing the life force directed toward transformation. Because Scorpio is the portal to the unseen realm, goddesses of death and rebirth are also included.

OCTOBER 23

Spider Woman

RELATIONSHIP

Spider Woman is a creation goddess known as She Who Creates from a Central Source. In the beginning, at the dawn of being, there was only dark purple light. Hopi Spider Woman spun threads to form the sacred directions of east, west, north, and south. Cherokee Grandmother Spider brought the sun and the gift of fire, and is similar to the goddess Biliku of the Andamanese Islanders. Spider Woman is the keeper of the primordial alphabet and teaches the mysteries of the past and how it will affect the future. To the Hopi, Spider Woman, or Kokyanwuthi, created and brought forth the people. She also has the power to give and take life.

Spider Woman is a wisdom holder who clasps the thread that connects the divine world to the human world. She has the ability to weave new energies into being from the substance of herself. Spiders combine gentleness and strength and are totems for those who weave magic with the written word.

CONTEMPLATION

I honor the great web that
connects and unites all things.

OCTOBER 24

Rati

PASSION

Rati (RAH-tee) is a Hindu goddess of passion and joyful sexuality. Her father was the sun god Daksha, and in her nature there is a sense of the contrast between the darkness and the light. Her consort and soul mate is Kama, the god of love, whose mother is Lakshmi, goddess of abundance. Rati's name in Sanskrit means "one who moves," and this perhaps suggests the rhythmic movement of passion. Rati is honored each year at the festival of colors, called Holi. Women offer her gifts of rice, coconut, and colorful bangles.

Her beloved Kama was once reduced to a pile of ashes when he had the misfortune to disrupt the meditation of Lord Shiva. Rati was devastated and appealed to the goddess Parvati to restore her lover. Kama was subsequently incarnated as Pradyumna. In the guise of Mayadevi, Rati then acted as Pradyumna's protector. In one story, Kama was swallowed by a fish and Rati saved him. Some versions say Kama was restored only as an ideal mental image, representing the true nature of love that exists beyond the physical.

CONTEMPLATION

*Where can I find the passion in
my life that moves me to create?*

Goddesses for Every Day

Panacea

HEALING

Panacea (pan-ah-SEE-ah) is a Greek goddess of healing. Her name comes from *panakes*, meaning "all healing," and survives in our language as *panacea*, a cure for all ills. She embodies the idea and wisdom of healing with herbs, and her specialty was creating poultices. She and her sisters, Hygeia, "health"; Iaso, "remedy"; and Acesis, "recovery," are daughters of the famed healer Asclepius, who was immortalized by Zeus as the constellation of the Serpent Bearer.

Panacea was also the granddaughter of Apollo, god of the sun. To this day physicians swear by the names of Panacea and Hygeia when taking their most sacred oath. Contained in the deeper meaning of this goddess and her sister Hygeia are the all-nurturing power of the Great Mother Goddess and the healing power of breast milk. Certainly, honoring the earth could be a great panacea for many of the world's woes.

CONTEMPLATION

I swear by Apollo Physician and Asclepius and Hygeia and Panacea and all the gods and goddesses, making them my witnesses, that I will fulfill according to my ability and judgment this oath and this covenant.

— FROM THE HIPPOCRATIC OATH,
GREEK MEDICAL TEXT, FOURTH CENTURY

OCTOBER 26

Mictecacihuatl

RECYCLING

Mictecacihuatl (mick-TEK-ah-see-WAH-til) is an Aztec goddess whose title is Lady of the Dead. She is responsible for the fifth hour of the night. Some sources say she died at birth. She resides in Mictlan, the Aztec land of the dead, at the ninth, and lowest, level of the underworld. In a vast cave filled with skeletons, Mictecacihuatl guards the bones of all the deceased, which may be required for use as recycled raw material to build new bodies in the next world or cycle of manifestation.

When the time comes to create a new world, part of the quest of the hero-god Quetzalcoatl will involve stealing these bones to create people for the next cycle. Mictecacihuatl also presides over Dias de los Muertos, "The Days of the Dead," which have become widespread ceremonies. During this celebration, Mictecacihuatl is believed to guide the souls of the dead back to their families for a visit so they can be honored.

CONTEMPLATION

*Everything in the universe is recycled
energy, and all forms of energy are imprisoned light.*

Mere-Ama

WATER

Mere-Ama (meh-ree-AH-mah), whose name means "mother of waters," is a Finnish water goddess. Her alternative name is Vedenemo. Oceans, rivers, and streams are her domain, and she is the queen of all the creatures who live in the element of water. Around the world, water is associated with the feminine principle. The ancient Egyptians worshipped a goddess named Mera, which means "waters." Mere-Ama is actually the spirit of the element of water and was imagined to have long, flowing silver hair that looked like waves.

All the ceremonies honoring Mere-Ama involved using water in a conscious way, as a blessing or a means of invocation. Evidently, she was also a great fan of brandy. As a way of expressing gratitude to her for all the blessings water provides to humanity, people would pour the brandy that she loved into the water. This was also meant to ensure good fishing, as many fish would gather after this offering.

CONTEMPLATION

Water is perhaps our most precious resource. I give thanks and use it wisely.

OCTOBER 28

Morgen

SURRENDER

Morgen (MORE-gun) is a Celtic goddess who appears as the half-sister of King Arthur. The origin of her name is *morigena*, which means "sea born." Although she is cast in the role of powerful magician and evil adversary in the famous Arthurian tales, her true nature originated in antiquity, when she was a powerful goddess. This is revealed in myth by her presence in triple form with her two sisters, Elaine and Morguase. She also appears as chief of nine sisters called Morgens, three groups of three, on the ship that carried Arthur to Avalon — which means "apple" — where they lived. The symbolism of the apple links her with many other goddesses who tended trees that grew this fruit in their gardens of immortality. In one of her aspects she is similar to the Irish Morrigan, the Great Queen, and Queen of Ghosts, who took the form of a raven as a goddess of battle.

In the older stories Morgen was a psychopomp death goddess, who helped the dying and eased their transition to the world beyond the veil. The cyclical nature of death was not feared in ancient cultures. Death was a natural part of life, and people believed the dead person returned in a new form. Mythically, it's not surprising that Morgen, as Queen of the Western Isle, was transformed into a figure of death who became the archenemy of the king. As we welcome the sacred feminine back into the world, Morgen's truer image is reemerging.

CONTEMPLATION

I willingly surrender all outworn forms when it is time.

Goddesses for Every Day

The Valkyries

DISCRETION

The Valkyries (VAL-kuh-reez) are beautiful Norse goddesses of fate sent into battle by the god Odin. Their name means "choosers of the slain," and they decided who lived and who died. Some were fully divine, and some were half-mortal, living among humans for a time. In the heroic tales, they were bands of warrior women whose leader was the beautiful daughter of a powerful king. That leader, Brunhilde, whose name means "victory bringer," was the most famous, and she also doubled as a human princess.

Like many goddesses, the Valkyries have a complex nature, and it sometimes seems contradictory. In their earlier and darker role, they wove the web of war and used their magic to influence the outcome and aid their favorites. In *Bulfinch's Mythology* we are told that "their armor emits a strange flickering light, which flares up over the northern skies, creating the Northern Lights." The Valkyries also serve as cupbearers in Valhalla, the Norse paradise. And they are related to the Norns and the Greek Fates as weavers of the threads of fate in the lives of humans.

CONTEMPLATION

War takes a heavy toll no matter the outcome.
I choose not to engage in needless battles.

OCTOBER 30

Cailleach Bheur

GHOSTS

Cailleach Bheur (COY-look beer) is an Irish crone goddess who is born anew as an old woman each year at the end of October and brings the cold of winter and snow. She is thought to be one of the oldest Celtic representations of the goddess. The Celtic goddesses are seen as sovereigns over different times of the year. On February 2, as the wheel of the year turns and the power of the goddess Brigid increases the light, Cailleach places her magic staff behind a holly bush. Then she turns into stone on Beltane, May 1, the time of Brigantia, until her rebirth the following October.

Carlin, her Scottish counterpart, is the spirit of Hallomas, the eve of Samhain, or the day we call Halloween. Samhain, pronounced "sowen," meant "Hallowtide" in the ancient Celtic language. This halfway point between the autumn equinox and the winter solstice was seen as the beginning of winter and also of the new year. The winter solstice was called midwinter. Spirits of the deceased were believed to wander the earth on this night. Using ears of corn, people made dolls in Carlin's image to protect themselves in the fields from unwanted ghostly apparitions.

CONTEMPLATION

What ghosts from my past still haunt me, keeping me from my full power? I take a deep breath and banish these ghosts.

Arianrod

PORTALS

Arianrod (AIR-ee-un-rod) is a Welsh sorceress whose name means "silverwheel." She was surrounded by women attendants and lived on the isolated coastal island of Caer Arianrhod. Her seasonal counterpart is Olwen, whose name means "goldenwheel." Olwen's time is the spring equinox, when the length of the day begins to increase. Arianrod's power is greatest as the nights grow longer during the celebration of the Celtic new year. Beautiful and pale of complexion, Arianrod was the most powerful of the mythic children of the Celtic mother goddess Danu. She was keeper of the Wheel of the Stars, a symbol of time that was also seen as the Wheel of Fate, which turned at the portal between the visible world and the unseen. Caer Arianrod, the "castle of Arianrod," is the constellation Corona Borealis, whose name means the "northern crown." The Welsh saw the stars of this constellation as Arianrod's home in the sky, where the dead went between incarnations.

Arianrod is a guardian of the gates of immortality, and she wields the magic of living outside of time and passing through the veil between the seen and unseen realms. This time of the year is set aside to honor the dead and pay attention to manifestations of the thinning veil.

CONTEMPLATION

*I am open to guidance from the unseen realms
and seek portals through which I can access this guidance.*

Selket

VIGILANCE

Selket (SELL-kut), sometimes called Serquet, is a scorpion goddess of Egypt and is usually depicted as a beautiful woman with a scorpion on her head. She became known in modern times from a golden statue of her that toured as part of the fabulous Tutankhamen exhibition. Along with Isis, Nephthys, and Neith, Selket was one of the four guardians of the canopic jars that contained mummified persons' essential internal organs required for the afterlife. Selket also assisted with the rebirth of the deceased in the afterlife.

Scorpions are known to be good mothers who carry their babies on their backs until they are able to manage on their own. They are nocturnal creatures, and during the seventh hour of night, as the boat of Ra makes its dangerous journey, it is Selket who confronts and subdues an evil serpent who tries to block the sun god's way on his nightly sojourn. Selket dispenses death to the wicked and protection to the deserving. She once sent seven scorpions to protect Isis. It is said that those who revere Selket will never feel the sting of a scorpion.

CONTEMPLATION

I have accorded you a place in the sacred land, that you may appear gloriously in heaven like Ra.

— WORDS OF SELKET WELCOMING NEFERTARI,
TRANSLATION OF INSCRIPTION ON THE WALL OF NEFETARI'S
TOMB IN THE VALLEY OF THE QUEENS, EGYPT,
House of Eternity: The Tomb of Nefertari, JOHN K. McDONALD

Maman Brigitte

CROSSROADS

Maman Brigitte (MAH-man bruh-GHEE-tay) is a *loa*, or goddess, of the belief system known as Vodun in Haiti, which is often referred to as Voodoo. She is seen as a white woman and is thought to be related in some way to the Celtic Brigid. Maman Brigitte is a guardian of graves in cemeteries that have been properly marked with a crossroads, meaning, in this case, the portal between the worlds. The grave of the first woman to be buried in Haiti was consecrated to Maman Brigitte. Each November 2, thousands of people dressed in black and white converge in cemeteries to honor her. Candles are burned and offerings of coffee, rum, and peanuts are made.

In Vodun, elaborate and intricate figures called *veves*, which resemble Hermetic sigils, designs based on numbers and letters that are thought to have magical properties, are drawn to invoke the *loas*. Each deity has his or her own *veve*. These are usually drawn on the floor using flour, cornmeal, red powder, or even gunpowder, depending on the nature of the ritual. The *veve* is a powerful invocation that requires the *loa* to manifest on the earth plane in response, and when Maman Brigitte is invoked, it is to bring healing to someone on the brink of death.

CONTEMPLATION
What's been buried and laid to rest in my life usually needs to stay that way.

Sheila Na-Gig

SIGNIFICANCE

Sheila Na-Gig (SHEE-lah NAH-gig), sometimes spelled Sheela, Sile, or Sila, is the name given to carved female figures with dramatically accentuated vulvas. The Sheilas, as they are called, have been found all over Europe, but mostly in Ireland. The figures are embedded in structures, and most of them were added to early monasteries and village churches. They are thought to act as guardians of gateways, warding off evil. There is controversy about their origin and significance, and embarrassment in modern times about their presence on churches. The figures are sometimes explained by clergy as representations of the evil nature of feminine lust and vilified as lustful hags.

The etymology suggests that the word *gig* refers to female genitals and that Sheila Na-Gig was the name for an old woman, a hag. The word *hag* is linked to ugly Halloween witches but has its roots in the Greek word *hagia*, which means "holy." Nu-gig was the name of the "Holy Ones," the sacred prostitutes at Ishtar's temple in Eresh, Babylon. There are Irish myths, as well as traditions from other cultures, that say only the goddess could confer kingship. In these symbolic stories, a "lustful hag" like a Sheila Na-Gig would appear to a young man. If he accepted her, looking beyond her surface appearance to see her inner beauty, wisdom, and power, then he would be deemed wise enough to rule.

CONTEMPLATION

I look beneath surface appearances and
discern inner beauty and hidden significance.

336   Goddesses for Every Day

NOVEMBER 4

Baalat

BENEFICENCE

Baalat (bah-ah-LOT), called the Lady of Byblos and Queen of the Gods, is a Phoenician goddess from the part of the world that is now Lebanon, where papyrus came from. Byblos is the Greek name for Baalat's city, which the Phoenicians called Gebal, and was also the name the Greeks gave to papyrus and then to books. Gebal was founded seven thousand years ago and is believed to be the oldest continuously inhabited city in the world. Remains of a temple built nearly five thousand years ago and dedicated to Baalat Gebal, the Lady of Gebal, can still be seen above the sparkling Mediterranean. The temple, with its nearby sacred pool, was in use for two thousand years.

Baalat was depicted as a generous goddess with a bountiful body and was shown holding her ample breasts to feed her children. She was the patroness of shipmasters who set sail from her port carrying what we now call the cedars of Lebanon. An image of her found on a cylinder seal is reminiscent of images of the Egyptian goddess Hathor.

CONTEMPLATION

No matter what I have suffered, I can endure and become stronger and more compassionate.

Tethys

FULLNESS

Tethys (TETH-is) is a pre-Hellenic goddess of ancient Greece whose name is related to the word for "grandmother." She was the nurse of the goddess Hera in one story. In the earliest myths, Tethys and her consort and brother, Oceanus, ruled the planet Venus. Although she is considered to be a Titan, one of the gods who preceded the Olympians, and the daughter of Gaia and Ouranos, evidence suggests Tethys is an even earlier creator goddess, Mother Creation, who appeared in the Orphic cosmogony. Orphism was a Greek religious movement that had its origins in Egypt. It was founded by the poet Orpheus, and its tenets were expressed in verse.

Tethys was called Mother of All Rivers and was seen as a personification of the sea. She is also thought to embody the idea of fertility. Indeed, in Greek stories, Tethys gave birth to thousands of Oceanids and three thousand rivers, including the river Styx in Hades. Oceanus's name is thought to mean "belonging to the swift queen." Most cultures have myths that envision the ordered world as having emerged from a primeval chaos, and the idea of "deep waters" is the manner in which this chaos is expressed.

CONTEMPLATION

Behind all outward manifestation the
waters of consciousness flow like a great river.

Hine Titama

RESOLVE

Hine Titama (HEE-nay tee-TAH-mah) is a Maori goddess and the only female among the pantheon of the indigenous people of New Zealand. She is the daughter of Tane Mahuta, god of birds and forests, and Hineahuone, a woman who was formed from earth. Hine Titama began her life as a goddess of dawn and light.

Her myth is a tale of deception by her father, who, because he desired her and wanted her only for himself, disguised himself and became her husband. They had many children, and later Hine Titama discovered the truth when a little bird whispered it to her. She was horrified and fled to the underworld in a mythic representation of the cycles of life. She declared that she would become a goddess of death and resolved to stay there. Like many other goddesses, she now lives in the underworld and cares for the souls of the dead. In this role she is called Hinenuitepo, and she waits to welcome earth's children at the end of their lives.

CONTEMPLATION

I will seek the concealed truth that could change my life forever, not giving up until I discover it.

Lilith

PRINCIPLES

Lilith (LIL-uth) is an ancient Mesopotamian goddess who ex-emplifies how powerful feminine deities became demonized by the emerging patriarchy. Lilith is thought to have emerged from the earlier goddess Baalat. Hebrew texts turned her into a demon, and, in the "Sepher ben Sira," an anonymous collection of Jewish proverbs, she was identified as the first wife of Adam, who refused to submit to him because, Lilith claimed, they were created equal. As a modern icon she has become a symbol for powerful, independent women.

In the ancient Akkadian language, spoken in Babylon, she is called Ardat-lili. Lilith is also identified with Ki-sikil-lil-la-ke, a female being mentioned in the Sumerian prologue to the Epic of Gilgamesh. The name Lilith is sometimes translated as "Lila's maiden companion" or the "beloved or maid" of Gilgamesh. She is called "beautiful maiden" and described as the "gladdener of all hearts" and "maiden who screeches constantly," which might relate to the owls who are her companions. She is said to live in a tree, with a dragon at the roots and a nesting bird at the top, linking her with intrinsic symbols of the sacred feminine that appear in many cultures. The male hero Gilgamesh chopped down the tree, killed the serpent, and caused Lilith to flee.

CONTEMPLATION

When my core values and honor are
at stake, I will not submit to tyranny.

Kadru

STEALTH

Kadru (KAH-dru) is the mother of the Nagas, a thousand beautiful serpent beings from Hindu myth, the most famous of which is their king, Sesha, the cosmic serpent whose coils turn the mill of life. When the gods churned the cosmic ocean, they used the coils of Sesha like a rope.

Kadru's myth tells of a wager she made with her sister and how she cheated to win. Much was at stake, but the truth won out. The story teaches a moral lesson about the inevitable outcome of dishonesty and concealment. Kadru and her children are related to the serpent god Mehen of Egypt, who undulates across the sky with the sun god Ra each day and takes him to the underworld at night. She is also connected to the Hindu serpent Kundalini, the goddess of enlightenment who lies coiled at the base of the spine until we awaken her and set our feet on the path to wisdom.

CONTEMPLATION

*Winning at any cost carries a
high price, so I always play fair and act openly.*

Hygeia

WELL-BEING

Hygeia (hi-JEE-ah) is a Greek goddess of healing whose name means "health." Our word *hygiene* comes from her name, and hygiene has far-reaching ramifications for both medicine and health. Along with her sisters — Panacea, whose name means "all healing"; Iaso, "remedy"; and Acesis, "recovery" — she is the daughter of the famed healer Asclepius and granddaughter of the sun god Apollo. Hygeia represents the state of health itself, while Panacea bestows the process of healing. Hygeia is often pictured with her father, and some authors say she is actually his wife. Hygeia is usually shown holding a cup containing a potent cure, and with a serpent twined around her arm. Sometimes the snake drinks from the cup.

The bowl of Hygeia is still the symbol of pharmacy, and the coiling serpents around the central staff of the caduceus form the symbol of modern medicine. Over time Hygeia was invoked for mental health as well as physical health, and she offered safety and protection in general, promoting an overall sense of well-being.

CONTEMPLATION

My surroundings, my food and water,
my thoughts and words, are pure and clear,
creating a sense of well-being.

Nicheven

MORTALITY

Nicheven (nick-EE-vun) is a Scottish goddess whose name means "brilliant" and "divine." According to the old Julian calendar, her special night fell on November 10, when she rode through the night with her followers at the time of Samhain, or All Hallows Eve. She was called Bone Mother, and, as the crone aspect of the triple goddess, she is linked to the Hindu Kali. Nicheven is the archetype who is born, ages, dies, and is reborn each year, showing the impermanent nature of physical form and the repeating cycles of time.

In northern climes, this is the time of year when life turns inward and the annual death of the year stalks the land. If we are awake we can contemplate our mortality in human form and the significance of eternity that is implied by the annual renewal of life that comes each spring. We gather the wisdom of our experiences and accept aging with grace.

CONTEMPLATION

*Life is eternal, but the world of form is
ephemeral. I identify with my inner life.*

Biliku

RESTRAINT

Biliku (BILL-uh-coo) is a goddess from the Andaman Islands, which are in the Bay of Bengal and are part of the territory of India. The indigenous inhabitants of these islands are thought to be among the oldest peoples of earth. Only thirty individuals remain, and they all live on one small island. They still follow their old ways and live as hunter-gatherers. Biliku is a powerful creator goddess who was the first being to possess the secret of fire; later the kingfisher stole this magic. Biliku can be both kind and fearsome. Sometimes she appears in the form of a giant female spider, very similar to Grandmother Spider of the Cherokee people half a world away. Before the world existed, Biliku wove complex webs and traveled the universe in darkness.

After a while she created the first people from her weavings and decided to live on earth. Her temper could be terrible and was unpredictable. Thunder was her anger, and fierce winds were her words of rage. Finally, she returned to her home in the sky, but the Andaman Islanders still fear her outbursts.

CONTEMPLATION

Where do I need to manage my anger
in order to respond appropriately?

Egle

METAMORPHOSIS

Egle (EEG-lay) is a Lithuanian goddess called Queen of the Serpents. Her story is a very old and much-loved Lithuanian fairy tale that incorporates the worldwide association of trees and serpents with the goddess. As a young girl, Egle married the prince of the serpents. While playing with her sisters, she found a green snake in her sleeve. The snake spoke to her, saying he would come out if she agreed to marry him. She gave her consent, and when he emerged she saw only a handsome prince, so she went to live with him at the bottom of the ocean. This seems to represent the journey from ordinary awareness to the depths of our being to find wisdom. Egle had four children, and, after a time, her sons wanted to know more about where their mother came from. Many stories of the goddess involve beings who are half human and half serpent, or who have dual natures.

Egle's tale is convoluted and, like all epic fairy tales, involves sorcery and deception. She finally managed to visit her natal family, but sadly her family deceived her and murdered her husband, whom she had grown to love. In her grief, Egle transformed her four children into ash, oak, birch, and aspen trees and herself into a spruce.

CONTEMPLATION

The price for deception is always high,
with consequences that may keep coming back.

NOVEMBER 13

Baubo

LAUGHTER

Baubo (BAU-boh) is a Greek goddess who plays a pivotal role in Demeter's search for Persephone. In despair over the loss of her daughter, who had been abducted and raped by the lord of the underworld, Demeter encountered Baubo, who told her bawdy jokes, the kind that tend to bring the most laughter. Demeter remained unmoved.

When Baubo lifted her skirts and exposed herself, Demeter finally laughed. A shaft of light had entered the darkness, and the healing power of laughter restored Demeter's equilibrium. Baubo is similar to the Japanese goddess Uzume, who coaxed Amaterasu out of her cave by doing a bawdy dance and making the other gods laugh. The deeper meaning of the story is the revelation of the life-giving power of the goddess, and of the feminine, which continually restores balance to nature. No matter how abused and defiled a woman has been, it is the essence of Woman that brings life into the world.

CONTEMPLATION

Sometimes the more outrageous the joke, the bigger the laugh and the deeper the healing.

Medusa

CONCEALMENT

The Greek goddess Medusa (muh-DOO-sah), whose stare had the power to turn men to stone, was a once-beautiful creature turned ugly by Athena's jealousy. Athena supposedly turned Medusa into a hideous creature called a Gorgon, which had snakes for hair. Feminine wisdom was symbolized in antiquity by a woman's face with serpent hair. A fierce face, like a frightful mask, conceals the mysteries from the profane. Medusa is another example of how the power of the goddess was turned into something dark and evil.

The presence of Medusa's face on the goddess Athena's aegis (her shield) suggests a stronger and older connection with the principle of feminine wisdom. Clues to Medusa's power are also revealed by the fact that the healer Asclepius used her blood to heal. A single drop could raise the dead. This blood was obtained when Perseus severed Medusa's head. The winged horse Pegasus, Poseidon's son, was born from that fatal wound. The stories say there were three Gorgons, including Medusa's sisters Stheno and Euryale, which indicates a link to the triple goddess archetype.

CONTEMPLATION

*What I seek lies within, and the illusion
of surface appearances must be pierced.*

Feronia

SIMPLICITY

Feronia (fir-OH-nee-ah) is a Latin goddess who was honored with the first fruits of the harvest in a Thanksgiving type of ritual thought to ensure a bountiful harvest for the following year. She was worshipped in Capena, at the base of Mount Soracte, a mountain ridge in a province of ancient Rome. Feronia's festival, which was like a lively fair or market, was celebrated each year on November 15 in a sacred grove at this site. Although woods and springs were especially sacred to her, and she preferred the peace of the country to the bustle of the city, Feronia also had a temple in Rome.

Feronia's followers were thought to perform magical acts such as fire walking. Slaves thought of her as a goddess of freedom, and they believed that, if they sat on a particular holy stone in her sacred sanctuary, they could attain freedom. One tradition says that newly freed slaves would go to her temple to receive the pileus, the special cap that signified their status as free people.

CONTEMPLATION

*I create a simple sanctuary within my heart and my home,
knowing I can enter this place of silence
and peace at any time.*

Itoki

PATIENCE

Itoki (ee-TOH-key) is a creator goddess of the Miskito people of Nicaragua in Central America. She is envisioned as a great Mother Scorpion who makes her celestial home in the Milky Way. Itoki is responsible for sending new souls, who are born in the stars, on their journey to earthly existence. She also waits patiently in the sky to welcome all the souls of the newly deceased when they are ready to return to her.

Her spouse is the father figure Maisahana. Together, they are seen as first mother and first father and are the founders of several tribes of indigenous peoples in Central America. Itoki is also seen as an abundant mother with many breasts, feeding countless children. Scorpions are known to be good mothers and carry their broods on their backs until they are ready to survive on their own.

CONTEMPLATION

Anything worth having is worth waiting for.

GOODNESS

Kla (claw), a goddess of goodness of the Ashanti people of Ghana in West Africa, is part of a complex ideological duality. The feminine Kla is the principle of goodness, and the masculine Kla is the force of evil in the world. Kla is similar to the idea of the eternal soul, journeying through life in a physical body. In the afterlife, Kla overcomes death and evil and is known as Sisa, in whom only goodness remains.

Ghana was previously known as the Gold Coast and was hard hit by the slave trade. Wrenched from a life where women were held in high esteem for their role in bringing life into the world, female slaves met harsh degradation. Their humiliation frequently included sexual violation by their white masters in order to breed more slaves. The evils of slavery must have confirmed for the Ashanti their beliefs about the duality of Kla.

CONTEMPLATION

Can I stand firm in the presence of evil
and not lose my own intrinsic goodness?

NOVEMBER 18

Yurlunger

SHADOW

Yurlunger (yoor-LUN-ger) is the great copper python, the Great Rainbow Serpent, who has a major role in the story of the Wawalag Sisters, goddesses of the Aborigines of northern Australia. Yurlunger is a powerful creator deity who brought forth the element of water and, as a result, much-needed rain. In the tradition of Vodun, a similar goddess is named Aida-Wedo, and she is a rainbow python with glistening iridescent scales.

The young Wawalag Sisters unknowingly trespassed into the cave of the serpent and bathed in her underground waters. Angered, Yurlunger was drawn to the sisters by the scent of their blood, which symbolically contained their creative power. Yurlunger consumed the girls but was later made to regurgitate them. The legend contains complex symbols from Aborigine culture that relate to coming of age for both boys and girls. The lesson for young boys is that the power of giving birth to new life is feminine and can't be overshadowed by might. Girls are taught respect for their reproductive power.

CONTEMPLATION

*Just because I refuse to acknowledge
something doesn't mean it isn't there.*

NOVEMBER 19

Uzume

SENSUALITY

Uzume (oo-ZOO-may) is a Shinto goddess who is still depicted in *kyogen*, a type of farce, in Japan. She is said to revel in her sensuality and is similar to the Greek goddess Baubo. Her name means "whirling," and she is always related to dancing. Uzume's dances, including a dance to awaken the dead and another that represents the planting of seeds, were traditionally performed in folk rites and have evolved into a type of Shinto theatrical dance known as Kagura. Uzume is also a goddess of health, perhaps because of her comic antics, and people are renewed by drinking holy water from her sacred stream.

She is best known for her role in bringing back the goddess of the sun, Amaterasu, who had hidden in a cave after a brutal attack on her garden by her brother the storm god. Uzume performed an outrageous dance, tearing off her clothes in a frenzy and making all the other gods laugh uproariously. Their laughter finally drew Amaterasu out of the cave and brought light back to earth.

CONTEMPLATION

*I remember to look on the light side and
put some earthy humor in my life.*

OATH

Styx (sticks) is the Greek goddess best known as the deity of the river in Hades. She is actually one of the Titans, the powerful deities who preceded the Greek Olympians, and is the daughter of Gaia and Ouranos. The river Styx, like the veil between the worlds, separates the living from the dead, and it symbolically transports us into another state of consciousness. The river wound seven times through the underworld. In Hebrew the number seven also meant "oath." Styx's children were named Zelos, meaning "rivalry"; Bia, "force"; Kratos, "strength"; and the most famous, Nike, "victory."

When Zeus revolted against his father, Kronos, Styx deserted her kin and, along with her children, stood with the new king of the gods. Zeus declared that, forever after, all oaths sworn by the gods had to be done on the waters of her river. Iris, messenger of the gods, brought water from the river Styx to the one taking the oath, making the oath sacred. In Greece until the eighteenth century, coins were placed in the mouths of the deceased to pay Charon, the ferryman, to transport loved ones to the afterlife.

CONTEMPLATION

I give my word as if my life
depended on it; in fact, it does.

SAGITTARIUS GODDESSES
The Bow and Arrow

AIM FOR THE STARS,
AND KEEP YOUR FEET ON THE GROUND

*S*agittarius is mutable fire and exemplifies the idea of illumination that results from power balanced between Libra and Scorpio. Sagittarian energy is philosophical in nature, seeking wisdom and an understanding of fundamental archetypal principles. While Gemini tends to gather information, Sagittarius looks for wide and varied experiences that ultimately lead to spiritual understanding. The path of Sagittarius is to learn the patterns that lie at the root of our challenges. This can lead to true perception and the ability to focus and direct the fire of aspiration.

The goddess sign for Sagittarius is the Bow and Arrow. In traditional astrology, Sagittarius is symbolized by the Archer, who is a centaur. Many goddesses, in fact some of the most ancient, are huntresses who live in primeval forests and guard the animals who live there. For these goddesses, hunting is not sport but a sacred act of reciprocity that is represented in women's lives and the earth herself. The Sagittarian hunt can also be seen as the quest for wisdom, engaging our aspirations and taking us into a larger view of the world. Sagittarius goddesses represent wisdom, dreams, providence, fortune, and the voices of oracles. Because Sagittarius is ruled in astrology by the sky god Jupiter, goddesses of light, wisdom, thunder, and lightning are also included here.

Diana

HUNTING

Diana is the Roman goddess of the hunt who is the equivalent of the Greek Artemis, although Diana is believed to actually be of earlier, rural Italian origin. The hunting aspect of her nature relates her to the destroying aspect of the crone. As a goddess of sacred groves and forests, Diana was seen as the protector of all the wild creatures. She is usually pictured with her bow and quiver of arrows and accompanied by her hunting dogs. Her name stems from the word for light, and she is also a goddess of the sun and moon, called the lights of heaven.

Diana was envisioned as riding across the sky in a chariot drawn by two white stags. In later myth she and her twin, Apollo, the male sun god, were born on the Greek island of Delos. Many temples devoted to Diana were later converted to churches dedicated to Mary. At the funeral of Princess Diana of Wales, as reported in the British newspaper the *Guardian*, her brother, Earl Spencer, linked the princess to this goddess, affirming that his sister had been "the most hunted person of the modern age."

CONTEMPLATION

Ready, aim, reconsider, and maybe then fire.

BOUNDLESSNESS

Danu (DAN-oo), or Dana, is the ancient mother goddess of the Celtic Tuatha De Danann, "people of the goddess Danu," a magical race of beings skilled in the lore of the Druids. These beings are linked to the Sidhe, called the "lordly ones," the legendary fairy folk who live beneath the hills. The Sidhe are said to fight beside mortals in battles of honor, wielding swords of blue flame like avenging angels. Danu is part of a trinity of goddesses that includes Brigid and Ana, or Anu.

The etymology of Danu's name indicates that it comes from a root meaning "overflowing abundance" and "bountiful," although the Celtic word is linked to "knowledge," suggesting an ancient origin. In fact, there is a Hindu goddess named Danu who is cited in the Vedas. Danu's name is also related to the principle of primeval waters, and certain rivers, such as the Danube, are named after her. The name Danes supports one theory that the Tuatha De Danann reached Ireland through Denmark.

CONTEMPLATION

The boundless light of ancient wisdom and feminine power runs through me like a mighty river at high tide.

Benzozia

FERVOR

Benzozia (ben-ZOH-zee-ah) is a Basque goddess of creation. It is said the Basques were born of "Benzozia's fire." The Basque people, who dwell in the Pyrenees Mountains, are an enigma culturally and linguistically. Their language is the oldest in Europe and is not related to any other language on earth. Some of their own legends say the Basques are descended from the centaurs, the horse-human creatures of Greek myth.

Benzozia lives beneath the surface of the earth as a great Mother Dragon. In the beginning she tossed and turned in restless sleep, churning up the peaks of the Pyrenees. Fire emerged from her seven heads, and clouds and steam rose into the air. Water fell from the sky and mixed with the fire, and all the green things of earth sprouted forth. Like other fiery or dragon goddesses who live in the earth, the sleeping Benzozia can still be restless at times, causing the ground to tremble.

CONTEMPLATION

*What stirs the fire in my belly
and moves me to creative acts?*

Bilquis

RIDDLES

Bilquis (BIL-quis) is an Arabian goddess from Yemen. Scholars equate her with the Queen of Sheba, the famous visitor of Solomon's who appears in the Quran and the Bible. Bilquis was half djinn, or genie, on her mother's side and was endowed with magical powers. Like Isis in Egypt, Bilquis was sometimes called Queen of the South. Bilquis ruled the land of Sheba, or Saba, where southern Yemen is today, when the land was rich with spices and jewels. The Queen of Sheba was called Makeda in Ethiopia and was worshipped as a goddess by the wisest of kings.

One lineage considers her to be the mother of Menelik, the king of Ethiopia, who was Solomon's son, part of a dynasty that extends to present-day Rastafarians. Modern Rastafarians use the Kebra Nagast, the "glory of kings," as their sacred text. Although its origins are unclear, scholars believe the collection of texts has existed for more than a thousand years.

Young girls are often named Bilquis in Yemen, where archaeological discoveries are bringing her legend to life. An enigmatic statement attributed to Jesus in the Bible says that the "Queen of the South will rise up in judgment with this generation and find it guilty" (Matthew 12:42).

CONTEMPLATION

Wisdom is sweeter than honey and brings more joy than wine.

— EXCERPT FROM THE KEBRA NAGAST,
TRANSLATED BY E. A. WALLIS BUDGE

Goddesses for Every Day

Aganippe

EPIPHANY

Aganippe (ah-gah-NIP-ee) is a naiad from Greek mythology. The origin of her name, however, is a word meaning "the mare who destroys mercifully," which links her to the goddesses Rhiannon and Demeter. Aganippe is also the name of a fountain at the foot of Mount Helicon in Boeotia, part of ancient Greece, that was sacred to the Muses. A sacred spring ran underground and rose from the mountain to fill a well shaped like a horseshoe. The well was supposedly created by the hoof of the winged horse Pegasus. People drank the magical waters to receive poetic inspiration.

According to scholar Robert Graves, Aganippe is the earlier and original name for Pegasus. Pegasus sprang from the severed head, or "wise blood," of the goddess Medusa, and his mythic creation of the well ties these waters of inspiration to a much older source. Pegasus, whose name means "of the springs of water," was named for the Pegae, priestesses who tended sacred springs.

CONTEMPLATION

*I honor the vast wellspring of my
inspiration and its deep and ancient source.*

Rauni

ASPIRATION

Rauni (RAH-nee) is an extremely powerful Finnish goddess of thunder. Her mate is Ukko, the lightning god. In earlier times people respected and revered the forces of nature and tried to order their lives so they would resonate with nature and continue to receive the blessings of the goddess. According to her myth, Rauni looked down from above and saw that the earth was dry and desolate. This caused her to grieve, as she loved plants and growing things, so she came to earth and took the form of a rowan tree, or mountain ash. Rauni called to her mate, and he responded by striking the tree with a powerful and enlivening bolt of lightning. All the green things of earth are said to be a result of this electric union.

Since every tree and other plant is thought to come from the lineage of the rowan tree, Rauni, according to this myth, is the mother of all plants. The red berries of the rowan are said to be sacred to her. Some scholars believe the word *rowan* comes from the same source as the word *rune* and so carries the idea of magic and wisdom. The Lapps, who were reindeer herders, honored the same goddess under the name of Raudna and offered her sacrifices of reindeer.

CONTEMPLATION

I let my roots grow deep so my branches can reach high into the sky.

NOVEMBER 27

Fortuna

FORTUNE

Fortuna (for-TOO-nah) is the Roman goddess of good fortune, as her name suggests. Her name is thought to derive from that of the earlier Roman goddess Vortumna, who was called She Who Revolves the Year. This wheel that Vortumna "revolves" is the same as the zodiac. Sometimes she was shown veiled, in which case her nature was seen as chance, and it was anyone's guess what the outcome might be. Blessings might be bestowed or withdrawn without apparent reason. It is from this aspect of her nature that the wheel of fortune in casinos derives.

Fortuna was worshipped far and wide in the Roman world, where people went to her shrines to appeal for her positive intervention in their changing fortunes. Lady Fortune was usually depicted on a grand scale, to underscore her significance. Fortuna asks us to ponder whether we are victims of fickle fortune or have a role in our fate. What is the relationship of choice and consequence, and what might tip the scales or move the ball on the roulette wheel in our favor?

CONTEMPLATION

*I play the hand that was dealt, but
I do so skillfully and with finesse.*

Minerva

PRECOGNITION

The Roman goddess Minerva (muh-NUR-vah) was the keeper or guardian of Rome itself. She is believed to be Etruscan in origin, and her name seems to derive from an Indo-European root that means "mind." She was thought to be the embodiment of wisdom, which always takes feminine form, and to have invented numbers and musical instruments. Her sacred animal is the antelope, which was known for its keen vision and relationship to prophecy. At the site of the hot healing waters of Bath, in England, she was worshipped as Sulis-Minerva and was an underworld goddess of both knowledge and prophecy. As Minerva Medica, in Rome, she was a goddess of physicians.

The Roman poet Ovid named Minerva the Goddess of a Thousand Works, as she was goddess of medicine, wisdom, peace, crafts, commerce, weaving, and magic. She, Juno, and Jupiter formed a powerful triad and were worshipped together in a temple on the Capitoline Hill in Rome. According to one legend, the queen of spades on playing cards represents Minerva.

CONTEMPLATION

*I clear my mind of judgment and see the chain
of consequences that flows from each choice.*

Pandora

POSSIBILITIES

Pandora (pan-DOR-ah) is a Greek goddess whose name means "all giver." This was also an ancient title of the Cretan goddess Rhea, whose body was seen to provide sustenance to all creatures. In a version of the story by the Greek poet Hesiod, Zeus ordered Hephaestus, the blacksmith god, to create Pandora, the first mortal woman. She was sent to earth as a punishment after Prometheus stole fire for humanity. She was very beautiful, but her hidden mission was to bring misery to the human race. In that version, compelled by curiosity, Pandora opened her infamous box, a gift from Hermes, releasing all the ills of the world, which had been placed inside by the Olympian gods. Only hope remained inside.

In earlier myths, Pandora was married to Prometheus, and she dispensed only good gifts to humanity. The identification of the box was a mistake in translation. The container was really a honey jar, a *pithos*, that poured sweet blessings upon the world. The *pithos* was an earthen vessel, suggesting that Pandora was the earth itself, offering all good gifts to her children. Blaming all the world's ills on female curiosity was a late invention of Greek myth, and her story bears resemblance to that of Eve, who was blamed for all the sins of humanity.

CONTEMPLATION

What blessings can I pour forth today to sweeten the world through spontaneous charity?

Dorje-Phagmo

ENLIGHTENMENT

Dorje-Phagmo (DOR-jay-POG-moh) is a Tibetan Buddhist goddess who represents the energy of all that is good and the power of right speech. *Dorje* means "indestructible" in the Tibetan language, and the *dorje* is a ritual tool, named after the goddess, that symbolizes a bolt of lightning, the flash of inspiration that is the beginning of enlightenment. In Sanskrit the word is *vajra*. Dorje-Phagmo is a *khadoma*, a female spirit being, and a bodhisattva, one who has attained enlightenment. One of her altar objects is a *kapala*, a cup made from a human skull.

She is known, too, as the Thunderbolt Sow. One story says that, when her monastery was once under attack, she transformed herself and those living there into pigs. The invaders found an empty monastery and decided not to loot the building. Before they left, however, Dorje-Phagmo shape-shifted herself and the others from pigs to humans and back to pigs again. This so terrified the attackers that they offered priceless gifts to the monastery. When invoked, Dorje-Phagmo can also bestow supernatural powers.

CONTEMPLATION
*I empty my mind of careless
thoughts so it can be filled with light.*

DECEMBER 1

Athena

REASON

Athena (ah-THEE-nah), or Pallas Athena as she is also called, is the Greek goddess of wisdom. When she is Pallas, she takes command of war, but she is cast in the role of mediator or strategist rather than combatant. Although her Greek myth is powerful, Athena is thought to have originated much earlier. Her mother is Metis, Greek goddess of wisdom. Her father, Zeus, feared that a child of their union would supplant him, so he swallowed the pregnant Metis. This gave him horrific headaches, and the result was the birth of Athena, who sprang fully formed from Zeus's forehead, clothed in her famous armor. As a result, Athena is said to be his favorite child.

Athena's icons were her golden helmet and her shield, on which an image of Medusa figured prominently. Romance and marriage were not part of Athena's paradigm. Her constant companion was Nike, goddess of victory, and the city of Athens was named for her in gratitude for her gift of the olive tree. One of the largest asteroids, now frequently used in astrological interpretation as an archetype of the Divine Feminine, is named for her.

CONTEMPLATION

If I am reasonable I can avoid most battles.

DECEMBER 2

Anna-Nin

EXPERIENCE

The Sumerian goddess Anna-Nin (AH-nah-neen), who is called Lady of Heaven, has also been known by many names through the ages, but she is always the grandmother of god. *An* is the Sumerian word for "heaven." She was Ana, mother of the goddess Mari, and much later of Anne, who was the mother of the biblical Mary. As Anatha she was the consort of Yahweh. Her name means "queen" or "goddess mother" and is sometimes connected to the moon. Historians believe the Sumerians used the name Anna as an honorific, bestowing divinity on the role of motherhood.

Because she is a grandmother goddess, she is a crone, and so she has often been shown in her destroyer guise. In her biblical role, she was, like her daughter, conceived without sin. This article of faith was later discarded by the Catholic Church, and although much is written on the subject in texts that are not considered by the church to be divinely inspired, the truth of the actual circumstances remains unknown. The power of the mythic archetype, however, lives on.

CONTEMPLATION

Often experience is the best school, and
I can pass my lessons on to children.

ECHOES

Rhiannon (ree-ANN-on) is a Welsh horse goddess whose name derives from Rigantona, which means "great queen." Rhiannon made an inroad into modern awareness by means of a popular song titled after her and written by Stevie Nicks. Nicks liked the name when she discovered it a novel, but was unaware of the goddess and her myth until after writing the song. ("Rhiannon" was voted one of the five hundred greatest songs of all time by *Rolling Stone* magazine.) The goddess Rhiannon traveled across the earth on her swift horse accompanied by three magical birds. These birds had the ability to wake someone who was dead or to put a seven-year sleeping spell on a living person.

Rhiannon is likely connected with the Cretan goddess Leukippe, which means "white mare." Rhiannon was later accused, falsely, of murdering her own son and was made to carry people on her back for seven years in punishment. The dark side of Rhiannon likely originated earlier, in the aspect of the crone who annually brings death, the Night Mare, a female spirit who comes in dreams. One aspect of the goddess Demeter, who took the form of the horse, was called the Mare Who Destroys Mercifully. Mythically, Rhiannon is usually seen in her benevolent aspect, as bringer of sweet dreams.

CONTEMPLATION

*Rhiannon rings like a bell through the night,
and wouldn't you love to love her?*

— STEVIE NICKS, FLEETWOOD MAC, "RHIANNON"

DECEMBER 4

Bona Dea

CRONES

Bona Dea (BOH-nah DEE-ah), whose name means "the good goddess," was a Roman goddess whose special rites were celebrated on December 4. Stories of Bona Dea related mostly to women, especially to older matrons. She was associated with healing, and sick people were tended in gardens of medicinal herbs that were dedicated to her. Bona Dea was worshipped in a temple in Rome located on the Aventine Hill and is usually shown seated on a throne holding a cornucopia. Her image appeared frequently on Roman coins.

Special rites for Bona Dea occurred in secret in the home of the presiding pontifex maximus, the supreme pontiff and high priest of the pontiffs of ancient Rome. These rites were conducted by his wife, who was assisted by vestal virgins. Men were not permitted to attend, and even drawings of men or male animals were prohibited. In 62 BCE, during the reign of Julius Caesar, a scandal occurred. As in the myth of Daphne, an unknown and heavily cloaked man sneaked into the proceedings disguised as a woman. Although his identity was never verified, a man named Publius Clodius Pulcher was tried for the incident. Little is known about details of the ceremony, but since it occurred annually at the approach of the winter solstice, it may have involved asking for the return of light.

CONTEMPLATION
Although the nights grow longer and darker,
on the other side of the world it is summer.

Goddesses for Every Day

Nanshe

OMENS

Nanshe (NON-she) is a Sumerian goddess of dreams and prophecy whose primary city was Nina. She was skilled in the art of oneiromancy, a form of divination based on dream symbols. This practice not only interprets dreams but also lets one see into the future. Some sources say special dreams were sent by Zaqar, a messenger of the gods who brought divine messages to mortals in their dreams. Nanshe was considered to be a prophet of such high caliber that she could see the future for deities as well as humans.

Nanshe also had a special connection with underground springs, which have often been linked with the gift of prophecy. The seers who presided at her rites and learned to interpret dreams were required to undergo an initiation that required a symbolic descent into the earth. Each year, at a symbolic review, Nanshe served as a judge of each person's acts.

CONTEMPLATION

I pay attention to my dreams, for my soul travels in that realm while I sleep.

Sarah

UNDERSTANDING

Sarah, or Sara, a figure described in the Bible and the Quran, is really a goddess in disguise. Her name is sometimes translated as "goddess" or "princess," and at the least it denotes a woman of extremely high rank. As described in rabbinic literature, Sarah's gifts of prophecy were greater than those of her husband, Abraham, since she received her prophecies directly from God rather than from angels. Hints of her true nature are revealed by the descriptions of her unrivaled beauty and the fact that Abraham says she is really his sister. The spouse-sister archetype mythically links Sarah to many ancient goddesses, such as Isis.

As a human woman, Sarah was a Chaldean princess who brought wealth and status to her husband. Revealing her nature as a goddess, Sarah also lived nearly a century before giving birth, according to her myth. And while she was alive, the land was fertile, but when she died the land became a desert. In the Bible story, God promises that Abraham will be the father of nations, and in the New Testament both Sarah and Jerusalem are called "free women."

CONTEMPLATION

In the stillness of silent meditation,
I hear the voice of the Divine.

Tyche

PROVIDENCE

Tyche (TIE-key), whose name means "fortune," is a Greek mother goddess who has dominion over fate and luck. She is usually depicted standing on a wheel, blindfolded and winged, carrying a scepter and wearing a crown. She was seen as the personification of providence, or random good fortune, and of the idea of "chance" that contributes to the success of any venture. When people invoked Tyche, they asked her to intervene in their favor. Tyche was called Fortuna in Roman mythology.

A statue that depicts Tyche's face within a zodiac, which is supported by a winged goddess Nike, was found at Petra in Jordan. The site of Petra was discovered in the early 1800s; before that, like Troy, the famous city of stone was thought to be only legend. The Petra zodiac seems to revolve in a unique manner, divided in half rather than moving in the familiar sequential order. The wheel that encircles Tyche's face shows the Arabian goddess Al Uzza in the place of Sagittarius. Tyche of Antioch, a statue whose image appeared on the coins of that ancient city located in Asia Minor, where southern Turkey is today, was considered one of the great works of antiquity. No ruler of Antioch had power to act without Tyche's favor.

CONTEMPLATION

I pay attention to what seems random
but may be a gift of providence.

VOICE OF THUNDER

Sodza (SAHD-zah) is goddess of lightning and thunder to the Hos people of Togoland on the coast of Guinea in western Africa. This area was formerly known as the slave coast. Sodza's bright flashes and loud noises are thought to drive away evil spirits and to keep everyone in the household safe from dark sorcery. She is married to Sogble, who is the male god of lightning, and their loud voices speak to each other in the sky.

Sodza is invoked to bless the land after it has been tilled and seeded, and to bring rain that allows the crops to grow. When the people hear her voice in heaven, bringing the much-needed rain, it is thought to be fortunate. Sodza is called by such names as Mother of Humans and Animals, Ship Full of Yams, and Ship Full of the Most Varied Fullness. Among her gifts is the blessing and protection of children.

CONTEMPLATION

Sometimes I must break my silence and speak my truth in a voice like thunder to banish dark energies from my life.

The Muses

INSPIRATION

The nine Muses are Greek goddesses of inspiration who were seen as overseeing all the arts and sciences. The nine sisters were daughters of Mnemosyne, whose name means "memory," and Zeus. The English words *music, museum, amuse,* and even *mosaic* come from the sisters' collective name. The Muses and their areas of responsibility, which have been assigned since the Renaissance, are Calliope, epic poetry; Clio, history; Erato, erotic poetry; Euterpe, lyric song; Melpomene, tragedy; Polyhymnia, sacred song; Terpsichore, dance; Thalia, comedy; and Urania, astronomy. A different goddess named Thalia is also one of the three Graces.

The Muses act as spirit guides who inspire people to create. They also act as sponsors for artists, embodying their specialties; in tradition, when a Muse was invoked by someone, that individual was required to state the area of endeavor within which he or she worked. In art the Muses were often depicted with an emblem of their specialty. For example, Euterpe carried a flute. Solon, the well-known Athenian poet and creator of laws, said in his "Prayer to the Muses," that the Muses were the "key to a good life."

CONTEMPLATION

I call upon my muse today,
knowing inspiration will flow.

Abeona

PARTING

Abeona (ah-bee-OH-nah) is a Roman goddess who safeguarded children as they took their first steps and when they left home for the first time, parting from their parents. She was also the goddess of all departures and farewells, even those that were temporary, so she was invoked whenever it was time to leave. Her name comes from the Latin verb *abeo*, which means "to depart or go forth." Knowing when it is time to leave is a valuable gift, which prevents us from wearing out our welcome.

The city of Rome was under Abeona's protection, perhaps because many people departed the gates of the city on journeys and adventures. She was likewise the protector of all travelers who set forth. The goddess is immortalized in the names Abeona Mons, a mountain on the planet Venus, and asteroid 145 Abeona.

CONTEMPLATION

*I recognize when it is time to leave
and make my departure gracefully.*

MYSTICAL UNION

Sapientia (sah-pee-EHN-tee-ah), whose name means "feminine wisdom" in Latin, is the archetype of wisdom. Whenever any reference to wisdom appears in either the Bible or Hebrew writings, the idea is expressed in the feminine gender and is understood to be divine wisdom. *Wisdom* was *sophia* to the Greeks, and *chockmah* to the Jews. Sapientia has been termed the "goddess of the Bible" by some scholars, indicating the presence of the Divine Feminine in monotheism. She was acknowledged up until medieval times but has been forgotten with the passage of time. In fact, she thrived as a hidden goddess of philosophical inquiry between the fifth and fifteenth centuries at a time when the sacred feminine was considered heresy.

Mystics spoke of her as dwelling in the heart of God and, in some cases, saw her as bringing all creation into being. She embodied the World Soul, or the collective of humanity, and the mystical union with the Divine sought by sages and spiritual pilgrims. A beautiful series of antiphons are still chanted as part of Advent liturgy, including: "O, Sapientia, O holy Word of God, you govern all creation with your strong yet tender care. Come and show your people the way to salvation."

CONTEMPLATION

*I, Wisdom, came out of the mouth of
the Most High, firstborn of all creation.*

— BIBLE, ECCLESIASTES 24:5

Tonantzin

MIRACLES

Tonantzin (toh-NAN-zin) is an Aztec goddess who was transformed into the now-famous Lady of Guadalupe, whose feast day is December 12. Ten million people make pilgrimages to Mexico City each year to honor her, making her basilica the second-most-visited Catholic site in the world; only the Vatican draws greater numbers. What prompts such profound adoration?

Her Christianized story is that of a peasant named Juan Diego who reportedly saw visions of the mother of God, who called herself Mother Tonantzin. She told him to build a church on the site where she appeared. This spot had once held a temple dedicated to the Aztec goddess. As a sign of proof to the bishop that his ongoing visions were genuine, Our Lady filled Juan Diego's cloak with roses in winter. In such a mysterious and miraculous way, the deep reverence for the Great Goddess continues through the adoration of a Catholic archetype.

CONTEMPLATION

I lovingly place red roses on my altar
today, knowing the goddess is always with us.

Sibyl

PROPHECY

The name Sibyl (SIH-bull) means "dweller in a cave." Sibyl is the origin of a tradition of divine prophets, called sibyls, who became an enduring lineage of priestesses. There is a demeaning Greek myth about how Sibyl tricked Apollo into giving her long life, which he did while making her grow old and ugly. But the more important story is the history of the sibylline oracles, who lived in oracular caves in ten important locations in the ancient world. The most notable and renowned sibyl lived outside Naples. Her prophecies were written on leaves, and if no one came to collect them, she cast them upon the wind.

The famous texts known as the Sibylline Prophecies were prophecies written on leaves in hexameter verse. These prophecies were highly regarded, and a portion of them was once purchased by a Roman king at a high price. They were often consulted for important matters of state. These books were largely destroyed in a fire and then rewritten by both Jewish and Christian writers and used for missionary purposes as if they were genuine.

CONTEMPLATION

*I still my mind and open my inner
ear to the voice of divine wisdom.*

Benzaiten

ELOQUENCE

Benzaiten (ben-sigh-TEN), sometimes called Benten, is a Japanese goddess whose name means "everything that flows," referring especially to knowledge and words. She is related to eloquence in speech and music, and so is also related to the geisha tradition. Benzaiten is thought to have originated in ancient India, however, and to have emerged in Chinese translations of the Sutra of Golden Light, which also made its way into Japan. She was seen as a protector and benefactor of the Japanese state, and she was invoked to keep the unstable Japanese islands safe from earthquakes. She is the only goddess among the Shichi Fukujin, the Seven Deities of Good Fortune, who has the capacity to bestow monetary wealth.

Benzaiten is often depicted riding on a dragon, who was her lover, and she is always dressed in elegant and ornate clothing. In another example of the link between goddesses and serpents, she has a retinue of white snakes.

CONTEMPLATION

My speech flows like an elegant lyric and is pleasing to the heart as well as the ear.

Sanja

CONSCIENCE

Sanja (SAN-jah) is a Hindu goddess of light, and the wife of the sun god Surya. Her name means "conscience," which suggests what we might see clearly in the light of wisdom. Sanja's myth illustrates the interplay of light and dark, and the interplay between her inner light and the brilliance of the sun. Her mate was so fiery and brilliant that at times Sanja asked her companion Chhaya, whose name means "shade," to take her place while she transformed herself from light into a spirited mare and cavorted in the dark coolness of the forest.

When Surya, the sun, discovered she was missing, he would take the form of a great stallion and pursue her. This myth suggests the rhythmic cycles of light and dark in the year. According to the stories, they enjoyed this game of hide-and-seek, which may also tell a story of eclipses. To help her cope with the sun, Sanja asked her father, the divine artificer Visvakarma, to periodically take away a portion of Surya's brilliance. This too may tell of a partial eclipse.

CONTEMPLATION

I cannot look directly at the sun, so my
deep insight usually comes during reflection.

Oya

TRUTH

Oya (OYE-yah) is the fiery storm-and-thunder goddess of the Yoruba people of western Africa, and her mate is the god of lightning. Her full name is Oya-Yansan. Although she is a warrior goddess adept with horses, she is also the goddess of the Niger River. In this role she is called Queen of the Nine, for there are nine tributaries of the river. Oya controls wind and fire but also brings hurricanes. The worship of the Orishas, the spirit beings or gods of the Yoruba people, spread to Brazil along with the slave trade, where Oya also guards the gates of death and cemeteries. To avoid further persecution, the Yoruba overlaid the Orishas with Catholic saints, and Oya is the goddess equated with Saint Theresa.

Oya is the patron goddess of justice and memory, and using her machete like a sword of truth, she reveals the buried essence in any matter presented to her. She embodies the force of change based on revelation, and she cuts through stagnation. She is sometimes depicted holding a flame. Along the river, people hang prayer flags honoring her.

CONTEMPLATION

Does my candle of truth burn brightly,
or is it hidden beneath a tarnished cover?

ILLUMINATION

Shekinah (shah-KYE-nah) is the feminine side of God, and she appears in the Talmud, a sacred book of the Jewish faith that contains traditional interpretations of Jewish laws found in the Hebrew Bible. *Shekinah* means "dwell," and the name comes from the Hebrew word *shakan*. *Shekinah* is also the word for the habitation of God, especially in the Jerusalem temple. Christian theologians used the feminine Greek word *Parousia* in a similar way to describe the divine presence. The essence of Shekinah is perceived as a feminine principle of light, whose nature and spirit are described as radiant. According to the Talmud, it was Shekinah who inspired David to write his psalms and who gave him his voice. Some stories in the Talmud tell how Shekinah argued with Yahweh on behalf of humanity. In Judaism she is also perceived as the "soul of the Divine" and is similar to the idea of the Christian Holy Spirit and the Hindu Shakti.

Some stories say Shekinah abandoned the world when it became too evil and unbalanced by an overabundance of masculine energy, especially in people's understanding of the Divine. Aspects of Kabbalah explore ways to reunite the separated masculine and feminine aspects of God and bring God back into equilibrium. To do this spiritual work, we must find Shekinah, bring her back into our consciousness, and restore balance.

CONTEMPLATION

*May the light of true wisdom radiate, filling
my mind and heart with compassion.*

Epona

PURPOSE

Epona (ee-POH-nah), who, like the goddess Demeter, was called the Great Mare, is a Celtic horse goddess. Most Celtic deities were associated with a specific location, but Epona's worship was widespread across the Roman Empire. She was the only Celtic goddess to have a Roman temple, and her Roman feast day was December 18. One of her more mundane roles was to oversee horse races, but Epona also had a more serious side as a psychopomp, leading the souls of the deceased on their final journey out of the visible world and into the unseen realm beyond the veil. In this aspect, we see her as one form of the Night Mare.

Epona was thought to be the daughter of a mare who mated with a man, and she could shape-shift into either human or equine form, depending on the need. In art, she is sometimes shown sitting sidesaddle on a horse, reminiscent of Lady Godiva, but usually she is shown seated on a throne and flanked by horses to show her status as a sovereign. In Ireland, kings were symbolically joined or mated with actual mares, symbols of Epona, to give them power.

CONTEMPLATION

I choose a guide carefully if I am
riding into unknown territory.

Chariklo

CANDOR

Chariklo (CHAR-ee-klo) is a goddess in the form of a centaur, *kentaur* in Greek, a mythical race of beings who were half human and half horse. She was the daughter of the sun god Apollo and the mate of the famous centaur Chiron. Chariklo was also the nurse of the hero Jason for a time. The centaurs were beautiful to look at, combining the best physical aspects of the two races of creatures, but they had a reputation for being serious "party animals." Chariklo, however, was known for her special grace and her truthfulness and served in the temple of Vesta as a much-beloved companion of Athena, the Greek goddess of wisdom.

Chariklo is now also one of the more intriguing members of our solar system, also called Centaurs, which orbit eccentrically between Jupiter and Pluto. Centaurs are neither comets nor asteroids, having the characteristics of both, and because of this dual nature, these celestial bodies have been named after the mythical centaurs.

CONTEMPLATION

When I feel torn between a wise choice
and an instinctual reaction,
I remember to be honest with myself
and choose the higher ground.

Cassandra

FORESHADOWING

Cassandra (kah-SAN-dra), the Greek goddess of prophecy, is the daughter of Hecuba and the king of Troy. Cassandra was taken prisoner after the fall of Troy, and she cursed the victorious king. In another story, which no doubt has a deeper meaning, Apollo desired her because she was the most beautiful of the daughters of Hecuba. She refused his advances, and so he cursed her. He gave her the gift of accurate prophecy but twisted the gift so that no one would believe her. As a result, Cassandra prophesied the fall of Troy, but no one listened.

An older and more symbolic story of how she received the gift of prophecy recounts that she and her twin spent the night in the temple of Apollo. While she slept, the temple snakes, oracle symbols, licked her ears clean so she would be able to hear the future. Although we refer to someone who speaks truthfully, but is disbelieved, as a Cassandra, the mythical Cassandra was vindicated after her death and worshipped as a goddess.

CONTEMPLATION

Some blessings, especially the gift of clairvoyance,
can seem more like a curse, so I use my gifts wisely.

CAPRICORN GODDESSES
The Spinning Wheel

THREADS OF DESTINY ARE SPUN
BY CHOICES AND DEEDS

*C*apricorn anchors the winter solstice and combines the principles of cardinal initiating energies with the grounding influence of earth. In this sign, matter organizes itself into perfect forms. Capricorn's energy expresses itself as governing and conserving, focused on achievement, integrity, recognition, and responsibility. Capricorn natives are fueled by tremendous ambition, and their lessons stem from learning the motive that underlies their drive to climb. Capricorn is the tenth sign, and it represents the stage of the spiritual journey in which our aspiration turns inward to the clear mountain air of our spiritual nature. It also represents the principle of ambition, whether this is directed outwardly to the world of accomplishment or turned toward the spiritual path.

The goddess sign for Capricorn is the Spinning Wheel,

representing crone goddesses who are weavers of fate. Spinning, weaving, and looms are the province of wise elder goddesses who pronounce our destiny and measure and cut the threads of our lives. While Scorpio spins the threads out of the substance of the goddess's belly, it is in Capricorn, the sign of form, that the threads take shape and are woven into the tapestry of our lives. Mountains symbolize the spiritual quest in numerous traditions, so Capricorn is traditionally symbolized by the Sea Goat, a mountain goat with the tail of a fish or dolphin. And so, ancient mountain goddesses are included in Capricorn, along with goddesses who embody structure, organization, time or duration, endings, the dark of winter, and the wisdom of old age.

DECEMBER 21

Chin Nu

BRIDGES

Chin Nu (chen new) is the Chinese goddess of spinners and weavers. She is the daughter of the Jade Emperor, Yu Hang. In her myth she came down from heaven to bathe in a stream, and a cowherd who desired her was informed of her presence by an intelligent ox. The cowherd stole her clothes and then convinced Chin Nu to marry him. The goddess agreed and didn't return to the sky for seven years. After she left, her husband longed for her, and so he followed her into the stars with their children. Chin Nu's father gave her husband a star in the western sky, and Chin Nu's star was placed to the east of the Milky Way.

The lovers are separated for the whole year, but on one night, the night of the seventh day of the seventh month in the Chinese calendar, they are reunited when flocks of magpies bring twigs and build a bridge across heaven. Chin Nu's star is in the constellation of Vega, known as the Weaving Sisters to the Chinese, and her husband's star resides in the constellation of the Herdsman.

CONTEMPLATION

*Are there bridges of healing
that need to be built in my life?*

Hekate

CONVERGENCE

The pre-Hellenic goddess Hekate (hay-CAH-tay) is the daughter of the Titans Asteria and Perses, both symbols of scintillating light. She has dominion over crossroads, especially those where three roads converge, and she is a guardian of the Gates of Immortality. Hekate is sometimes depicted with three bodies, whose faces look in three directions at once, and she is shown with these bodies standing back to back, each sighting down one of three roads. She also protects travelers, especially solitary ones in lonely places.

As a goddess of the underworld, Hekate was said to wait on Queen Persephone and to associate with spirits, ghosts, and hounds. She also had great powers of magic and witchcraft. On earth, she was known to haunt tombs and places where crimes had occurred and was followed by her ghostly train of ethereal light and baying spectral hounds. Those who honor her today believe Hekate still roams these places, and although most humans cannot sense her presence, earthly dogs seem to.

CONTEMPLATION

*I look at past, present, and future
simultaneously and light the
lamp of my inner sight.*

Acca Larentia

GENEROSITY

Acca Larentia (AH-cah la-REN-tee-ah) is a Roman goddess who acted as the foster mother of the famous twins Romulus and Remus. It was also her role to watch over the dead. She was a major goddess of the Etruscans before her later Roman role. Her festival, called the Larentalia, which sounds like a New Year's Eve party, was celebrated on December 23.

The stories of Acca Larentia are varied, but one of the most popular is that Hercules won her in a game of dice. He was not able to collect his prize, as someone had locked her in a room, so in a snit he said she would have to marry the first man she met in the morning. Acca Larentia was blessed, as the man she married was kind and very wealthy. Later, when she became a full-fledged goddess, she bequeathed all her money to Rome. The Romans gratefully celebrated her generosity each year at her lively festival.

CONTEMPLATION

What I share generously comes
back to me a hundredfold.

Holda

GIFTS

Holda (HOL-dah) is a Germanic or Teutonic goddess whose annual job is the same as that of Santa Claus. In the more familiar story of Christmas Eve, Mrs. Claus stays home while Santa and his reindeer make an overnight journey. But in Germany, Austria, and Switzerland, it's Holda who flies through the night in a magical carriage on the 24th of December, the time of Yule, bringing gifts and spreading her boundless joy. Holda dresses in the familiar red and white and wears a cape made from goose feathers. It's her job to decide who deserves gifts.

One of her titles is the White Lady, because she comes at the snowy time of year. On Christmas morning a fresh bowl of milk is set out for her to thank her for her gifts. If some of the milk disappears, the people believe that Holda has acknowledged their gratitude. Whatever is left after the goddess drinks her fill is thought to hold special power. Holda also gave women the gift of flax and knowledge about spinning. Many women spin during the long, dark nights of winter to earn extra money. Bestowing knowledge about spinning is the domain of crone goddesses of fate whose time is the dark period of the year.

CONTEMPLATION

Tonight I have the eyes of a child
and believe in magic and wonder.

Juno Lucina

REVERSAL

Juno Lucina (JOO-noh loo-CEE-nah), called Mother Light, is a Roman goddess who bestows the gifts of vision and enlightenment. Her festival was celebrated in Rome in December with torches and bonfires. Each year at the winter solstice, the sun appears to rise and set in the same place for three days. The astronomical term for this phenomenon in Latin is *sol sticere*, which means "sun stands still." Then, on December 25, the sun seems to start moving again in the opposite direction. So this day begins the annual "return of the light" in the Northern Hemisphere. Many mythical solar kings are reborn each year on this day.

Juno Lucina was seen as the midwife of the annual rebirth of the light, bringing the year out of darkness. She was also thought to open the eyes of each newborn child after nine months in the darkness of the womb. At the festival of Matronalia, women past menopause wore loose clothes and let their hair hang down, symbolizing that they were no longer subject to the hazards of childbirth. Juno Lucina was later Christianized in the form of Saint Lucy.

CONTEMPLATION

Is there something in my life that has been gestating in the darkness of a womb and is ready to come to light?

Yellow Corn Girl

AWARENESS

Yellow Corn Girl, or Takus Mana (TAH-koos MAH-nah) to the Hopi, is a spirit being, one of the Hopi *katsinas*, who represent the forces of life. She comes each year in December, after the winter solstice, and helps open the kivas, the circular underground areas where sacred ceremonies are held. She blesses the corn during the yearly festival called the Soyalangwu ceremony. Yellow Corn Girl, her hair styled in corn rolls — a style in which the hair is wound into "balls" on either side of the head — also often appears with another long-haired *katsina*.

The Hopi say the *katsinas* once came personally but now take the form of clouds, coming down from the San Francisco Peaks or up from inside the earth. The *katsinas* arrive each year in December and depart in July. In the cold months, Hopi dances are performed underground in the kivas, but in warmer weather the dances are held outside and can last all day. The Hopi sacred calendar and ceremonial dances are linked to the annual growing cycles, and the dances are performed as part of the prayers for the blessing of rain that nourishes the corn.

CONTEMPLATION

I welcome and gratefully acknowledge the intercession of the spirit beings in my life.

DECEMBER 28

The Zorya

MIDNIGHT

The Zorya (ZOR-yah) are three Slavic goddesses honored mostly in Russia. They express the triple aspect of the goddess — maiden, mother, and crone — and are responsible for morning, noon, and night, respectively. *Zorya* means "star" in Russian. The Zorya are guardians of life and time and are charged with keeping watch over a giant doomsday hound that is chained to the North Pole. The dog constantly pursues the constellation of Ursa Minor, the Little Bear, as it circles around the vault of heaven, a star group that contains the North Star, or polestar. Due to the apparently slow movement of the heavens relative to earth, the polestar changes over time. With the passage of time, a new star takes the honor of being the polestar. If the chain should ever break, and the hound should catch the bear, the cycle of time would close and the universe come to an end. Myths of doomsday curses, which can be uttered only by crones, appear in many cultures.

In the morning, the first aspect of Zorya opens the gates of heaven and welcomes the sun. In the evening, the second closes the gates and secures everything for the night. The Midnight Zorya is the crone aspect of this trinity, and each night the sun dies in her arms and is reborn the following morning. Midnight Zorya is a goddess of death, rebirth, and the mystery of the gestating power of darkness.

CONTEMPLATION

What rich, dark secrets and deep mysteries lie dormant in the midnight side of my psyche?

Ariadne

INITIATION

Ariadne (ar-ee-ODD-nee), whose name means "very holy," is known to us from Greek myth, but she originated much earlier, in Crete, where she was the daughter of King Minos and the goddess Parsiphae. In the familiar story, Ariadne aided the hero Theseus in the labyrinth, where the Minotaur, the "bull monster," hid, by giving him a ball of thread to mark his path so he could make his way back out. The Cretan labyrinth was a dancing-ground, created for Ariadne rather than for Minos. In *The Iliad*, Homer relates that the pattern the god Hephaestus inscribed on a shield was a dancing-ground, "like the one Daedalus designed in the spacious town of Knossos for Ariadne of the lovely locks."

Greek stories omit the detail that in Crete there was a "lady" who presided over the labyrinth. But a tablet inscribed in Linear B, a type of script, found at Knossos, in ancient Crete, records "a gift to all the gods of honey; to the mistress of the labyrinth honey." The mistress of the labyrinth received as much honey as all the rest of the gods combined. A true labyrinth had a single route to the center and was an ancient symbol. The journey into the labyrinth was a process of initiation, one that included a ritual death and rebirth. The goddess leads the hero in all of us through this secret process.

CONTEMPLATION

When entering an unfamiliar forest, it is always wise to leave a trail of bread crumbs.

Al Menat

TEMPERANCE

Al Menat (al MEN-not) is a Chaldean and pre-Islamic Arabian goddess of fate and good fortune. Her name is derived from the Arabic word *maniya*, which means "fate or doom," and the word *menata*, which means "portion." She was part of a triple-goddess archetype from ancient Arabia, which included Al Uzza and Al Lat, and which represented the phases of the moon, the year, and a woman's life. These goddesses are mentioned in the Quran and were the source of the controversy in Salman Rushdie's notorious book *The Satanic Verses*.

Al Menat is the aged and wizened crone, who is depicted as an old woman with a cup, and like other goddesses of fate and time, she is responsible for destiny and the length of life. Her symbol is the waning crescent moon. She was worshipped in the form of an uncut, black meteoritic stone at Quidad, near Mecca. Some scholars speculate that this same stone may actually now rest in Mecca, as the original stone was stolen from Quidad when Al Menat's shrine was destroyed.

CONTEMPLATION

I drink deeply from the cup of my life,
both the bitter waters and the sweet.

Kali Ma

RESURRECTION

Kali Ma (KAH-lee mah), the Dark Mother, is a beloved Hindu goddess of India. Her name comes from the Sanskrit word *kal*, which means "time." Her nature is complex and can be frightening at first glance, when we see her wearing a necklace of fifty-two skulls, holding a severed head, and dancing on the corpse of her consort, Shiva, the Destroyer. Kali is both womb and tomb, reveling in an eternal dance of transformation. She also represents the death of the ego, which is a vital step forward in our growth. We are meant to identify not only with our body but also with our eternal soul.

In Hinduism this Great Goddess is a trinity — maiden, mother, and crone — and has relationships with Brahma, the Creator, and Vishnu, the Preserver, as well as with Shiva, the Destroyer, as all existence is a balance of these three principles. In his book *Erotic Art of the East*, Philip Rawson relates that Vishnu remarked in a poem that the "Universe rests upon Her." She is the "Ocean of Blood" from the beginning of the world that eternally regenerates all of existence.

CONTEMPLATION

Death is an illusion. The form dissolves, but life is eternal, and tomorrow we are born again.

ACKNOWLEDGMENTS

I thank my agent, Lisa DiMona, for her long-term faith and support. Tremendous thanks, coupled with a sense of awe, goes to Georgia Hughes and the editorial staff at New World Library for seeing the possibilities and challenging me to reach for deeper meaning and greater clarity. Special thanks are due to Mariko Layton for years of writing partnership and critiquing, and to Janet Miller for her creative vision.

I am so blessed by the gift of my daughters, Emily and Elizabeth, and my granddaughters, Matraca, Natasha, and Meredith. The empowering presence of all the beautiful and strong women who have inspired and supported me, listened to me, and laughed and cried with me on this incredible journey of discovery is priceless. Each of you is a precious archetype of the Divine Feminine, and this book would not have been possible without you.

INDEX OF GODDESSES

INDEX OF ATTRIBUTES AND KEY WORDS

RESOURCES

Books

Allen, Paula Gunn. *Grandmothers of the Light*. Boston: Beacon, 1991.

Arrowsmith, Nancy, and George Moorse. *A Field Guide to the Little People*. New York: Wallaby, 1977.

Baigent, Michael. *Holy Blood, Holy Grail*. New York: Dell, 1982.

————. *The Jesus Papers*. New York: HarperCollins, 2006.

Baigent, Michael, and Richard Leigh. *The Dead Sea Scrolls Deception*. New York: Summit Books, 1991.

Baring, Anne, and Jules Cashford. *The Myth of the Goddess*. New York: Arkana, Penguin Group, 1993.

Baring, Anne, and Andrew Harvey. *The Divine Feminine*. Berkeley: Conari, 1996.

Barnes, Craig S. *In Search of the Lost Feminine*. Golden, CO: Fulcrum, 2006.

Begg, Ean. *The Cult of the Black Virgin*. London: Penguin, 1985.

Blair, Nancy. *Goddesses for Every Season*. Ringwood, U.K.: Element, 1995.

Bolen, Jean Shinoda. *Goddesses in Everywoman*. New York: Harper and Row, 1985.

Bonheim, Jalaja. *Goddess*. New York: Stewart, Tabori and Chang, 1997.

Budge, E. A. Wallis. *The Egyptian Book of the Dead*. New York: Dover, 1967.

————. *The Gods of the Egyptians*. Vol. 1. New York: Dover, 1969.

————. *The Gods of the Egyptians*. Vol. 2. New York: Dover, 1969.

Bulfinch, Thomas. *Bulfinch's Mythology*. New York: Avenel, 1979.

Bunson, Margaret. *The Encyclopedia of Ancient Egypt*. New York: Random House, 1991.

Buxton, Simon. *The Shamanic Way of the Bee*. Rochester, VT: Destiny, 2004.

Byrne, Sean. *The Tragic History of Esoteric Christianity*. Hollywood, CA: Age-Old Books, 2001.

Campbell, Joseph. *The Hero with a Thousand Faces*. Princeton, NJ: Princeton University Press, 1972.

————. *The Inner Reaches of Outer Space*. New York: Harper and Row, 1986.

————. *Myths to Live By*. New York: Bantam, 1972.

————. *Transformations of Myth through Time*. New York: Harper Perennial, 1990.

Campbell, Joseph, with Bill Moyers. *The Power of Myth*. New York: Doubleday, 1988.

Cirlot, J. E. *A Dictionary of Symbols*. New York: Dorset, 1971.

Clapp, Nicholas. *Sheba*. Boston: Houghton Mifflin, 2001.

Coulter, Charles Russell, and Patricia Turner. *Dictionary of Ancient Deities*. New York: Oxford University Press, 2000.

Daly, Mary. *Beyond God the Father*. Boston: Beacon, 1973.

Dever, William G. *Did God Have a Wife? Archaeology and Folk Religion in Ancient Israel*. Grand Rapids, MI: Eerdmans, 2005.

Doresse, Jean. *The Secret Books of the Egyptian Gnostics*. Rochester, VT: Inner Traditions, 1958.

Dunwich, Gerina. *The Wicca Book of Days*. New York: Citadel, 1995.

Ehrman, Bart. *Misquoting Jesus*. New York: HarperCollins, 2005.

Eisenman, Robert, and Michael Wise. *The Dead Sea Scrolls Undiscovered*. New York: Barnes and Noble, 1992.

Estes, Clarissa Pinkola. *Women Who Run With the Wolves*. New York: Ballantine, 1992.

Ferguson, V. S. *Inanna Returns*. Seattle: Thel Dar, 1995.

Fraser, Antonia. *The Warrior Queens*. New York: Alfred A. Knopf, 1988.

Frazer, James G. *The Golden Bough*. New York: Avenel, 1981.

Freke, Timothy, and Peter Gandy. *Jesus and the Lost Goddess*. New York: Three Rivers, 2001.

Gadon, Elinor W. *The Once and Future Goddess*. New York: HarperCollins, 1989.

Gaffney, Mark H. *Gnostic Secrets of the Naassenes*. Rochester, VT: Inner Traditions, 2004.

Gillentine, Julie. *The Hidden Power of Everyday Things*. New York: Pocket Books, 2000.

————. *Tarot and Dream Interpretation*. Saint Paul, MN: Llewellyn, 2003.

Gilligan, Carol. *In a Different Voice*. Cambridge, MA: Harvard University Press, 1982.

Gimbutas, Marija. *The Language of the Goddess*. San Francisco: Harper and Row, 1989.

Gleadow, Rupert. *The Origin of the Zodiac*. London: Dover, 1968.

Gordon, Stuart. *The Encyclopedia of Myths and Legends*. London: Headline, 1993.

Graves, Robert. *The White Goddess*. London: Faber and Faber, 1948.

Grimal, Pierre. *The Penguin Dictionary of Classical Mythology*. New York: Penguin Books, 1986.

Hallam, Elizabeth. *Gods and Goddesses*. New York: Simon and Schuster, 1996.

Hamilton, Edith. *Mythology*. New York: New American Library, 1940.

Haskins, Susan. *Mary Magdalen*. Orlando, FL: Harcourt Brace, 1993.

Hirshfield, Jane. *Women in Praise of the Sacred*. New York: HarperCollins, 1994.

Hoeller, Stephan A. *The Gnostic Jung and the Seven Sermons to the Dead*. Wheaton, IL: Quest, 1982.

Hoffman, Curtiss. *The Seven Story Tower*. Cambridge, MA: Perseus, 1999.

Jegen, Carol Francis. *Mary According to Women*. Kansas City: Leaven, 1985.

Jennings, Sue. *Goddesses*. Carlsbad, CA: Hay House, 2003.

Johnson, Buffie. *Lady of the Beasts*. San Francisco: Harper and Row, 1981.

Jones, V. S. Vernon. *Aesop's Fables*. New York: Avenel, 1912.

Kasser, Rodolphe, Marvin Meyer, and Gregor Wurst. *The Gospel of Judas*. Washington, DC: National Geographic Society, 2006.

King, Karen. *The Gospel of Mary of Magdala*. Santa Rosa, CA: Polebridge, 2003.

Kinstler, Clysta. *The Moon Under Her Feet*. New York: HarperCollins, 1989.

Knappert, Jan. *Indian Mythology*. London: Diamond, 1991.

Knight, Christopher, and Robert Lomas. *The Hiram Key*. London: Arrow, 1997.

Knight, Gareth. *The Rose Cross and the Goddess*. New York: Destiny, 1985.

La Croix, Mary. *The Remnant*. Virginia Beach, VA: A.R.E. Press, 1981.

Lapatin, Kenneth. *Mysteries of the Snake Goddess*. Cambridge, MA: Da Capo, 2002.

Larrington, Carolyne. *The Feminist Companion to Mythology*. London: Pandora, 1992.

Leeming, David Adams. *The World of Myth*. New York: Oxford University Press, 1990.

Leloup, Jean-Yves. *The Gospel of Mary Magdalene*. Rochester, VT: Inner Traditions, 2002.

Long, Asphodel P. *In a Chariot Drawn by Lions*. Freedom, CA: Crossing Press, 1993.

Longfellow, Ki. *The Secret Magdalene*. Brattleboro, VT: Eio, 2005.

Lurker, Manfred. *The Gods and Symbols of Ancient Egypt*. London: Thames and Hudson, 1980.

Markale, Jean. *The Church of Mary Magdalene*. Rochester, VT: Inner Traditions, 1989.

Mascetti, Manuela Dunn. *The Song of Eve*. New York: Simon and Schuster, 1990.

Matthews, John, and Caitlin Matthews. *British and Irish Mythology*. London: Diamond, 1988.

Mead, G. R. S. *Pistis Sophia: A Gnostic Gospel*. Blauvelt, NY: Garber Communications, 1984.

Meyer, Marvin W. *The Secret Teachings of Jesus*. New York: Vintage, 1984.

Mollenkott, Virginia Ramey. *The Divine Feminine*. New York: Crossroad, 1983.

Monaghan, Patricia. *The Book of Goddesses and Heroines*. Saint Paul, MN: Llewellyn, 1993.

————. *The Goddess Companion*. Saint Paul, MN: Llewellyn, 2000.

Morris, Desmond. *Body Guards*. Boston: Element, 1999.

Muten, Burleigh. *Goddesses: A World of Myth and Magic*. Cambridge, MA: Barefoot, 2003.

————. *The Lady of Ten Thousand Names*. Cambridge, MA: Barefoot, 2001.

Nelson, Kirk. *Edgar Cayce's Hidden History of Jesus*. Virginia Beach, VA: A.R.E. Press, 1995.

Newman, Barbara. *God and the Goddesses*. Philadelphia: University of Pennsylvania Press, 2005.

Newman, Sharan. *The Real History Behind the Da Vinci Code*. New York: Berkley, 2005.

Pagels, Elaine. *Beyond Belief: The Secret Gospels of Thomas*. New York: Random House, 2005.

————. *The Gnostic Gospels*. New York: Vintage, 1979.

————. *The Origin of Satan*. New York: Vintage, 1995.

Pennick, Nigel. *The Pagan Book of Days*. Rochester, VT: Destiny, 1992.

Picknett, Lynn. *Mary Magdalene*. New York: Carroll and Graf, 2004.

Picknett, Lynn, and Clive Prince. *The Templar Revelation: Secret Guardians of the True Identity of Christ*. New York: Touchstone, 1997.

Platt, Rutherford H. *The Lost Books of the Bible and the Forgotten Books of Eden*. Berkeley, CA: Apocryphile, 2005.

Poynder, Michael. *The Lost Magic of Christianity*. London: Green Magic, 2000.

Ralls, Karen. *The Templars and the Grail*. Wheaton, IL: Theosophical Publishing, 2003.

Robbins, Trina. *Eternally Bad: Goddesses with Attitude*. Berkeley, CA: Conari, 2001.

Robinson, Herbert Spencer, and Knox Wilson. *Myths and Legends of All Nations*. Totowa, NJ: Littlefield, Adams, 1976.

Robinson, James M. *The Nag Hammadi Library*. New York: HarperCollins, 1978.

————. *The Secrets of Judas*. New York: HarperCollins, 2006.

Rogers, Lynn. *Edgar Cayce and the Eternal Feminine*. Palm Desert, CA: We Publish Books, 1993.

Schaberg, Jane. *The Resurrection of Mary Magdalene*. New York: Continuum International, 2002.

Schaef, Anne Wilson. *Women's Reality*. Minneapolis: Winston Press, 1981.

Smith, Jerry E., and George Piccard. *Secrets of the Holy Lance: The Spear of Destiny in History and Legend*. Kempton, IL: Adventures Unlimited, 2005.

Goddesses for Every Day

Spretnak, Charlene. *Lost Goddesses of Early Greece*. Boston: Beacon, 1978.

———. *The Politics of Women's Spirituality*. New York: Doubleday, 1982.

Starbird, Margaret. *The Goddess in the Gospels*. Rochester, VT: Bear and Company, 1998.

———. *Magdalene's Lost Legacy*. Rochester, VT: Bear and Company, 2003.

———. *Mary Magdalene, Bride in Exile*. Rochester, VT: Bear and Company, 2005.

———. *The Woman with the Alabaster Jar*. Rochester, VT: Bear and Company, 1993.

Stassinopoulos, Agapi. *Conversations with the Goddesses*. New York: Stewart, Tabori and Chang, 1999.

Stein, Diane. *The Goddess Book of Days*. Saint Paul, MN: Llewellyn, 1988.

Stephenson, June. *Women's Roots*. Napa, CA: Diemer, Smith, 1981.

Stone, Merlin. *When God Was a Woman*. Florida: Harcourt Brace, 1976.

Stoneman, Richard. *Greek Mythology*. London: Diamond, 1991.

Tate, Karen. *Sacred Places of Goddess*. San Francisco: Consortium of Collective Consciousness, 2006.

Taylor, Joan E. *Jewish Women Philosophers of First-Century Alexandria*. New York: Oxford University Press, 2003.

Telesco, Patricia. *365 Goddesses*. San Francisco: HarperCollins, 1998.

Tenneson, Joyce. *Wise Women*. New York: Hachette, 2002.

Todeschi, Kevin J. *Edgar Cayce on the Reincarnation of Biblical Characters*. Virginia Beach, VA: A.R.E. Press, 1999.

Tribbe, Frank C. *I, Joseph of Arimathea*. Nevada City, CA: Blue Dolphin, 2000.

Trobe, Kala. *Invoke the Gods*. Saint Paul, MN: Llewellyn, 2001.

Valtos, William M. *La Magdalena*. Charlottesville, VA: Hampton Roads, 2002.

Waldherr, Kris. *The Book of Goddesses*. New York: Harry N. Abrams, 2006.

Walker, Barbara G. *The Crone*. New York: HarperCollins, 1985.

———. *The I Ching of the Goddess*. San Francisco: Harper and Row, 1986.

———. *The Woman's Dictionary of Symbols and Sacred Objects*. New York: HarperCollins, 1988.

———. *The Woman's Encyclopedia of Myths and Secrets*. New York: Harper and Row, 1983.

———. *Women's Rituals*. New York: Harper and Row, 1990.

Warner, Rex. *Men and Gods*. New York: Farrar, Straus and Giroux, 1959.

Wilbert, Johannes, and Karin Simoneau, eds. *Folk Literature of the Chorote Indians*. Los Angeles: University of California, Latin American Institute, 1985.

———. *Folk Literature of the Toba Indians*. Los Angeles: University of California, Latin American Institute, 1982.

Willis, Roy. *World Mythology*. New York: Oxford University Press, 1993.

Young, Serinity. *An Anthology of Sacred Texts by and about Women*. New York: Crossroad, 1993.

Resources

Websites

The following is a diverse sampling of the numerous pertinent websites I encountered in my research. Please visit www.julieloar.com for more links and information.

http://www.altreligion.about.com
http://www.ancientworlds.net
http://www.beliefnet.com
http://www.celtnet.org
http://www.earlywomenmasters.org
http://www.egyptianmyths.net
http://www.festivaloftara.org
http://www.fromoldbooks.org
http://www.gallae.com
http://www.gatewaytobabylon.com
http://www.godchecker.com
http://www.goddessgift.com
http://www.goddessmyths.com
http://www.kingarthursknights.com
http://www.kstrom.net
http://www.online-mythology.com
http://www.pantheon.org
http://www.queenofcups.com
http://www.religionfacts.com
http://www.sangraal.com
http://www.thaliatook.com
http://www.themystica.com
http://www.theo.com
http://www.timelessmyths.com
http://www.wicca.com
http://www.wikipedia.org

ABOUT THE AUTHOR

*J*ulie Loar (formerly Gillentine) has been a student of metaphysics, mythology, and symbolism for more than thirty years. She has traveled to sacred sites around the world researching material for her award-winning books and teaching. She conducts workshops and lectures nationally, and each year she leads a sacred journey to Egypt. She was an executive in two major corporations before turning to writing full-time. Julie lives in Colorado.

Please contact Julie at her website,
www.julieloar.com.